$34.30

The Ethnography of Communication

Language in Society

GENERAL EDITOR
Peter Trudgill, Professor in the Department of Language and Linguistics,
University of Essex

ADVISORY EDITORS
Ralph Fasold, Professor of Linguistics, Georgetown University
William Labov, Professor of Linguistics, University of Pennsylvania

Titles in Print

The Ethnography
of Communication

AN INTRODUCTION

Second Edition

Muriel Saville-Troike

BLACKWELL
Oxford UK & Cambridge USA

First published 1982
Reprinted 1984

Second Edition 1989
Reprinted 1990, 1993, 1994

Blackwell Publishers
108 Cowley Road, Oxford, OX4 1JF, UK

238 Main Street
Cambridge, Massachusetts 02142, USA

British Library Cataloguing in Publication Data

A CIP catalogue record for this book is available from the British Library.

Library of Congress Cataloging in Publication Data

Saville-Troike, Muriel, 1936–
    The ethnography of communication: an introduction/Muriel
Saville-Troike.—2nd ed.
    p. cm.—(Language in society; 3)
    Bibliography: p.
    Includes index.
    ISBN 0–631–16678–5
    1. Sociolinguistics. 2. Language and culture. I. Title.
II. Series: Language in society (Oxford, England);
3. P40.S26 1989
401′.9—dc19

Typeset in Times on 11pt by Columns Typesetters of Reading
Printed in Great Britain by T.J. Press (Padstow) Ltd., Padstow, Cornwall

This book is printed on acid-free paper.

Contents

Preface

I would like to express my sincere appreciation to graduate students at Georgetown University and the University of Illinois who have served as both source and trial audience for most of this book. The names of those who have provided examples for the languages or countries indicated are listed at the beginning of the bibliography. In a few cases where the information might be politically sensitive, I have intentionally omitted the source; any other omissions are with my regrets and apologies.

Any attempt such as this to present a synthesis of the field of the ethnography of communication is indebted to many people, as the bibliography will attest. I would specifically like to acknowledge the useful comments I received from Richard Bauman, Nico Besnier, Ralph Fasold, Joel Sherzer, Deborah Tannen, Rudolph Troike, and Peter Trudgill. Most of all I am indebted to Dell Hymes, who is truly the father of the field. While I have drawn heavily on the ideas of Hymes and others, responsibility for the formulation presented here must remain my own.

A number of scholars have made substantial contributions to the development and application of the ethnography of communication since the first edition of this book was published in 1982. These advances are reflected in this revised edition by new citations for all of the topics covered, by updated references for work that was in progress at the time of the original release, and by the broadening of the comparative base for the analysis of patterns of communicative phenomena in the languages of the world. The most extensive revision has been made in the discussion of the components of

communication (Chapter 4), primarily as a result of comments
and questions from students and colleagues. I have restored
the component *key* to the set which Hymes originally
suggested, and expanded considerably on discussions of
message form and *message content* in response to an expressed
need for further clarification of those concepts. Finally, my
continuing experience in teaching a course on the ethnography
of communication has also led me to add references which
illustrate the application of this methodological perspective in
a number of different domains. It is my hope that these added
references will be helpful to instructors and readers who wish
to supplement the book with readings that are appropriate to
specific disciplinary applications.

Series Editor's Foreword

The ethnography of communication studies the norms of communicative conduct in different communities, and deals with methods for studying these norms. In her comprehensive treatment of the field in this book, Muriel Saville-Troike combines linguistic expertise with a wide range of anthropological insights. She draws on a large number of the world's language communities for exemplification, and one of the great pleasures of the book is the way in which it exposes the reader to the many different ways of speaking that can be found around the world, and to the very varied mechanisms human societies have developed for regulating communicative behaviour. The first edition of this book was the first general introduction to the ethnography of communication to appear; this revised edition brings this introduction up to date and represents a skilful synthesis of the different types of approach and of the wide range of findings that work in this area has produced in the last fifteen years or so. The ethnography of communication is still a relatively new topic within the field of sociolinguistics, but it is becoming increasingly clear that it is a topic of considerable importance, not only to linguists and anthropologists, but also to language teachers, educationists, language planners, international business people, and anyone else involved in cross-cultural communication. The recognition by the academic community, and now increasingly by the wider community also, that human societies may differ dramatically from one another in the way they communicate, is an important step.

Peter Trudgill

1

Introduction

Ethnography is a field of study which is concerned primarily with the description and analysis of culture, and linguistics is a field concerned, among other things, with the description and analysis of language codes. In spite of widespread awareness of the interrelationship of language and culture, the descriptive and analytic products of ethnographers and linguists traditionally failed to account for such a relationship. Even anthropological linguists and linguistic anthropologists until recently gave little attention to the fact that the uses of language and speech in different societies have patterns of their own which are worthy of ethnographic description, comparable to, and intersecting with, patterns in social organization and other cultural domains. The realization of this omission led Dell Hymes to call for an approach which would deal with aspects of communication which were escaping both anthropology and linguistics.

With the publication of 'The enthnography of speaking' in 1962, Hymes launched a new synthesizing discipline which focuses on the patterning of communicative behavior as it constitutes one of the systems of culture, as it functions within the holistic context of culture, and as it relates to patterns in other component systems. The *ethnography of communication*, as the field has come to be known since the publication of a paper by Hymes with this title, has in its development drawn heavily upon (and mutually influenced) sociological concern with interactional analysis and role identity, the study of performance by anthropologically oriented folklorists, and the work of natural-language philosophers. In combining these various threads of interest and theoretical orientation, the enthography of communication has become an emergent discipline, addressing a largely new order of information in the structuring of communicative behavior and its role in the conduct of social life.

As with any science, the ethnography of communication has two foci: particularistic and generalizing. On the one hand, it is directed at the description and understanding of communicative behavior in specific cultural settings, but it is also directed toward the formulation of concepts and theories upon which to build a global metatheory of human communication. Its basic approach does not involve a list of facts to be learned so much as questions to be asked, and means for finding out answers. In order to attain the goal of understanding both the particular and the general, a broad range of data from a large variety of communities is needed.

A major early contribution to the field included an outline of information to be collected in doing ethnographies of communication, by Dell Hymes, Joel Sherzer, Regna Darnell, and others (1967), and this has served as a guide to the scope and organization of this book. Other major contributors to the development of the field have included John Gumperz, Dan Slobin, Richard Bauman, Susan Philips, Susan Ervin-Tripp, Shirley Brice Heath, and Ben Blount. Hymes' influence has been so pervasive that it is impossible to specifically credit each of the concepts and visions for which he was initially responsible, and which inform this book and the work of others in various ways.

SCOPE AND FOCUS

The subject matter of the ethnography of communication is best illustrated by one of its most general questions: What does a speaker need to know to communicate appropriately within a particular speech community, and how does he or she learn? Such knowledge, together with whatever skills are needed to make use of it, is *communicative competence*. The requisite knowledge includes not only rules for communication (both linguistic and sociolinguistic) and shared rules for interaction, but also the cultural rules and knowledge that are the basis for the context and content of communicative events and interaction processes. Each of these components will be further delineated in the chapters which follow.

The focus of the ethnography of communication is the *speech community*, the way communication within it is patterned and organized as systems of communicative events, and the ways in which these interact with all other systems of culture. A primary aim of this approach is to guide the collection and analysis of descriptive data about the ways in which social meaning is conveyed: 'If we ask of any form of communication the simple question what is being communicated? the answer is: information from the social system' (Douglas 1971:389). This makes the ethnography of communication a mode of inquiry which carries with it substantial content.

Among the basic products of this approach are ethnographic descriptions of ways in which speech and other channels of communication are used in diverse communities, ranging from tribal groups in Africa and the Amazon regions, to nomadic herdsmen, to highly industrialized peoples in Europe, Asia, and North America. The priority which the ethnography of communication places on modes and functions of language is a clear point of departure from the priorities announced for linguistics by Chomsky (1968:62): 'if we hope to understand human language and the psychological capacities on which it rests, we must first ask what it is, not how or for what purpose it is used'.

Hymes repeatedly emphasizes that what language is cannot be separated from how and why it is used, and that considerations of use are often prerequisite to recognition and understanding of much of linguistic form. The ethnography of communication takes language first and foremost as a socially situated cultural form, while recognizing the necessity to analyze the code itself and the cognitive process of its speakers and hearers. To accept a lesser scope for linguistic description is to risk reducing it to triviality, and to deny any possibility of understanding how language lives in the minds and on the tongues of its users.

METHOD

'Doing ethnography' in another culture involves first and foremost field work, including observing, asking questions, participating in group activities, and testing the validity of one's perceptions against the intuitions of natives. Research design must allow an openness to categories and modes of thought and behavior which may not have been anticipated by the investigator. The ethnographer of commmunication cannot even presuppose what a speech community other than his own may consider to be 'language', or who or what may 'speak' it: 'language' for the Ojibwa includes thunder; dogs among the Navajo are said to understand Navajo; the Maori regard musical instruments as able to speak; and drums and shells are channels through which supernatural forces are believed to speak to members of the Afro-Cuban Lucumí religious cult.

Ethnography by no means requires investigating only 'others': one's own speech community may be profitably studied as well. Here, however, discovering patterned behavior which operates largely unconsciously for the native investigator presents quite different problems for 'objectivity'. One of the best means by which to gain understanding of one's own 'ways of speaking' is to compare and contrast these ways with others, a process that can reveal that many of the communicative practices assumed to be 'natural' or 'logical' are in fact as culturally unique and conventional as the language code itself. A valuable by-product which emerges from this process is an essential feature of all ethnography: a sense of cultural relativism.

Complete escape from subjectivity is never possible because of our very nature as cultural animals; however, the constraints and guidelines of the methodology are intended to minimize our perceptual and analytical biases. The tradition of participant-observation is still basic for all ethnography, but it may be augmented by a variety of other data collection and validation procedures depending on the focus of investigation and the relation of the investigator to the speech community being studied. Many of these other procedures will be discussed in some detail in Chapter 4.

Ethnographic study has been made at the core of anthropology virtually since its inception, both in Britain and America. The American tradition, begun by Franz Boas and Alfred Kroeber, tended toward a somewhat static presentation of cultural patterns and artifacts which was sometimes criticized as the 'trait list approach'. The British tradition, which came to be called 'functionalist', was developed along two rather different orientations by A. R. Radcliffe-Brown and Bronislaw Malinowski, both of which strongly influenced American anthropology. The British tradition, especially following Malinowski, was much concerned with the social and cultural 'meaning' of actions, events, objects, and laws as they functioned within the immediate or larger cultural context.

North American anthropologists beginning with Boas were primarily concerned with preparing ethnographic descriptions of Native American cultures before they were destroyed or assimilated by the European settlers. Even before Boas, however, the Bureau of American Ethnology (BAE) under John Wesley Powell had placed a priority on describing Native American languages and collecting texts, which still serve as a major source of data for comparative studies of languages on the North American continent. Few of the linguistic descriptions from this period go beyond a sketch of the phonological system and grammatical structures (as outlined in Powell 1877; 1880; Boas 1911) and a list of vocabulary items collected according to a schedule distributed by the BAE (cf. Powell 1880), but accompanying reports often include observations which are relevant to understanding patterns of communication. In his *Introduction to the Study of Indian Languages* (1880:vi), Powell clearly states his intent to relate the description of language to other aspects of culture:

It has been the effort of the author to connect the study of language with the other branches of anthropology, for a language is best understood when the habits, customs, institutions, philosophy – the subject-matter of thought embodied in the language – are best known. The student of language should be a student of the people who speak the language; and to this end the book has been prepared, with many hints and suggestions relating to other branches of anthropology.

One of the earliest sociolinguistic descriptions I can find within this tradition was prepared by a physician, J. B. White, who described Apache greeting behavior in the 1880s:

Kissing which seems to us natural [as] an expression of affection is never practised by the Apaches – and they seem to have no form of salute or of greeting – when meeting or of taking leave of each other. On one occasion the writer of this – being curious to know what kind of reception an Indian would give his wife and family after an absence from them of several months – placed himself in a position, where he could overlook (without himself being noticed) an Apache's entrance into his dwelling after a long absence. In this instance the Indian simply rode up to his little brush dwelling and dismounted. One of his wives took charge of the horse. [He] approached a fire along side of his hut where his family were collected without exchanging a word to any of them – not even to the wife who had taken the horse. There he stood motionless and speechless for some ten to fifteen minutes when at last he took a seat on the ground and engaged in ordinary conversation without having observed any form of greeting. (Cf. the more recent description of Apache greetings in Basso 1970.)

Occasionally, descriptions of traditional educational practices contained references to training in 'speaking well', as in this brief mention of sociolinguistic constraints imposed on girls of the Carrier Indian tribe of Canada: 'The stone labret worn by the noble maiden was a perpetual reminder to her that she should speak slowly and with deliberation' (Jenness 1929:26). Most information on communication beyond the vocabulary lists and structural sketches of the language codes was limited to listings of kinship terms, reflecting social organization and role-relationships within the groups; ethnological dictionaries, indicating plants and animals in the environment and of importance to the culture; and accounts of language origins and attitudes toward language reflected in creation myths and other folkloristic texts.

The American tradition of descriptive linguistics in conjunction with anthropological fieldwork continued with such notable figures as Edward Sapir, and (in spite of the divergence of an 'autonomous linguistics') more recently in the work of such Amerindian language scholars as Floyd Lounsbury, Mary Haas, Carl Voegelin, Paul Friedrich, and Dell Hymes.

Ethnography underwent a period of decline within anthropology during the middle years of this century as values began to favour more 'scientific' studies of social structure and issue-oriented research. There has been a resurgence of interest, however, deriving from Goodenough's cognitive reformation of the concept of culture, and in the wave of growing disenchantment with behaviorism. Observed behavior is now recognized as a manifestation of a deeper set of codes and rules, and the task of ethnography is seen as the discovery and explication of the rules for contextually appropriate behavior in a community or group; in other words, culture is what the individual needs to know to be a functional member of the community.

Concurrent with this latter development in anthropology was the introduction of interactionist and cognitive orientations in sociology by Goffman (1974) and Cicourel (1974), which have focused attention on the processes by which members of a community negotiate relations, outcomes, and meanings, and construct new realities and meanings as they do so. The convergent interest in sociology and linguistics, and the description of language use in a social context (most notably by Halliday in the British school) raised serious questions about the autonomy of linguistics and the 'ideal speaker-hearer' in the 'completely homogeneous speech-community' (Chomsky 1965:3), central concepts in the dominant theoretical model of the 1960s. By the end of that decade, merely accounting for *what* can (and cannot) be said in a language, but not what can be said when, where, by whom, to whom, in what manner, and under what particular social circumstances, came to be considered inadequate as a goal for linguistics by many linguists, and by all identifying themselves as 'sociolinguists'.

SIGNIFICANCE

While the goals of ethnography are at least in the first instance descriptive, and information about diverse 'ways of speaking' is a legitimate contribution to knowledge in its own right, the potential significance of the ethnography of communication goes far beyond a mere cataloging of facts about communicative behavior.

For anthropology, the ethnography of communication extends understandings of cultural systems to language, at the same time relating language to social organization, role-relationships, values and beliefs, and other shared patterns of knowledge and behavior which are transmitted from generation to generation in the process of socialization/enculturation. Further, it contributes to the study of cultural maintenance and change, including various acculturation phenomena in contact situations, and may provide important clues to culture history.

For psycholinguistics, the ethnography of communication means that studies of language acquisition must now not only recognize the innate capacity of children to learn to speak, but must account for how particular ways of speaking are developed in particular societies in the process of social interaction. Experimental design can no longer presume that mothers are primary caregivers in all societies, for example, nor can a researcher assume that the presence of an observer (and a tape recorder) will distort data comparably in all settings among all groups. Any study of language pathologies outside of one's own speech community must include culture-specific information on what is considered 'normal' and 'aberrant' performance within the other group. Claims about universal strategies and processes need to be tested against descriptive data from other cultures, and such cross-cultural research requires the openness and relativism of ethnographic methods.

For sociolinguistic research, which generally involves recording naturalistic speech in various contexts, the potential contribution of this perspective was noted by Gumperz:

> Even after the material has been recorded, it is sometimes impossible to evaluate its social signficance in the absence of ethnographic knowledge about social norms governing linguistic choice in the situation recorded. (1970:9)

Again, the qualitative information which forms an essential part of ethnographies of communication should become an important prerequisite for sampling, data collection, and interpretation. Experimental design which is based only on the researcher's own cultural presuppositions has no necessary validity in a different speech community.

For the field of applied linguistics, one of the most significant contributions made by the ethnography of communication is the identification of what a second language learner must know in order to communicate appropriately in various contexts in that language, and what the sanctions may be for various communicative shortcomings. There are also important applications for contrasting whole communicative systems in cross-cultural interaction and translation, and for recognizing and analyzing communicative misunderstandings.

For theoretical linguistics, the ethnography of communication can make a significant contribution to the study of universals in langauge form and use, as well as to language-specific and comparative fields of description and analysis. Its approach and findings are essential for the formulation of a truly adequate theory of language and linguistic competence.

Throughout this book, an attempt has been made to relate the methods and products of the ethnography of communication to the other disciplines which are concerned with the description, explanation, and application of various aspects of communication. Because the book is included in a series on sociolinguistics, particular emphasis is placed on the relationship of the ethnography of communication to other developments in this field. In particular, the position is taken here that qualitative and quantitative approaches to the study of culturally situated communication are not mutually exclusive, and that each can and should inform the other. While ethnography has tended to be identified exclusively with qualitative approaches, many practitioners today are recognizing the need to extend the boundary to include quantitative data in ethnographic descriptions. Gumperz and others have also stressed the need to look at the larger socio-political contexts within which culturally situated communication takes place, as these contexts may determine features of communication in ways that are not evident from a focus on coummunicative patterns alone.

Thus while the ethnography of communication has a unique contribution to make in terms of the questions it asks and its relativistic perspective, its contribution to the description and understanding of culturally constituted patterns of communication will be limited if its methods and findings are not integrated with other descriptive and analytical approaches. It is the nature of ethnography to be holistic in nature, and this should also characterize the disciplinary orientation of its practitioners.

A well-known fable tells of three blind men describing an elephant: to one (feeling the tail) it is like a rope; to one (feeling the side) it is flat and leathery; and to one (feeling the trunk) it is like a long rubber hose. While each perception is accurate so far as it goes individually, they fail to provide an accurate picture of the total animal because there is no holistic perspective. Such an integrative approach seems essential if we are to fulfill Hymes' call to develop an ethnographic model for the study of communication which will help us more fully to understand its role in human affairs.

2

Basic Terms, Concepts, and Issues

The principal concerns in the ethnography of communication, as these have been defined by Hymes and as they have emerged from the work of others, include the following topics: patterns and functions of communication, nature and definition of speech community, means of communicating, components of communicative competence, relationship of language to world view and social organization, and linguistic and social universals and inequalities.

PATTERNS OF COMMUNICATION

It has long been recognized that much of linguistic behavior is rule-governed, i.e. it follows regular patterns and constraints which can be formulated descriptively as 'rules'. Thus, sounds must be produced in language-specific but regular sequences if they are to be interpreted as a speaker intends; the possible order and form of words in a sentence is constrained by the rules of grammar; and even the definition of a well-formed discourse is determined by culture-specific rules of rhetoric.

Sociolinguists such as Labov (1963; 1966), Bailey (1976), and Trudgill (1974) have demonstrated that what earlier linguists had considered irregularity or 'free variation' in linguistic behavior, can be found to show regular and predictable statistical patterns. The ethnography of communication is concerned with discovering regularities in language use, but while sociolinguists focus on variability in pronunciation and grammatical form, ethnographers are concerned with how communicative units are organized and how they pattern in a much broader sense of 'ways of speaking', as well as with how these patterns interrelate in a systematic way with and derive meaning from other aspects of culture.

Some common patterns are so regular, so predictable, that a very low information load is carried even by a long utterance or interchange, though the social meaning involved can be significant. For instance, greetings in some languages (e.g. Korean) may carry crucial information identifying speaker relationships (or attitudes toward relationships). An unmarked greeting sequence such as 'Hello, how are you today? Fine, how are you?' has virtually no referential content. However, silence in response to another's greeting in this sequence would be marked communicative behavior, and would carry a very high information load for speakers of English.

Greetings in many languages are far more elaborate than in English (e.g. Arabic, Indonesian, Igbo), but even a lengthy sequence may convey very little information as long as it is unmarked. In all cases patterned variations can be related to aspects of the social structure or value and belief systems within the respective cultures.

The potential strength of a pattern may be illustrated by the opening sequence of a telephone conversation in English (Schegloff 1968). The ring of the telephone is a summons, and the person who answers must speak first even though the caller knows the receiver has been picked up. (Many people will not pick up the telephone in the middle of a ring because they feel it is an interruption of the summons.) Even an obscene telephone caller generally waits for the person who is answering to say something before the obscenities begin. If someone picks up the telephone and does not say anything, the caller cannot proceed. He or she can either say something like 'Hello, hello, anybody there?' as a second summons, or else hang up. The caller may dial back again to repeat the sequence, but not continue if there has not been an appropriate response.

The relationship of form and function is an example of communicative patterning along a different dimension. Asking someone in English if he or she has any cigarettes is readily recognized as a request rather than an information question, for instance, because it is part of the regular structural pattern for requesting things in English; the person who answers 'Yes, thanks', without offering one is joking, rude, or a member of a different speech community.

Patterning occurs at all levels of communication: societal, group, and individual (cf. Hymes 1961). At the societal level, communication usually patterns in terms of its functions, categories of talk, and attitudes and conceptions about language and speakers. Communication also patterns according to particular roles and groups within a society, such as sex, age, social status, and occupation: e.g. a teacher has different ways of speaking from a lawyer, a doctor, or an insurance salesman. Ways of speaking also pattern according to educational level, rural or urban residence, geographic region, and other features of social organization.

Finally, communication patterns at the individual level, at the level of expression and interpretation of personality. To the extent emotional factors such as nervousness have a physiological effect on the vocal mechanism, they are not considered part of 'communication', but there are many conventional symbols which are part of patterned communication. An example of conventional expression of individual emotion is the increased volume meaning 'anger' in English. A Navajo expressing anger uses enclitics not recognized as emotion markers by speakers of other languages, and a friendly greeting on the street between Chinese speakers may have surface manifestations corresponding to anger for speakers of English. Similarly, American Indian students often interpret Anglo teachers' 'normal' classroom projection level as anger and hostility, and teachers interpret students' softer level as shyness or unfriendliness. Perceptions of individuals as 'voluble' or 'taciturn' are also in terms of cultural norms, and even expressions of pain and stress are culturally patterned: people in an English speech community learn withdrawal or anger, in Japanese nervous laughter or giggling, and in Navajo silence.

Although I have listed these levels of patterning separately, there is an invisible web of interrelationships among them, and indeed among all patterns of culture. There may very well be general themes that are related to a world view present in several aspects of culture, including language. There are societies that are more direct than others, for instance, and this will be manifested in ways of speaking as well as in belief and value systems. The notion of a hierarchy of control seems to be pervasive in several cultures, and must first be understood in order to explain certain language constraints as well as religious beliefs and social organization (cf. Thompson 1978; Watkins 1979; Witherspoon 1977).

The concern for pattern has always been basic in anthropology (cf. Benedict 1934; Kroeber 1935; 1944), with interpretations of underlying meaning dependent on the discovery and description of normative structure or design. More recent emphasis on processes of interactions in generating behavioral patterns (cf. Barth 1966) extends this concern to explanation as well as description.

COMMUNICATIVE FUNCTIONS

At a societal level, language serves many functions. Chief among these, perhaps, is that of creating/reinforcing boundaries, unifying its speakers as members of a single speech community, and excluding outsiders from intragroup communication. Many languages are also made to serve a social identification function within a society by providing linguistic indicators which may be used to reinforce social stratification. Linguistic features are often employed by people, consciously or unconsciously, to identify themselves and others, and thus serve to mark and maintain various social categories and divisions.

At the level of individuals and groups interacting with one another, the functions of communication are directly related to the participants' purposes and needs (Hymes 1961; 1972). These include such categories of functions as expressive (conveying feelings or emotions), directive (requesting or demanding), referential (true or false propositional content), poetic (aesthetic), phatic (empathy and solidarity), and metalinguistic (reference to language itself).

This list is similar to Searle's (1977a) classes of illocutionary acts (representatives, directives, commissives, expressives, declarations), but there are differences in perspective and scope which separate the fields of ethnography of communication and speech act theory or pragmatics. Among these are the latters' primary focus on form, with the speech act almost always coterminus with sentences in analysis; for ethnographers, the functional perspective has priority in description, and while function may coincide with a single grammatical sentence, it often does not, or a single sentence may serve several functions simultaneously. Further, while speech act theorists and pragmaticists generally exclude the metaphorical and phatic uses of language from basic consideration, these constitute a major focus for ethnographic description. Phatic communication conveys a message, but has no referential meaning. The meaning is in the act of communication itself. Much of ritual interaction is included in this category, fully comprising most brief encounters, and at least opening and closing most longer ones (Goffman 1971). Not accounting for such functions of communication is ignoring much of language as it is actually used.

The distinction between intent and effect in function (Ervin-Tripp 1972) is comparable to the difference between illocutionary and perlocutionary acts in pragmatics (cf. Searle 1969; 1977b). The difference between the functional intent of the speaker and the actual effect on the hearer is part of the notion of functional relativity (Hymes 1972). Both are relevant to the description and analysis of a communicative event.

While many of the functions of language are universal, the ways in which communication operates in any one society to serve these functions is language specific. The same relative status of two speakers may be conveyed by their choice of pronominal forms in one language; in another, by the distance they stand apart or their body position while speaking; and between bilinguals, even by their choice of which language is used in addressing one another.

The functions of language provide the primary dimension for characterizing and organizing communicative processes and products in a society; without understanding why a language is being used as it is, and the consequences of such use, it is impossible to understand its meaning in the context of social interaction.

To claim primacy of function over form in analysis is not to deny or neglect the formal structures of communication; rather it is to require integration of function and form in analysis and description. Sentences and even longer strings of discourse are not to be dealt with as autonomous units, but rather as they are situated in communicative settings and patterns, and as they function in society.

SPEECH COMMUNITY

Since the focus of the ethnography of communication is on the speech community, and on the way communication is patterned and organized within that unit, clearly its definition is of central importance. Many definitions have been proposed (cf. Hudson 1980:25–30), including such criteria as shared language use (Lyons 1970), frequency of interaction by a group of people (Bloomfield 1933; Hockett 1958; Gumperz 1962), shared rules of speaking and interpretation of speech performance (Hymes 1972), shared attitudes and values regarding language forms and use (Labov 1972), and shared sociocultural understandings and presuppositions with regard to speech (Sherzer 1975).

Linguists are generally in agreement that a speech community cannot be exactly equated with a group of people who speak the same language, for Spanish speakers in Texas and Argentina are members of different speech communities although they share a language code, and husbands and wives within some speech communities in the South Pacific use quite distinct languages in speaking to one another. Speakers of mutually unintelligible dialects of Chinese identify themselves as members of the same speech community (they do indeed share a written code, as well as many rules for appropriate use), while speakers of Spanish, Italian and Portuguese are not members of the same speech community although their languages are to some degree mutually intelligible. Questions arise in deciding if speakers of English from Britain and the United States (or Canada and Australia, or India and Nigeria) are members of the same speech community. How different must rules of speaking be to be significantly different? Are deaf signers and hearing interpreters members of the same speech community? Answers to such questions are based on history, politics, and group identification, rather than on purely linguistic factors. It is thus useful to distinguish between participating in a speech community and being a member of it; speaking the same language is sufficient (yet not necessary) for some degree of participation, but membership cannot be based on knowledge and skills alone.

All definitions of *community* used in the social sciences include the dimension of shared knowledge, possessions, or behaviors, derived from Latin *communitae* 'held in common', just as the sociolinguistic criteria for speech community enumerated above all include the word 'shared'. The key question is whether our focus in initially defining communities for study should be on shared language form and use, or on common geographical and political boundaries, culture traits, and perhaps even physical characteristics (e.g. a particular skin color may be considered a requirement for membership in some communities, a hearing impairment for others). Since patterns of language use and interpretation, rules of speaking, and attitudes concerning language are part of the product of ethnographic investigation, it is somewhat circular to use them as basic criteria for defining a group to study.

If circularity is to be minimized, ethnographers of communication should begin with an extra-linguistically defined social entity, and investigate its communicative repertoire in terms of the socially defined community: the nature and distribution of linguistic resources, how they are organized and structured, how they relate to the social organization, how they function as a patterned and integrated component of the community as a whole.

Part of the difficulty we have in defining speech community must be attributed to the differential scope which 'community' has according to different criteria:

1   It is any group within a society which has anything significant in common (including religion, ethnicity, race, age, deafness, sexual orientation, or occupation, but not eye color or height)
2   It is a physically bounded unit of people having a full range of role opportunities (a politically organized tribe or nation, but not a single-sex, single-age, or single-class unit like a monastery, home for the aged, or ghetto).
3   It is a collection of similarly situated entities that have something in common (such as the Western World, developing countries, European Common Market, or the United Nations).

Depending on the degree of abstraction desired, social units may be selected at different levels; virtually any community in a complex society might be considered part of another larger one, or subdivided into smaller groups. While one can focus on a single school, a neighborhood, a factory, or the gay 'community', an integrated ethnographic approach would require relating such subgroups to the social and cultural whole, with its full complement of roles. There is no expectation that a community will be linguistically homogeneous, but as a collectivity it will include a range of language varieties (and even different languages) that will pattern in relation to the salient social and cultural dimensions of communication, such as role and domain. From this perspective, patterns of language use do not define a community to be investigated, but their description is part of the outcome of an ethnographic study which focuses on a community selected according to non-linguistic criteria. Also a product of investigation is the determination of whether a community is a 'speech community' according to selected linguistic criteria. To the ones already mentioned, I would add that language must be found to play a significant role in identifying the boundary of a speech community, at least from the perspective of its own members.

At any level of speech community selected for study, the societal functions of language will include the boundary functions of separating, unifying, and stratifying. The interactional functions which are present will be dependent on the level of community studied, with a full complement of language functions and domains present only at the level defined as including a range of role opportunities. At this more inclusive level, a speech community need not share a single language, and indeed it will not where roles are differentially assigned to monolingual speakers of different languages in a single multilingual society (e.g. speakers of Spanish and Guaraní in Paraguay, discussed in Chapter 3).

An informal typology of speech communities as 'soft-shelled' versus 'hard-shelled' may be distinguished on the basis of the strength of the boundary that is maintained by language: the 'hard-shelled' community has of course the stronger boundary, allowing minimal interaction between members and those outside, and providing maximum maintenance of language and culture.

Speech communities which primarily use one of the world languages are more likely to be 'soft-shelled', because it will be known as a second language by many others, and interaction across the boundary will be relatively easy in both directions. A speech community speaking Japanese or other language with limited distribution would more likely be 'hard-shelled', because few outside the community learn to use it. Educated Japanese learn a world language for interaction across the boundary, but this is unidirectional, with outsiders still very restricted in their linguistic participation with Japan. The most extreme form of a 'hard-shelled' community would be one like Mongolia, where members speak a language outsiders do not know, yet few learn a world language for wider communication; another would be the Tewa-speaking San Juan pueblo in New Mexico, where outsiders are forbidden even to hear the language, and only a few insiders learn either English or Spanish.

Language often serves to maintain the separate identity of speech communities within larger communities, of which their speakers may also be members. Within the United States, for instance, Armenian continues to function in some areas as the language of home, religion, and social interaction among members of the group. Because the Armenians are bilingual and also speak English, they participate fully in the larger speech community, but because outsiders seldom learn Armenian, the language is a barrier which keeps others from participating in their internal social and religious events. A similar situation exists in Syria, where Armenians bilingual in their native language and Arabic participate in two speech communities; these remain separate entities because of the one-way boundary function the Armenian language serves. In cases where individuals and groups belong to more than one speech community, it is useful to distinguish between primary and secondary membership.

Individuals, particularly in complex societies, may thus participate in a number of discrete or overlapping speech communities, just as they participate in a variety of social settings. Which one or ones a person orients himself or herself to at any moment – which set of rules he or she uses – is part of the strategy of communication. To understand this phenomenon, it is necessary to recognize that each member of a community has a repertoire of social identities, and each identity in a given context is associated with a number of appropriate verbal and nonverbal forms of expression. It is therefore essential to identify the social categories recognized in a community in order to determine how these are reflected linguistically, and how they define and constrain interpersonal interaction in communicative situations.

Traditional anthropological and sociological definitions of a community frequently contain language–related criteria, so circularity frequently cannot by entirely avoided. Having a shared culture, having a native name with which members identify, having a social network for contact, and having common folklore or history are all largely dependent on having a common mode of communication.

COMMUNICATIVE COMPETENCE

Hymes (1966a) observed that speakers who could produce any and all of the grammatical sentences of a language (per

Chomsky's 1965 definition of linguistic competence) would be institutionalized if they tried to do so. Communicative competence involves knowing not only the language code, but also what to say to whom, and how to say it appropriately in any given situation. It deals with the social and cultural knowledge speakers are presumed to have to enable them to use and interpret linguistic forms. A child who uses a taboo expression in public and causes embarrassment is said not to 'know better', i.e. not to have acquired certain rules for social conduct in the use of language (the embarassment itself presupposes the existence of this competence). The concept of communicative competence (and its encompassing congener, social competence) is one of the most powerful organizing tools to emerge in the social sciences in recent years.

Communicative competence extends to both knowledge and expectation of who may or may not speak in certain settings, when to speak and when to remain silent, whom one may speak to, how one may talk to persons of different statuses and roles, what appropriate nonverbal behaviors are in various contexts, what the routines for turn-taking are in conversation, how to ask for and give information, how to request, how to offer or decline assistance or cooperation, how to give commands, how to enforce discipline, and the like – in short, everything involving the use of language and other communicative dimensions in particular social settings.

Clear cross-cultural differences can and do produce conflicts or inhibit communication. For example, certain American Indian groups are accustomed to waiting several minutes in silence before responding to a question or taking a turn in conversation, while the native English speakers they may be talking to have very short time frames for responses or conversational turn-taking, and find silences embarrassing. Conversely, Abrahams (1973) has pointed out that among Blacks conversations may involve several persons talking at the same time, a practice which would violate White middle-class rules of interaction. And as mentioned earlier, even such matters as voice level differ cross-culturally, and speaker intent may be misconstrued because of different expectation patterns for interpretation.

The concept of communicative competence must be embedded in the notion of cultural competence, or the total set of knowledge and skills which speakers bring into a situation. This view is consonant with a semiotic approach which defines culture as meaning, and views all ethnographers (not just ethnographers of communication) as dealing with symbols (cf. Geertz 1973; Douglas 1970). The systems of culture are patterns of symbols, and language is only one of the symbolic systems in this network. Interpreting the meaning of linguistic behavior requires knowing the meaning in which it is embedded.

Ultimately all aspects of culture are relevant to communication, but those that have the most direct bearing on communicative forms and processes are the social structure, the values and attitudes held about language and ways of speaking, the network of conceptual categories which results from shared experiences, and the ways knowledge and skills (including language) are transmitted from one generation to the next, and to new members of the group.

Shared cultural knowledge is essential to explain the shared presuppositions and judgements of truth value which are the essential undergirdings of language structures, as well as of contextually appropriate usage and interpretation.

While referential meaning may be ascribed to many of the elements in the linguistic code in a static manner, situated meaning must be accounted for as an emergent and dynamic process. Interaction requires the perception, selection, and interpretation of salient features of the code used in actual communicative situations, integrating these with other cultural knowledge and skills, and implementing appropriate strategies for achieving communicative goals.

The phonology, grammar, and lexicon which are the target of traditional linguistic description constitute only a part of the elements in the code used for communication. Also included are the paralinguistic and nonverbal phenomena which have conventional meaning in each speech community, and knowledge of the full range of variants in all elements which are available for transmitting social, as well as referential, information. Ability to discriminate between those variants which serve as markers of social categories or carry other meaning and those which are insignificant, and knowledge of what the meaning of a variant is in a particular situation, are all components of communicative competence.

The verbal code may be transmitted on oral, written, or manual (signed) channels. The relative load carried on each channel depends on its functional distribution in a particular speech community, and thus they are of differential importance in the linguistic repertoire of any individual or society. Full participation in a deaf speech community requires ability to interpret language on the manual channel but not the oral, for instance; a speech community with a primarily oral tradition may not require interpretation of writing; and a speech community which relegates much information flow to the written channel will require literacy skills for full participation. Thus, the traditional linguistic description which focuses only on the oral channel will also be too narrow to account for communicative competence in most societies. Although it may cause some terminological confusion, references to 'ways of speaking' and 'ethnography of speaking' usually include a much broader range of communicative behavior than merely speech.

The usual descriptive focus on oral production has tended to characterize language as a unidirectional phenomenon. In considering the nature and scope of communicative competence, it is useful to distinguish between receptive and productive dimensions (Troike 1970); only shared receptive competence is necessary for successful communication. Knowledge of rules for appropriate communicative behavior entails understanding a wide range of language forms, for instance, but not necessarily the ability to produce them. Members of the same community may understand varieties of a language which differ according to the social class, region, sex, age, and occupation of the speaker, but only a few talented mimics will be able to speak them all. In multilingual speech communities, members often share receptive competence in more than one language but vary greatly in relative ability to speak one or the other.

The following outline summarizes the broad range of

shared knowledge that speakers must have in order to communicate appropriately. From the ethnographer's perspective, this inventory also indicates the range of linguistic, interactional, and cultural phenomena which must ultimately be accounted for in an adequate description and explanation of communication (see also Duranti 1988, Gumperz 1984, Hymes 1987, and Saville-Troike 1989). These, then, are essentially the components of communication:

1   Linguistic knowledge
    (a)   Verbal elements
    (b)   Nonverbal elements
    (c)   Patterns of elements in particular speech events
    (d)   Range of possible variants (in all elements and their organization)
    (e)   Meaning of variants in particular situations
2   Interaction skills
    (a)   Perception of salient features in communicative situations
    (b)   Selection and interpretation of forms appropriate to specific situations, roles, and relationships (rules for the use of speech)
    (c)   Discourse organization and processes
    (d)   Norms of interaction and interpretation
    (e)   Strategies for achieving goals
3   Cultural knowledge
    (a)   Social structure
    (b)   Values and attitudes
    (c)   Cognitive maps/schemata
    (d)   Enculturation processes (transmission of knowledge and skills)

Since communicative competence refers to knowledge and skills for contextually appropriate use and interpretation of language in a community, it refers to the communicative knowledge and skills shared by the group, although these (like all aspects of culture) reside variably in its individual members. The shared yet individual nature of competence reflects the nature of language itself, as expressed by von Humboldt (1836):

While languages are in the ambiguous sense of the word
. . . creations of nations, they still remain personal and
individual creations of individuals. This follows because
they can be produced in each individual, yet only in such
a manner that each individual assumes a priori the
comprehension of all people and that all people,
furthermore, satisfy such expectation.

Problems arise when individual competence is judged in
relation to a presumed ideal speech community, or assessed
with tests given in a limited subset of situations which do not
represent the true range of an individual's verbal ability
(Hymes 1979b). The problems are particularly serious ones
when such invalid judgements result in some form of social
discrimination against the individuals, such as unequal or
inappropriate educational treatment. Awareness of the complex nature of communicative competence and the potential
negative consequences of misjudgements is leading to major
changes in procedures and instruments for language assessment, but no simple solutions are forthcoming (see Milroy
1987; Philips 1983a).

THE COMPETENCE OF INCOMPETENCE

Part of communicative competence is being able to sound
appropriately 'incompetent' in the language when the situation
dictates. This may be done to signal deference when
interacting with someone of higher rank: e.g. in Burundi,
lower ranking persons are expected to speak in a bumbling
and hesitating manner to those of higher rank, but the same
individuals speak fluently with peers or others of lower rank
than they (Albert 1972). Similarly, members of a subordinate
group in the community may adopt a 'powerless speech style'
with members of the dominant group, including women with
men, ethnic minorities with majorities, and children with
adults (Giles, Scherer, and Taylor 1979). Conversely, in
Wolof 'for the highest of the nobles incorrectness in certain
aspects of speech is considered appropriate, since high-

ranking persons are not supposed to be very skilled at speaking, at least in terms of superficial elaboration' (Irvine 1973:40–1).

On some occasions, proving 'incompetence' may have practical benefits. Actors or actresses may cultivate a 'sexy' foreign accent to increase box office receipts, and applicants to at least one federally funded training project for which limited English proficiency was an entry criterion were caught cheating downward on the language test used for admission.

In a religious context, such as 'speaking in tongues' among charismatic Christian groups, inarticulateness may be taken as evidence of divine inspiration, proof that the speaker is not in conscious control of what is being said (Douglas 1970:109–10), just as 'I don't know what to say' may be interpreted as the most sincere expression of deep emotion to someone who is bereaved.

Speakers of a second language are often well advised not to try to sound too much like a native. A foreign accent will often allow as yet imperfectly learned rules of etiquette to be excused as such, while a speaker who has mastered the phonology of a language is assumed to have also mastered all other aspects of its use, and violations are more likely to be interpreted as rudeness. Additional consequences of perfecting pronunciation in a second language may be suspicion or resentment from native speakers if they do not welcome new members, or feelings from the primary speech community that one is disloyal to it.

UNITS OF ANALYSIS

In order to describe and analyze communication it is necessary to deal with discrete units of some kind, with communicative activities that have recognizable boundaries. The three units suggested by Hymes (1972) are *situation*, *event*, and *act*.

The *communicative situation* is the context within which communication occurs. Examples include a religious service, a court trial, a cocktail party, an auction, a train ride, or a class in school. The situation may remain the same even with a change of location, as in a train, plane, bus, or car, or it may change in the same location if very different activities go on there at different times. A busy street corner at noon would not provide the same communicative context as that corner at midnight, nor would the auction place if closed for business, nor the site of a cocktail party when functioning as a family dwelling. A single situation maintains a consistent general configuration of activities, the same overall ecology within which communication takes place, although there may be great diversity in the kinds of interaction which occur there.

The *communicative event* is the basic unit for descriptive purposes. A single event is defined by a unified set of components throughout, beginning with the same general purpose of communication, the same general topic, and involving the same participants, generally using the same language variety, maintaining the same tone or key and the same rules for interaction, in the same setting. An event terminates whenever there is a change in the major participants, their role-relationships, or the focus of attention. If there is no change in major participants and setting, the boundary between events is often marked by a period of silence and perhaps change of body position.

Discontinuous events are possible, if one is interrupted and then resumed without change in major components. A conversation between student and professor in an office may be interrupted by a telephone call, for instance. The professor then participates in a different event with the caller, leaving the student on 'hold'. They may say 'Now where were we?' before resuming the first event, but participants can usually continue from the point of interruption. In this case the student has not been an active participant in the intervening event, generally looks elsewhere, and at least pretends not to listen. He or she has essentially left the situation, although physically still present.

Discovering what constitutes a communicative event and what classes of events are recognized within a speech community are part of doing ethnography of communication. The designation of some may be inferred from the fact they are given different labels in the language, and may be identified as categories of talk, but some are not neatly differentiated.

The *communicative act* is generally coterminous with a single interactional function, such as a referential statement, a request, or a command, and may be either verbal or non-verbal. For example, not only may a request take several verbal forms (*I'd like a cigarette* and *Do you have a cigarette?* as well as *May I please have a cigarette?*), but it may be expressed by raised eyebrows and a 'questioning' look, or by a longing sigh. In the context of a communicative event, even silence may be an intentional and conventional communicative act, and used to question, promise, deny, warn, insult, request, or command (Saville-Troike 1985). The same observable behavior may or may not constitute a communicative act in different speech communities. A burp at the end of a meal is not a communicative act if it is merely a sign of indigestion, but it is a communicative act in societies where one burps to symbolize appreciation and thanks for the meal; the way stones, shells, or bones configurate when thrown is considered communicative in many parts of the world, but they are not considered potential elements of commuication in others.

The study of speech acts within linguistic theory is the basis for this level of analysis, but must be extended to account for a broader range of phenomena within the ethnography of communication, and to allow for possible differences with regard to what segments of language are considered basic functional units by members of different speech communities.

The following examples illustrate the three different units of analysis:

First, a religious service is a communicative situation which might include these discrete events:

1 Call to worship
2 Reading of scriptures
3 Prayer
4 Announcements
5 Sermon
6 Benediction

Even though a single set of participants is involved (perhaps even a single speaker), and the setting and general purpose remain the same, the change between events is clearly marked by different ways of speaking, different body position for both leader and congregation, and periods of silence or musical interludes. Within the event labelled 'prayer', the sequence of communicative acts predictably includes the summons, praise, supplication, thanks, and closing formula.

It is possible for an event to occur which is outside the general configuration of activities in a religious service, but this will create a discontinuous situation and often be difficult to interpret. The event labelled 'announcements' includes introduction of visitors in one Washington DC church, and on an occasion when two visitors from the city of Dallas, Texas, were introduced, the minister asked them 'Do you know J.R.?' A question about a character in the TV program *Dallas* was so removed from the immediate context, that when the visitors had recovered from their surprise and responded, the minister signalled the resumption of the event with 'Well, now back to church'.

An elementary school class is another communicative situation. Discrete events in such a situation might include:

1 Pledge to the flag
2 Roll call
3 Collection of milk or lunch money
4 Show and tell (or 'sharing time')
5 Motivational activity (often background discussion of the topic to be studied)
6 Presentation of new information
7 Question and answer period
8 Transition period (changing groups, subjects, or teachers)

Although setting and participants usually remain the same, each event involves different ways of speaking and different rules for interaction. In bilingual classes, a shift in languages is often involved at event boundaries.

The 'pledge to the flag' is a ritual oath of allegiance to the United States, which is often repeated on ceremonial occasions, and sometimes included in the opening activities of each school day for students in kindergarten and elementary school. Students typically stand and place their right hands on their hearts, reciting the pledge in unison as a frozen routine.

'Show and tell' is a common performance event in classes for young children (the rules for appropriate speaking are discussed in Chapter 6). Hands must be raised to request permission to speak and strict turn-taking is observed, as it is for the question and answer period. This is not the case for collection of lunch money and transition periods, which are generally much more informal.

Acts within the event labelled 'roll call' are cyclic recitation of names by the teacher (functioning as requests for information about the presence or absence of each child) and responses by the students named. These responses may be verbal (often *here* or *present*), or may be in the form of a raised hand or bringing homework up to the teacher, depending on the specific classroom procedure that has been established.

'Roll call' is also a discrete event in other situations, including military and prison contexts, and in memorial services for the dead; each would be described and analyzed as a separate 'situated event' (Malinowski 1923), and then compared and contrasted for more general patterns. The common English label used for the events suggests that we consider them the same in some significant respects, but such classification of kinds of communicative events is culture-specific.

CATEGORIES OF TALK

As with the identification of communicative events, labels used by a speech community for categories of talk provide a useful clue to what categories it recognizes and considers salient. The elicitation of labels is one aspect of ethno-semantics (also called ethnoscience, ethnographic semantics, and new ethnography).

As a procedure to discover categories of talk, on various occasions when verbal interaction is observed, the ethnographer may ask an informant the equivalent of 'What are they doing?' Frake (1969) provides an excellent example in his study of the Philippine Yakan. Their native categories of talk elicited in this manner include *mitin* 'discussion', *qisun* 'conference', *mawpakkat* 'negotiation', and *hukum* 'litigation'. Frake then analyzes each of these categories in terms of their distinctive communicative features, which in this case contrast on the dimensions of focus, purpose, roles, and integrity (the extent to which the activity is perceived as an integral unit).

In a collection of studies on categories in the domain of political oratory (Bloch 1975), ethnographers have elicited labels as part of their procedure for segmenting and organizing political activities into meaningful units for analysis. A listing of some of these illustrates the diverse dimensions along which such units occur: the Melpa speakers in Mt Hagan, New Guinea, reportedly categorize types of oratory as *el-ik* 'arrow talk' or 'war talk' (the most formal), *ik ek* 'veiled speech' or 'talk which is bent over or folded', and *ik kwun* 'talk which is straight' (Strathern 1975); categories of talk in Malagasy include *resaka* 'informal conversation' or *teny andavanandro* 'everyday talk' or *teny tsotra* 'simple talk', and *kabary* 'ceremonial speech' (Keenan 1975); communicative event labels for the Maori of New Zealand include *mihimihi* 'greeting speeches', *whai koorero* 'exchange of speeches', and *take* or *marae* 'discussion of serious matters' (Salmond 1975); and labels for speech acts in Balinese include *mebetènin ngeraos* 'self-abasement', *nyelasang* 'statement of common knowledge', *ngèdèngang pemineh pedidi* 'statement of current speaker's opinion', and *nyerahang tekèn banjar* 'commitment to follow what the assembly decides' (Hobart 1975). Listings of category labels in English include *conversation, lecture, oratory, gossip, joking, story telling*, and *preaching*.

Categories of talk in each language have different functional distribution, and most are limited to a particular situation, or involve constraints on who may speak them, or what topic may be addressed. Their description is thus of interest not only because of the linguistic phenomena which distinguish one from another, but also because these categories may provide clues to how other dimensions of the society are segmented and organized.

Since we cannot expect any language to have a perfect metalanguage, the elicitation of labels for categories of talk is clearly not adequate to assure a full inventory and must be supplemented by other discovery procedures, but it is basic to ethnography that the units used for segmenting, ordering, and describing data should begin with the categories of the group which uses them, and may include, but should not be limited to, the a priori categories of the investigator (see Wierzbicka 1985).

LANGUAGE AND CULTURE

The intrinsic relationship of language and culture is widely recognized, but the ways in which the patterning of communicative behavior interrelates with that of other cultural systems are of interest both to the development of general theories of communication, and to the description and analysis of communication within specific speech communities. Virtually any ethnographic model must take language into account, although many relegate it to a separate section and do not adequately consider its extensive role in a society. The very concept of the evolution of culture is dependent on the capacity of humans to use language for purposes of organizing social cooperation.

There are still questions regarding the extent to which language is shaping and controlling the thinking of its speakers by the perceptual requirements it makes of them, or the extent to which it is merely reflecting their world view, and whether the relationship (whatever it is) is universal or language-specific. There is no doubt, however, that there is a correlation between the form and content of a language and the beliefs, values, and needs present in the culture of its speakers. The vocabulary of a language provides us with a catalogue of things considered important to the society, an index to the way speakers categorize experience, and often a record of past contacts and cultural borrowings; the grammar may reveal the way time is segmented and organized, beliefs about animacy and the relative power of beings, and salient social categories in the culture (cf. Hill 1988; Taylor 1987; Whorf 1940; Witherspoon 1977).

Hymes suggests a second type of linguistic relativity which sees in grammar evidence not only of static social categories, but also of speakers' social assumptions about the dynamics of role-relationships, and about what rights and reponsibilities are perceived in society. While the first type of linguistic relativity claims that cultural reality in part results from linguistic factors, Hymes contends:

> people who enact different cultures do to some extent experience distinct communicative systems, not merely the same natural communicative condition with different customs affixed. Cultural values and benefits are in part constitutive of linguistic relativity. (1966b:116)

The interrelationship of patterns in various aspects of culture is pervasive enough in many cases for us to call them *themes*, or central organizing principles which control behavior. Opler (1941) exemplifies this concept with the Apache theme of male superiority, which is realized in patterns of communication as well as in religious and political domains. At tribal meetings, for instance, only a few older women may speak before all of the men have been heard, and it is very unusual for a woman to pray out loud in public. The Manus of New Guinea have been characterized in part as having an anti-sex theme in their culture: there are no purely social dances, no love songs, no romantic myths – and no word for 'love' in their language (Mead 1930).

Where directness or indirectness are cultural themes, they are always language-related. As defined in speech act theory, *direct acts* are those where surface form matches interactional function, as 'Be quiet!' used as a command, versus an *indirect* 'It's getting noisy in here' or 'I can't hear myself think', but other units of communication must also be considered.

Indirectness may be reflected in routines for offering and refusing or accepting gifts or food, for instance. A *yes* or *no* intended to be taken literally is more direct than an initial *no* intended to mean 'Ask me again'. Visitors from the Middle East and Asia have reported going hungry in England and the United States because of a misunderstanding of this message; when offered food, many have politely refused rather than accept directly, and it was not offered again. English speakers have the reverse problem in other countries when their literal *no* is not accepted as such, and they are forced to eat food they really do not want.

An indirect apology is illustrated by Mead (1930), who reports a situation where a Manus woman fled to her aunt's home after being beaten by her husband. His relatives, coming to retrieve her, engaged her relatives for an hour of desultory chatter about such topics as market conditions and fishing before one made a metaphorical reference to men's strength and women's bones. Still without saying a word, the wife joined the husband's relatives in their boat, and returned with them.

The use of metaphors and proverbs is a common communicative strategy for depersonalizing what is said and allowing more indirectness. Criticism is often couched in this form, as when chiefs of the San Blas Cuna Indian tribe of Panama express opinions in metaphoric songs (Sherzer 1974; 1983), or when an English speaker reproves another with 'People who live in glass houses shouldn't cast stones'.

Joking is also a common way of mitigating criticism that might not be acceptable if given directly. This has reached the level of art in Trinidad, where ritual verbal protests culminate in the song-form of the calypso. 'It is a means of disclaiming responsibility for one's words. It is only because the norms of the event are shared by members of the community – political leaders included – that many a calypsonian does not end up with a law suit filed against him' (Sealey).

At the level of the grammatical code, using passive rather than active voice, or using impersonal pronouns, are yet other common means of indirectness, Talmy (1976) illustrates the difference this may make in directness with his example of a Yiddish story in which a boy invites a girl to the woods. In English, she would have to respond with embarrassingly direct pronouns, *I can't go with you. You'll have to kiss me.* In Yiddish this is avoided with a nonspecific pronoun, *Me torništ geyn ahin. Me vet zix vein kušn.* 'One mustn't go there. One will want to kiss another.'

While it may be easier to be indirect in some languages than others, communicative patterns are not necessarily tied directly to language forms. The native speaker of Arabic, Yiddish, Farsi, Indonesian, or Japanese often uses English more indirectly than does a native speaker of English, for instance. There is no intrinsic reason that the structures and vocabulary for one language cannot be used in many domains of communication within other speech communities to express the cultures of those communities, and in ways in keeping with their rules of appropriate behavior. As it is developed and used creatively as an auxiliary language in Nigeria, India, and elsewhere in the world, English becomes 'Englishes' (Kachru 1980; 1986) in the enactment of different cultural values and beliefs.

Although language is unquestionably an integral part of culture, to assume specific cultural experiences and rules of behavior as invariable correlates of specific linguistic skills is a naive oversimplification of the relationship of language and culture. The issue of their relationship is one which pervades the whole of the ethnography of communication.

COMMUNICATION AND SOCIAL STRUCTURE

The role of language is not the same in all societies, but it often includes the identification or marking of social categories, the maintenance and manipulation of individual social relationships and networks, and various means of effecting social control.

The relationship is not a static one, but varying and constitutive in nature. Social categories are primarily part of the social system, but also become embedded in the language system as it is used to mark them; the use and valuation of the linguistic markers in turn may affect the nature and persistence of the categories themselves.

Societies vary in the extent to which communicative behavior is bound up with the definition of social roles. In some, such as that of the Cuna Indians of San Blas, Panama, speaking ability is an integral and necessary part of role achievement and validation (Sherzer 1974; 1983). In others, communicative ability may have little or no significance in terms of roles, although certain social categories (such as age and sex) may be marked by characteristic communicative behavior. Also, societies may recognize distinctive role types, such as Abrahams' (1983) 'man of words' in Black culture, which are defined primarily in terms of communicative behavior.

There are many in US society who feel that language markers help perpetuate inequalities in the social system, and that language can be changed to eliminate the inequality. It is felt, for instance, that using generic terms like *policeman* rather than *law enforcement officer*, or calling all doctors *he* and all nurses *she* perpetuates occupational inequality between men and women by influencing thought and perception. Some feel that the way to break down social categories is to break down the language distinctions that mark them; others feel that the symbols would only be replaced by new ones unless the underlying social structure is itself changed in some more basic way. Still others believe that changing labels may have little effect on present beliefs and values, but will prevent their being transmitted as readily to the next generation.

Similarly, there is widespread belief in both the United States and England that speaking nonstandard English is a causal factor in the low economic status of large segments of minority group populations, and that learning 'good' English will automatically erase class boundaries and prejudice. This view is epitomized in Shaw's *Pygmalion*, where Henry Higgins succeeds in changing Eliza Doolittle's social class status by changing her speech patterns.

Major changes in categories in the social structure, as in social revolutions, usually entail change in communicative patterns as well. Movement to the political left may be accompanied by changing terms of address or titles and pronominal forms to symbolize class leveling (cf. Brown and Gilman 1960; Fang and Heng 1983; Paulston 1976). Since the communist revolution in Cuba, a rural, once nonstandard variety of Spanish has become prestigious, and the variety once considered an educated standard has been disparaged and devalued, although to be sure, differential pronominal distinctions are creeping back into Hungarian, and the Indonesian language, originally adopted as more democratic than Javanese, has developed the capacity to make most of the same social distinctions.

Change in language use caused by changing ideologies is illustrated by the decline in Cuba of such exclamatory terms as *Jesús* and *Dios mío*, which are now used almost exclusively by the older generation. This change is attributed to the influence of Marxist attitudes towards religion. Another illustration of this relationship is the ban on the Bavarian greeting *Grüss Gott* during Hitler's reign in Germany.

The effect of social change on language use is clearly evident when we contrast a sociolinguistic domain such as address terminology among Mandarin Chinese speakers in Mainland China and in Taiwan. On the basis of interviews with students in the US from both locations, Jin (1987) found two significant differences in current patterns of address. During the Cultural Revolution in Mainland China (1966–78), the use of *tongzhi* 'comrade' largely replaced professional titles. The usage has diminished with subsequent social change, however, and *tongzhi* is now used only with (1) strangers, (2) those whose occupations are unknown, and (3) those whose occupations carry no title and with whom the speaker is not familiar. It is also noteworthy that while the introduction of *tongzhi* served to neutralize male–female distinctions (in accordance with political ideology), the gender distinction has been reintroduced with the invention of *nu tongzhi* 'female comrade' and *nan tongzhi* 'male comrade'. A more recent change is in the use of *shifu* 'master' as a general title in Mainland China, contrasted with a narrower use of the term in Taiwan to refer to individuals who actually teach skills (such as a locksmith or a Kungfu instructor). *Shifu* is apparently beginning to replace *tongzhi* when addressing members of the working class in Mainland China, in order to signal their higher position.

The differences found in norms of address terms between Mainland China and Taiwan thus reflect differing social organization and political values, while the far more extensive similarities suggest there is still more shared culture. The changes within Mainland China in recent years are evidence of the responsiveness of language use to the dynamics of social development, even within a relatively short time span.

The wider acceptance in US society of male–female cohabitation without marriage, and increased recognition of the validity of homosexual relationships, has been accompanied by pressure for change in the English language. A major etiquette problem of our day, judging from letters for advice submitted to such newspaper columnists as Ann Landers and Miss Manners (*Washington Post*), may well be what term of reference to use for the person with whom someone lives, but is not married to. *Mistress* is considered condescending, *boy friend* or *girl friend* childish, *partner* too businesslike, and *roommate* confusing. *Consort* makes Miss Manners 'think of Prince Philip walking three paces behind', and *coviviant* of someone 'who will only cook on copper pots', and so the problem continues. The response that it should not be necessary for people to declare their sexual affiliation is sociolinguistically naive; if the relationship does not have a label, others cannot be sure of how to interact appropriately.

The White House Conference on Families in 1980 began with arguments over the definition of *family*, which were never resolved. Much of the controversy focuses on whether or not the term refers to homosexual as well as heterosexual relationships, an issue of profound social and legal consequence. One case which went to the US federal appeals courts charged discrimination against a male alien because his 'marriage' to a male citizen was rejected for giving him immigrant status. Some social changes have been made by changing terminology, and with beneficial effect, as when the American Psychiatric Association officially did away with all *neurosis* by voting the word meaningless.

The maintenance and manipulation of social relationships are importantly served by greeting events in many communities, which for first encounters may include questions about

family, income, occupation, place of origin, or where one
went to school. This is usually interpreted as 'friendly'
behavior, but it also provides information for assignment of
the new acquaintance to a social category. What is considered
'appropriate' interactional behavior is largely determined by
such categorization.

The first questions traditional Navajo speakers ask another
on meeting are usually 'What clan are you born of?' and
'What clan are you born for?' in order to place that person in
the network of existing relationships, and to know how to
behave appropriately, including how to speak and what terms
of address to use. When Navajo language instruction was first
implemented in bilingual kindergarten and first grade classes
by the Bureau of Indian Affairs, a number of parents were
interviewed to find out what they considered most important
for their children to learn about the Navajo language that
they might not already know. Without exception, every
parent responded that most important would be how to ask
and respond to questions about clan membership, since many
children would encounter people from outside the family unit
for the first time on school entry, and there could be serious
social and religious consequences if they did not know how to
behave appropriately.

Language most obviously serves a role in social control by
providing a medium for telling people directly what to do, but
it also allows for such indirect control forms as threats, curses,
teasing, and gossip. One of the strongest control forms in
many societies is silence, or 'shunning', which is also part of
the communicative system.

Stories told to children are often intended to control their
behavior: Aesop's fables in Western tradition, Anancie tales
of Africa, Monkey tales of Japan, Coyote stories of North
American Indians, and Uncle Remus stories of New World
Blacks all serve this function, as the Trickster's antisocial
behavior focuses attention on the social norms, and allows for
the verbalization of morals and collective group wisdom.

Rights and responsibilities involved in such systems as law,
medicine, and religion cannot be fulfilled without language.
Its importance is perhaps most clearly seen in situations

where the social systems are thwarted because of a breakdown in communication. A man who was jailed in the state of Illinois, for instance, could not be tried because he could not hear or speak. He had to be taught sign language first so that he could defend himself. More problematic are people on trial in a speech community other than their own, or through the medium of a language in which they lack fluency, who may be equally unable to defend themselves.

Language also serves in social control by the way it is used in politics. Much attention has been given to the thought control potential of 'Newspeak' in George Orwell's *Nineteen Eighty-Four*, and a standing committee of the National Council of Teachers of English in the US is devoted to 'Doublespeak'. It gives annual awards for paticularly flagrant euphemistic or evasive language use by government agencies or representatives to justify or minimize the impression of negatively-perceived actions, such as 'terminate with extreme prejudice' (meaning 'to kill') and 'collateral damage' (meaning 'civilian casualties during war') (Shearer 1988). During the Nazi regime, the Office of the Press in Germany issued 'Language Regulations' stipulating the terms to be used or abandoned in newspaper reporting, or redefining them: e.g. on 14 January 1937, 'According to the new government, the term "propaganda" is a legally protected one, so to speak, and cannot be used in a derogatory sense. . . . In short, "propaganda" only if it serves us; "agitation" for those who are against us' (Mueller 1973:31).

A different dimension of the effect of patterns of communication on political thought and activity has been explored extensively by Maurice Bloch (1974), whose general thesis is that political language should be studied as a preliminary to studying politics, that the intentions of speakers may be inferred by the implications of the type of speech they use.

Bloch distinguishes between formal language and informal language, or formal speech situations and everyday speech situations, and their relative degree of social control. When a speech event is formalized, there are fewer options for participants; thus, as language becomes more formalized, more social control is exerted on participants. In formalizing a situation, the propositional content, the logic, is essentially removed. What is said is accepted because it is the right thing to say, and not because it is true or false. Bloch and others claim that in societies where there is more emphasis on ritual events, there is less freedom and more direct control than in societies where there is less emphasis on ritual. The control may be in both directions, controlling those in authority as well as those being governed: i.e. the speaker also gives up some freedom in ritual, even if he has power.

Ritual events are much more likely to be important to closed social groups than to those that are open. In making this point, Douglas (1970) contrasts the lack of ritual among the mobile Ituri pygmies of Africa (cf. Turnbull 1961) and the Basseri nomads of Persia (cf. Barth 1964b) with the pervasive ritual activity among the Navajo, which demands exact ordering in fixed cermonial events (cf. Aberle 1966).

Both Bloch and Douglas relate the formal–informal communicative situations to the ritual and anti-ritual in types of religion, and to Bernstein's (1971) distinction between positional and personal family structures and their relation to strong boundary maintenance and weak boundary maintenance in education. According to them, Bernstein's restricted code is appropriate in a ritualized situation where the context is highly coded, roles are rigidly delineated, meanings are local and particular, and there is a small range of alternative form. An elaborated code is appropriate in a less structured context where meanings must be made more explicit, and speakers have a wide range of choice. The restricted code serves the social function of control as well as communication, and creates solidarity. Bloch and Douglas interpret Bernstein's general distinction as essentially one of context, with the structural characteristics of the two types of code in any one speech community a matter for investigation: 'the distinction between restricted and elaborated codes must be relative within a given culture or within the speech forms of a given group' (Douglas 1970:77).

The relationship of social structure and communication patterns suggests dimensions for a typology of speech communities which might allow the analysis and display of patterns at a more abstract level, and thus contribute to general theory of communiction. I earlier suggested a 'hard-shelled' versus 'soft-shelled' dimension with reference to the degree of permeability in the boundary of a speech community; Douglas's closed versus open social group distinction refers to degree of group cohesiveness, and Bloch's formal versus informal dimension to degree of individual freedom. All of these are related, and relate in turn to the distinction Bloomfield (1927) makes in the types of interaction which take place in primitive groups and literate societies because of different levels of shared experience. Since there are groups which are both 'primitive' and open (such as the pygmies of Ituri), and literate and closed (such as the Japanese), to claim communicative patterns and social structure are in-variable coordinates would again be an oversimplification of the relation of language and culture.

ROUTINES AND RITUALS

Linguists are very interested in man's ability to be creative with language as part of defining competence, but also in how, when, and why man chooses *not* to be creative, to repeat what has been heard and said many times before, often in exactly the same form. The relation of ritual to social control has already been discussed, but the general nature of routines and rituals requires further consideration.

Linguistic routines are fixed utterances or sequences of utterances which must be considered as single units, because meaning cannot be derived from consideration of any segment apart from the whole. The routine itself fulfills the communicative function, and in this respect is performative in nature. Such communication essentially defines the situation.

Routines must be learned, as well as analyzed, as single units, although they may vary in length from single syllables (*Hi*) to phrases (*How do you do, April fool*, and *Have a nice day*) to a sequence of sentences (the well-rehearsed pitch of a door-to-door salesman). They may be uttered by an individual, or require cooperation between two or more persons, as in a greeting sequence or minister/congregation alternation in the reading of scriptures.

Non-native speakers of English often complain that native speakers do not really care about the state of their health when they ask *How are you?* The non-natives are not recognizing that this question is part of a greeting routine, which by nature has no meaning apart from its phatic function in communication. If English speakers *really* want to know how someone is feeling, they repeat the question after the routine is completed, or they mark the question with contrastive intonation to indicate it is for information, and not part of the routine.

Understanding routines requires shared cultural knowledge because they are generally metaphoric in nature, and must be interpreted at a non-literal level. They include greetings, leave takings, curses, jokes, condolences, prayers, complements, and other formulaic language. Sneezes, hiccoughs, or other involuntary noises may require routines to repair the situation, as may simultaneous talking or spontaneous silence in a group. In Japan or Korea, a sneeze means someone is talking about you, and many English speakers say *Bless you* to a sneezer because of traditional beliefs that it is the soul or spirit escaping, or a sign of illness. Someone who hiccoughs in Germany makes a wish, and in Puerto Rico, a common response is 'Did you steal something?'

Speech communities place differential value on knowledge of routines versus creativity on the part of individual speakers, with oral versus literate traditions a significant factor (cf. Tannen 1979a), along with degree of formalization and ritualization of other aspects of culture. English speakers are often quite opposed to routines and rituals at a conscious level, because they are 'meaningless' and depersonalize the ideas expressed. One occasion where a prescribed routine is considereed too impersonal is the bereavement of a friend; condolence therefore often takes a form of *I don't know what to say*, which has itself become a routine. This contrasts sharply with other speech communities where fixed condoling routines are considered an essential component of funerary ritual.

Ritual is made up of routines, but these are given far greater cultural significance for being part of a ritual context, rather than everyday encounters. Its context bound nature was noted by Malinowski (1935), who found in studying ritual that the meaning of symbols could not be interpreted in isolation, but only in the context of the meaning of the ritual situation. This observation creates serious problems for any discipline of autonomous semantics, which requires individual units of meaning to carry a semantic load in themselves. On the other hand, because the total meaning is already known to the group from the context, we can explain why it is the case that even though 'the receiver of a ritual message is picking up information through a variety of different sensory channels simultaneously (and these over a period of time), all these different sensations add up to just one "message"' (Leach 1976:41).

Magical incantations provide one example of ritual: the language is fixed, and the linguistic formulae themselves are expected to exert some control over the supernatural. Parts of a spell have no meaning uttered by themselves; the whole must always be recited in full to have effect. Paralinguistic features of production are clearly differentiated from 'normal' language, with spells often recited in a sing-song manner, and with distinctive rhythm and pitch.

Comparable to the sing-song of magical incantation, intoned speech (or 'wailing') is common for expressing grief, and both intoned speech and chanting are often used in religious rituals. These varieties of language are on a speech-song continuum, with the song end of the continuum used in more formal contexts (Bloch 1974).

As routines often mark the boundaries of speech events by opening and closing them, rituals serve as boundary markers for major changes in social status: puberty rites, weddings, funerals, and graduation ceremonies. Perhaps the most important characteristic of routines and rituals is that truth value is largely irrelevant. Their meaning is dependent on shared beliefs and values of the speech community coded into communicative patterns, and they cannot be interpreted apart from social and cultural context.

UNIVERSALS AND INEQUALITIES

It is precisely because the ritual use of language encodes cultural beliefs and reflects community social organization that it has been of primary interest to ethnographers, but this has led to the criticism that the field has focused on the ceremonial or 'special' uses of language to the neglect of more everyday communication.

Bloch (1976) asserts that nonritual communication has much more in common cross-culturally, while ritual communication reflects 'strange other ways of thinking', which may explain why such researchers as Levi-Strauss, Geertz, and Douglas stress differences in systems of classification which link systems of cognition to social structure, while such researchers as Berlin and Kay find universal criteria for classification. The former concentrate almost exclusively on ritual communication, the latter on nonritual. 'Only concentrating on the picture of the world apparent in ritual communication obscures the fact of the universal nature of a part of the cognitive system available in all cultures' (Bloch 1976:285).

The nature of language cannot be described or explained without both perspectives. Hymes considers the type of explanatory adequacy proposed by Chomsky and that of a socially constituted linguistics to have complementary goals:

Chomsky's type of explanatory adequacy leads away from speech, and from languages, to relationships possibly universal to all languages, and possibly inherent in human nature. The complementary type of explanatory adequacy leads from what is common to all human beings and all languages toward what particular communities and persons have made of their means of speech. (1974:203)

To be sure, the ethnographer is concerned with such constructs as a universal framework of conversational maxims (cf. Grice 1975), but as working hypotheses against which conversational patterns in different speech communities may be tested and compared rather than as facts. Keenan (1976) has reported that speakers of Malagasy regularly violate the maxim to 'be informative', for instance, as do Kaingáng speakers in Brazil (Kindell), and undoubtedly speakers of many other languages. In fact, in many communities (including the most technologically advanced societies) '. . . it may be one's obligation to lie, successfully, or avoid giving pertinent information' (Hymes 1987:222). The degree to which Grice's maxims hold in a particular community, and in relation to what particular sociocultural conditions, is important for the ultimate understanding of all human communication as well as for descriptions of conversational patterns in particular communities.

Similarly, while there is a finite general set of functions which language may serve in a society, and it is indeed universal that language serves a plurality of functions in each community, it is fundamental to the ethnography of communication that research begin from the perspective that *functions are problematic rather than given*. Hymes contends

> that the role of language may differ from community to community; that in general the functions of language in society are a problem for investigation, not postulation. . . . If this is so, then the cognitive significance of a language depends not only on structure, but also on patterns of use. (1967:116)

It is quite probable that some aspects of language function will prove to be universal, although perhaps in a hierarchy of importance which is relative to particular communities, but this remains a topic for empirical investigation. Clearly in multilingual societies, different languages often serve differential functions, and a single a priori assumption regarding Language might obscure enlightening sociolinguistic data.

A related issue which this raises is that of the inequality of languages: not all languages are equally capable of serving the same functions in a society. This assertion violates most pronouncements of linguists made during the last half century that all languages are adequate as communicative systems for members of a social group, but it will be accepted by most administrators concerned with education and economics in developing countries. While all languages are inherently capable of expressing all concepts and fulfilling all functions, they have evolved differently through processes of variation, adaptation, and selection. The fact that each language may retain the *potential* to serve all functions does not alter this conclusion.

> The official preference is to stress the potentiality of a language and to ignore the circumstances and consequences of its limitations. Yet every language is an instrument shaped by its history and patterns of use, such that for a given speaker and setting it can do some things well, some clumsily, and others not intelligibly at all. The cost, as between expressing things easily and concisely, and expressing them with difficulty and at great length, is a real cost, commonly operating, and a constraint on the theoretical potentiality of language in daily life. (Hymes 1973:73)

It therefore remains central to our concerns to describe what a community has made of its language, and why, and how – not only as part of our scientific inquiry, but because one of the responsibilities and motivations of a socially constituted study of language is the welfare of its human speakers. Ethnographers, who by the nature of their perspective reach beyond the 'facts' of observable behavior to interpret meaning/culture, have an ethical responsibility to the 'subjects' of investigation.

The question of inequality is also raised with respect to the degree to which individual speakers are competent in the language(s) of their group. The concept of possible 'semi-lingualism' (cf. Cummins 1979) in some language contact situations is rejected by many on philosophical grounds, yet it may be one of the social problems to which findings from ethnography of communication may be applied. Bloomfield in a study of the North American Menomini noted:

White-Thunder, a man around forty, speaks less English than Menomini, and that is a strong indictment, for his Menomini is atrocious. His vocabulary is small; his inflections are often barbarous; he constructs sentences of a few threadbare models. He may be said to speak no language tolerably. His case is not unknown among younger men, even when they speak but little English. (1927:437)

We are thus concerned with the obsolescence and loss of ways of speaking as well as with their development and maintenance. Of central interest will be the community's attitudes towards these phenomena, and ultimately the potential applications of our findings in furtherance of its goals.

3

Varieties of Language

Within each community there is a variety of language codes
and ways of speaking available to its members, which is its
communicative repertoire. This includes 'all varieties, dialects
or styles used in a particular socially-defined population,
and the constraints which govern the choice among them'
(Gumperz 1977). Any one speaker also has a variety of codes
and styles from which to choose, but it is very unlikely any
individual is able to produce the full range; different
subgroups of the community may understand and use
different subsets of its available codes.

The means of communication used in a community thus
include different languages, different regional and social
dialects of one or more of the languages, different registers
(generally varying on a formal-informal dimension which
cross-cuts dialect dimensions), and different channels of
communication (e.g. oral, written, manual). The nature and
extent of this diversity is related to the social organization of
the group, which is likely to include differences in age, sex,
and social status, as well as differences in the relationship
between speakers, their goals of interaction, and the settings
in which communication takes place. The communicative
repertoire may also include different occupational codes,
specialized religious language, secret codes of various kinds,
imitative speech, whistle or drum language, and varieties used
for talking to foreigners, young children, and pets.

Identification of the varieties which occur in any community
requires observation and description of actual differences in
pronunciation, grammar, lexicon, styles of speaking, and
other communicative behaviors which are potentially available

for differentiation, but it must ultimately depend on the discovery of which differences are recognized by members of the group as conveying social meaning of some kind. In addition, the communicative repertoire of a group includes the variety of possible interaction strategies available to it. These are most commonly used to establish, maintain, or manipulate role-relationships. Speakers' choices of interaction strategies provide a dynamic connection between the language code, speakers' goals, and the participant structure in specific situations.

LANGUAGE CHOICE

Given the multiple varieties of language available within the communicative repertoire of a community, and the subset of varieties available to its subgroups and individuals, speakers must select the code and interaction strategy to be used in any specific context. Knowing the alternatives and the rules for appropriate choice from among them are part of speakers' communicative competence. Accounting for the rules or system for such decision-making is part of the task of describing communication within any group, and of explaining communication more generally.

The concept of *domain* developed by Fishman (1964; 1966; 1971; 1972) is useful for both description and explanation of the distribution of means of communication. He defines it as:

> a socio-cultural construct abstracted from topics of communication, relationships between communicators, and locales of communication, in accord with the institutions of a society and the spheres of activity of a speech community. (1971:587)

Factors determining domains may thus include the general subject area under discussion (e.g. religion, family, work), the role-relationships between the participants (e.g. priest–parishioner, mother–daughter, boss–secretary), and the setting of the interaction (e.g. church, home, office).

No fixed set of domains can be posited a priori for all speech communities, since the set of activities which will constitute a cluster of purpose, role-relations, and setting will be culture-specific. Different levels of *focus* have also proved to be salient in different communities: e.g. societal–institutional (family, school, church, government) versus social–psychological (intimate, informal, formal, intergroup). These levels tend to coincide (family with intimate, for instance, and church with formal), but provide an interesting additional dimension for investigation (Fishman 1971).

Topic is often a primary determinant of language choice in multilingual contexts; bilinguals have often learned about some topics through the medium of one language and other topics through the medium of the second, and thus only know the vocabulary to discuss a topic in one of their languages, or feel it is more 'natural' to use one language for a particular topic.

Linguists from non-English speaking countries who were trained in an English-medium university provide a good example: they sometimes continue to discuss, lecture, and publish about linguistics in English, often even when their students are not fluent in that language. This may be because they do not know the necessary terminology in their national language, or because they have come to believe it is more appropriate to use English to talk about such subjects as grammatical analysis, and even to use English examples rather than their own Chinese, Arabic, or Japanese.

In bilingual education programs in the United States, native speakers of other languages find it easier to teach in English if they themselves are products of English-only education. For this reason, university training programs are recognizing the need to teach methods and content area courses in the language the teachers will be teaching the subject in. Some teachers have asserted it is impossible to teach a subject like American History in languages other than English because 'only English can be used to express American concepts'. A similar belief is held even more strongly by many Navajo teachers, that Navajo history and culture cannot be taught adequately in English. In this case, the Navajo language is believed to be so integrally related to the culture that religious beliefs must be understood in order to know how to use the language correctly, and the beliefs can be fully expressed only in Navajo.

In addition to topic, appropriate language choice may depend on *setting* (including locale and time of day) and *participants* (including their age, sex, and social status). A bilingual child may regularly use English at school with a grandmother if she has come to observe the class, and English at home with the teacher if he or she has come to visit.

Choice of varieties within a single language is governed by the same factors. Speakers may select from among regional varieties in their repertoire depending on which geographic area and subgroup of the population they wish to express identity with, or as they travel from one area to another. On a paralinguistic dimension, whispering is likely to be chosen for conversation in a church, or when the topic is one that should not be overheard by others, while shouting may be chosen for greeting out of doors, and from a distance. Shouting may be an appropriate choice even in this setting only for males under a certain age, and only when greeting other males of the same or lower age and status, or with other restrictions (including perhaps time of day). Choice of channel may depend on environmental conditions: drums may be used in jungle regions, signal fires where there are barren bluffs, and whistle languages or horns where there is low humidity. Choosing oral or written channels is usually dependent on distance, or the need for a permanent record.

Choice of register depends on the topic and setting, and also on the social distance between speakers. The possible complexity of levels of formality may be illustrated by different forms which would be chosen in a single speech event, a Japanese woman offering tea. According to Harumi Williams, the act of offering a cup of tea in upper- and middle-class homes demonstrates how Japanese place each other in society, and so requires careful choice of language forms and manner of speaking. The hierarchy of forms used with addressees of lower to higher status is usually as follows:

1 *Ocha?* (to own children) [tea]
2 *Ocha dō?* (to own children, friends who are younger
   than self, own younger brothers and sisters) [tea
   how-about]
3 *Ocha ikaga?* (to friends who are the same age, own
   older brothers and sisters) [tea how-about (polite)]
4 *Ocha ikaga desu ka?* (to husband, own parents, own
   aunts and uncles, husband's younger brothers and
   sisters) [tea how-about (polite) is Q]
5 *Ocha wa ikaga desu ka?* (to own grandparents) [tea
   topic how-about (polite) is Q]
6 *Ocha ikaga deshō ka?* (to husband's elder brothers
   and sisters) [tea how-about (polite) is (polite) Q]
7 *Ocha wa ikaga deshō ka?* (to teachers, husband's
   parents, husband's boss, husband's grandparents)
   [tea topic how-about (polite) is (polite) Q]

Williams reports that ranking varies with such factors as
how often she sees the people, and the level of respect form
used for her husband would be different if the marriage were
miai 'arranged marriage' rather than *renai* 'love marriage'.

Nonverbal alternatives are also important in this event:
when tea is offered in a Japanese *tatami* room it should not be
offered standing, but standing is appropriate if the room is
Western style. If there is a picture on the tea cup, the picture
side should face the receiver; the cup should be held with the
right hand on the body of the cup and the left supporting the
base. When offering tea to people ranking higher than her
own husband, a woman should bow slightly. Vocally,
increased formality not only involves choice of higher level
respect forms, but a higher pitched voice. In general, the
longer the sentence, the more polite; but the most honorific
expression is silence, which would be the appropriate choice
when offering tea to a guest of a very high position in the
society.

The choice of appropriate language forms is not only
dependent on static categories, but on what precedes and
follows in the communicative sequence, and on information

which emerges within the event which may alter the relationship of participants.

Rules for language choice are usually not consciously formulated by native speakers, as they are in the Japanese example above, and must be inferred by the ethnographer from a variety of observation and interview techniques (which will be discussed in Chapter 4). Essentially, the questions of language choice we are seeking answers to are: who uses what (variety of) language; with whom; about what; in what setting; for what purpose; and in what relationship to other communicative acts and events. Relating patterns of language choice within a speech community to these dimensions of context is discovering and describing rules of communication.

DIGLOSSIA AND DINOMIA

The clearest example of language choice according to domain is *diglossia*, or a situation in which two or more languages (or varieties of the same language) in a speech community are allocated to different social functions and contexts. When Latin was the language of education and religious services in England, for example, English and Latin were in a diglossic relationship.

The term was coined by Charles Ferguson (1959), who used it initially to refer only to the use of two or more varieties of the same language by speakers under different conditions. He exemplified it in the use of classical and colloquial varieties of Arabic, Katharevousa and Demotike varieties of Greek, Haitian Standard French and Creole, and Standard German and Swiss German. In each case, there is a high (H) and low (L) variety of a language used in the same society, and they have the following relationship:

1 There is a specialization of function for H and L.
2 H has a higher level of prestige than L, and is considered superior.
3 There is a literary heritage in H, but not in L.
4 There are different circumstances of acquisition; children learn L at home, and H in school.

5 The H variety is standardized, with a tradition of grammatical study and established norms and orthography.

6 The grammar of the H variety is more complex, more highly inflected.

7 H and L varieties share the bulk of their vocabularies, but there is some complementary distribution of terms.

8 The phonology of H and L is a single complex system.

Diglossia was extended by Fishman (1972) to include the use of more than one language, such as the situation in Paraguay where Spanish is the H language of school and government, and Guaraní is the L language of home (cf. Rubin 1968). Since the term diglossia refers to language distribution in the whole society and not in the usage of individuals, the fact that only a relatively small percentage of the population of Paraguay speaks both H and L does not affect the designation; only those who speak Spanish have traditionally participated in education and government, although this situation may be changing with the advent of bilingual education. To distinguish societal and individual language distribution, Fishman suggests a four-way designation; both bilingualism and diglossia, diglossia without bilingualism, bilingualism without diglossia, and neither bilingualism nor diglossia.

Regional distribution is not a determining factor in identifying a diglossic society. French and Flemish are in complementary regional distribution in Belgium, but each is used for a full range of functions in each part of the country; this is characterized as bilingualism without diglossia. The situation in Paraguay is characterized as diglossia without bilingualism.

Most (but not all) of the features by which Ferguson characterized monolingual diglossia are also true of multilingual situations. There is a comparable specialization of function for H and L languages; the H language generally has more prestige; and L is learned at home and H at school. Also, although the L language in a multilingual society may well have a literary heritage, tradition of grammatical study and established norms and orthography, these often are not known to its speakers in a diglossic situation. The only clear

differences between monolingual and multilingual diglossia
are those that relate to the structures of the codes themselves:
i.e. the relationship of their grammars, vocabularies, and
phonological systems.

Because our interest in communicative behavior includes
not only language structures, but also the social and
cultural systems which govern how they are used, I have
added the concept of *dinomia* (Saville-Troike 1978), which
translates roughly from Greek as 'two systems of laws'. There
are clear analogies between language domains and choice,
and cultural domains and choice, and obvious parallels with
language in the appropriate use of cultural rules, and in
switching between alternative cultural systems. The minority
culture first learned by many Spanish speakers in the United
States, for instance, is comparable to the L variety of a
language in a diglossic situation, and the dominant US
'mainstream' culture to the H variety of a national language.
Just as with L and H language varieties, the L culture is
generally learned by children at home, and H at school; the H
culture has more prestige in the society than the L; and there
is a specialization of function for H and L. Dinomia may thus
be defined as *the coexistence and complementary use within
the same society of two cultural systems*, one of which is the
dominant culture of the larger society and the other a
subordinate and less prestigious subculture from within that
same society. (See figure 3.1.)

Dinomia, like diglossia, is a societal state of affairs;
biculturalism, like bilingualism, refers to individual distribution. A society in which an entirely different set of cultural
norms governs behavior in home and school, for example, is
considered dinomic. This is the case in many African and
Asian communities where Western educational systems (often

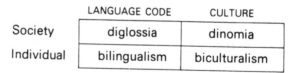

	LANGUAGE CODE	CULTURE
Society	diglossia	dinomia
Individual	bilingualism	biculturalism

Figure 3.1

including Western teaching and administrative personnel, as well as curriculum and instructional material) have been incorporated without adaptation into the indigenous cultures. This is also the case in the Navajo community, where the dominant US culture governs behaviors in most educational contexts, but a different culture governs behaviors at home (even though one language – either English or Navajo – may be used in both domains). Individual Navajos who are both bilingual and bicultural, and travel off the reservation, may change ways of speaking as well as language codes, including greeting forms, nonverbal behavior, and timing between questions and responses. A complete switch of rules for appropriate communicative behavior involves more than language; otherwise, the switch is only a partial one which identifies speakers as bilingual, but not bicultural.

Nonverbal aspects of communication are likely to prove more closely associated with dinomia and biculturalism than with bilingualism, since most individuals who can switch language codes with ease still use the gestures and proxemics of their native language, as well as its interactional strategies.

Part of my intent in coining the term 'dinomia' is to separate language code from patterns of use of the language code (and other means of communication) at the societal level; it is quite possible for language codes and rules of communicative behavior (as part of culture) to be distributed differently in the society. Fishman (1980) has accepted the analogy of *diglossia/bilingualism:dinomia/biculturalism* given here, but suggests a narrower concept would be more useful, which he terms *di-ethnia*. However, a concept relating to ethnicity is not coordinate with the *language:culture* distinction envisioned here. To adapt his suggestion in turn, one may find cases of biculturalism with or without dinomia, as well as dinomia with and without either bilingualism or diglossia.

CODE-SWITCHING AND STYLE-SHIFTING

Because of the proliferation of terms and inconsistent usage in the field, it is neccesary to begin any discussion of this topic with definitions. I have been intentionally vague in using *varieties* to indicate any patterned or systematic differences in language forms and use which are recognized by native speakers as being distinct linguistic entities, or 'different' from one another in some significant way. More precise distinctions must be made about types of varieties within any one speech community, but their nature cannot be presumed for all languages prior to investigation. *Variety-changing* would perhaps be a useful term to adopt in order to remain at this level of generality, but that is one term that has not yet been suggested by others, and I do not wish to add yet another to the catalogue.

We first require a definition of *codes*, by which I will mean different languages, or quite different varieties of the same language (comparable to classical versus colloquial Arabic, or Katharevousa versus Demotike Greek). *Code-alternation* (Gumperz 1976) refers to change in language according to domain, or at other major communicative boundaries, and *code-switching* to change in languages within a single speech event. *Style-shifting* will refer to change in language varieties which involves changing only the *code-markers*; these are variable features which are associated with such social and cultural dimensions as age, sex, social class, and relationship between speakers (discussed in the next section).

The distinction among these three types of code-variation is illustrated in the following sequence of speech acts (reported by Silverio-Borges) at the Cuban interest section office in an embassy in Washington, DC prior to official political recognition of the Castro government and full embassy status. To begin with, the receptionist is talking to a visitor in Spanish when the telephone rings. This *summons* marks a major boundary point, a change in events, and the receptionist changes to English (an example of *code-alternation*). The conversation begins:

1 Receptionist (R): *Cuban Interest Section.*
2 Caller (C): ¿Es la embajada de Cuba? (Is this the Cuban embassy?)
→3 R: *Sí. Dígame.* (Yes, may I help you?)

This is an example of the receptionist *code-switching* (→) from English to Spanish, changing languages within the same speech event, because she had identified the caller as a Spanish speaker.

> 4 C: *Es Rosa.* (This is Rosa.)
> ↓5 R: *¡Ah, Rosa! ¿Cóma anda eso?* (Oh, Rosa! How is it going?)

This is downward *style-shifting* (↓) from formal to informal Spanish as the receptionist identifies the caller as a friend, still in the same event. There is a shift to more marked intonation and faster speed, as well as use of the informal *¿Cóma anda eso?* rather than formal *¿Cómo le va?* or *¿Cómo está usted?* There is also a change to louder voice volume because the call is recognized as long distance, which may also be considered a kind of style-shifting. [I am introducing here an 'arrow convention' to distinguish between code-switching (→) and style-shifting (↑) or (↓), indicating shifts to higher or lower level, respectively.]

On another dimension, we may distinguish between *situational code-switching* and *metaphorical code-switching* (Blom and Gumperz 1972), a distinction which applies to style-shifting as well.

Situational code-switching occurs when the language change accompanies a change of topics or participants, or any time the communicative situation is redefined. Within a single conversation, Navajo teachers usually speak English to one another when discussing matters related to school, for instance, but may switch to Navajo to discuss their families, or rodeos and other community activities. They may also situationally switch into English if non-Navajo speakers join the conversation, so the new arrivals will not be excluded.

Style may also shift situationally within a conversation, perhaps as the addressee shifts from female to male, or adult to child, or with a shift in topic from personal to work-related: e.g. D. H. Lawrence employs style-shifting as a literary device to redefine situations in *Lady Chatterley's*

60   VARIETIES OF LANGUAGE

Lover as Mellors shifts from standard English to a 'broad Derbyshire dialect' with changes in topic and addressee (Shuy 1975a).

Metaphorical code-switching occurs within a single situation, but adds meaning to such components as the role-relationships which are being expressed. Since speaking different languages is an obvious marker of differential group membership, by switching languages bilinguals often have the option of choosing which group to identify with in a particular situation, and thus can convey the metaphorical meaning which goes along with such choice as well as whatever denotative meaning is conveyed by the code itself.

An example of such metaphorical switching was reported by Tuladhar, who described an event which occurred at a border checkpost between India and Nepal. A woman was stopped by the guard, accused of carrying too much tea, and threatened with a heavy fine. The woman first used Nepali (the official language) to make an appeal to the law, and to argue on legal grounds that she was within her limits of legitimate allowances. From the guard's accent in Nepali she inferred he was also a native speaker of Newari and switched into that language to make an entreaty on the grounds of common ethnic identity, an appeal to solidarity. She finally switched into English 'for formulation of thought above the system', which was both an implicit attack on the corruption of the system, and an assertion that she belonged to an educated class in society which had no intent or need of 'smuggling' across a few packages of tea. She consciously used code-switching as a verbal strategy in this instance, and was successful.

Even young children make use of the choices in their linguistic repertoire for a variety of communicative purposes. They commonly use intrasentential code-switching (i.e., code-switching within a sentence), for instance, to give additional force to part of an utterance, such as highlighting the object of a claim or the thrust of an insult. The following insults were uttered by two four-year-old boys, the first Korean and the second Chinese, each in talking to his younger brother:

1 *He is a* → *baba.*
        [idiot]
   (He is an idiot.) [Referring to a third Korean child
                      they were playing with]
2 *Ni shi* → *rug.*
   [you are]
   (You are a rug.)

In both of these cases, the child also knew the switched lexical item in the other language.

This strategy is in contrast to the intersentential code-switching (i.e., code-switching between sentences) that children often use to speak disparagingly about speakers of other languages who are within hearing when they do not wish them to understand. For example, a four-year-old Chinese girl spoke disrespectfully of two nearby nursery school teachers, knowing they did not understand Chinese:

3 *Tamen hao taoyan ei. Taoyande laoshi.*
   (They are very disgusting. Disgusting teachers.)

A final example of this strategy involved a twelve-year-old Korean boy who was speaking to his brother disapprovingly about an Icelandic girl who was trying to talk to him:

4 *Zigo mueonde?*
   (Who is she [to tell me]?)

Code-switching may be quite unconscious, and the fact of switching itself may be as meaningful in expressing a closer or more informal relationship as the referential content or specific language forms used. Blom and Gumperz (1972) report that speakers in Norway could not accurately recall their own changes between Ranamal, the local dialect, and Bokmal, the standard, and census takers in India have found segments of the population who are not even aware of being bilingual although they can converse in more than one language, depending on the addressee (Kachru 1977).

Metaphorical style-shifting occurs in such situations as

faculty meetings, where professors may address each other formally by title when making motions and conducting other official business, but shift to a first name level when trying to win the support of a colleague for their point of view. In some universities a ritual shift occurs at the end of a successful dissertation defense, when professors address the (former) student as *Doctor* and invite first names in return.

Metaphorical shifting may accomplish distancing as well as solidarity, of course, as when a German girl shifts from *du* to *Sie* with a boy to indicate the relationship has cooled, or when a wife calls her husband *Mr (Smith)* to indicate her displeasure.

Mohammed Abdulaziz (personal communication) reports policemen in Kenya switch from Swahili to Pidgin English to establish authority in a confrontation situation, and professors may switch into English if someone comes into their office at an inconvenient time. They may say in English, 'Oh, did we have an appointment at this time?', but different rules would be in operation if they used Swahili, and a referentially comparable expression would be considered rude. (If the visitor dropped by their house instead of their office, the professors would be constrained from switching into English, and would have no choice but to take time to visit.)

Yet another dimension to be distinguished is the scope of switching, or the nature of the juncture at which language change takes place (as illustrated in examples above). The basic distinction in scope is usually between *intersentential switching*, or change which occurs between sentences or speech acts, and *intrasentential switching*, or change which occurs within a single sentence. Some sociolinguists refer to the latter type as 'code-mixing', but I reject that term because of the pejorative connotation it carries that intrasentential switching involves a random or unprincipled combination of languages.

In conversations between Spanish and English bilinguals, Poplack (1979) reports half of the switching is of each type. The most common intrasentential switching involves the insertion of a single noun from the other language, and next in frequency is switching for such major constituents as full noun or verb phrases, independent clauses, or tag questions. Factors which influence the scope of switching in these data are sex (women favor intrasentential switching), age of acquiring the second language (those bilingual from early childhood used the highest percentage of intrasentential switching, those from adolescence or adulthood much less), and attitudes toward ethnic identity (positive feelings yield more intrasentential switching).

I have found intrasentential switching for nouns or noun phrases the most common form for Navajo–English and Chinese–English bilinguals. The following utterances were made by Navajo children (Saville-Troike 1980):

1 *The boy → łééchaa'í biłanné.*
    [dog   with-him-playing]
    (The dog is playing with the boy.)
2 *Table → yaa   sidá.*
    [under-it seated]
    ((He) is seated under the table.)
3 *Table → tł'ááhi → dollie → dóó → drum →*
    [under]   [and]
    sinił.
    [are (in position)]
    (The doll and drum are under the table.)

Switches at other constituent boundaries occur, but with much less frequency, e.g.

4 *Boy is → łééchaa'í yiłaané.*
    [dog   with-it-playing]
    (The boy is playing with the dog.)

Similarly, Chinese children typically switch to English for nouns and noun phrases or for unanalyzed chunks or routines, as in the following examples:

5 *Neige → fox → yao chi ta.*
    [that]   [want eat him]
    (That fox wants to eat him.) [Telling a story]

6   *Ta yong yi ge* → *picture of a fox.*
    [he use a]
    (He used a picture of a fox.) [Another child telling
                                      the same story]
7   *Clean up time* → *le.*
                [aspect marker]
    (It's already clean up time.)

Gunarwan recorded informal conversation among Bahasa Indonesian (I), Dutch (D), and English (E) trilinguals, including the following sentences:

1   (I) *Akan ada rapat* → (D)*van avond.*
    [will   be   meeting   this evening]
    (There will be a meeting this evening.)
2   (D) *Samengaan,* → (I)*yok?*
    [go-together   let's]
    (Shall we go together?)
3   (I) *Berapa   panjangnya* → (E)*this side?*
    [how-many length-the]
    (How long is this side?)
4   (I) *Jam berapa* → (E)*New Year's Eve's party* → (I)-*nya?*
    [clock how-many]   [the]
    (What time is the New Year's Eve party?)

The greatest number of his examples are also of switching for a noun phrase, but some are at other constituent boundaries (e.g. the tag in 2), and some even within words (e.g. the article in 4, which is a suffix). Gunarwan reports some utterances in which all three languages were used by the same speakers within a single turn:

5   (I) *Ini, ini.* → (D)*Tien* → (E)*centimeter.*
    [this this   ten]
    (This, this. Ten centimeters.)

6 (I) *Ee,* → (D)*Tante, je   hebt verkeerd*
    [hey   aunt   you have mistake
gedaan. → (I)*Kan harus begini.* → (E)*You see?*
made   ?   must like-this]
(Hey, Aunt, you have made a mistake. It should be
like this. You see?)

When the two languages used in intrasentential switching
do not share the same word order, an additional distinction is
needed between *guest* and *host* languages in an utterance
(Sridhar and Sridhar 1980; Nishimura 1986). The host
language is the one to which the basic grammatical structure
is assigned; elements of the guest language are switched into
it following placement rules of the host language. In the
following sentence, for instance, a child inserted an English
noun while maintaining Korean Subject–Object–Verb word
order (Korean–English examples from Oh 1988):

Na → *toy* → *chueyo.*
[me]   [give]
(Give me a toy.)

Korean is also considered the host language in the following
example, where a Korean inflection (s.m. = subject marker)
is attached to an English noun:

Bird → *-ga wasseyo.*
      [s.m. came]
(The bird came.)

The guest language component maintains its own integrity of
word order, as in the following sentence (in this case, Korean
is guest and English is host):

I'm → *ppalli wa* → *-ing.*
     [quick come]
(I'm coming quickly.)

The integrity of guest language structures is further illustrated in the following utterance by an adult Arabic speaker from Jordan, who was receiving technical training in electronics in the US (Al-Rusan):

Es → *circuit* → *lat ṭandhīm,* → *but you can bypass it*
[the]   [this regulator]
→ *bidūn mushkileh idha kān el* → *voltage* → *9adi.*
[without problem if was the]   [normal]
(This is a regulator circuit, but you can bypass it without any problem if the voltage is normal.)

There is need to distinguish further between code-switching and *borrowing*, in which lexical items from one language are adapted phonologically to the sound system of the other, and are frequently subject to is morphological inflections. If someone says *I'm going to Los Angeles* (pronounced as Anglicized [las ænjıləs]), the place name is a borrowing from Spanish. If someone says *I'm going to* → [*los ánheles*], using Spanish pronunciation, they are code-switching. Similarly, *He's going to work on one of the kibbutzes next year* includes a lexical borrowing from Hebrew because the term *Kibbutz* has been used with an English plural inflection. *He's going to work on one of the* → *kibbutzim* → *next year* is code-switching for some, because the Hebrew plural inflection is used along with the lexical item.

This is not an absolute distinction, because there are lexical borrowings in English such as *datum, data, alumnus,* and *alumni* where these have included the morphological inflection and they have been incorporated as exceptions in English grammar; this does not mean they involve code-switching into Latin. *Kibbutzim* is a borrowing in English for those who are not consciously using a Hebrew inflection. Speakers' attitudes about how 'native' a word is must be taken into account, as well as formal criteria. It is possible that a word which is a borrowing for the person speaking may be perceived as code-switching by the listener, or vice versa, depending on subgroup membership within the speech community. A New York may use Yiddish words like *schlemiel* and *schlok* quite natively, but the initial consonant sequence is considered non-English in most other parts of the country, and thus code-switching.

Intrasentential style-shifting occurs when the variety of language being used changes within a sentence, as in *Hi,* ↑ *Mr President*, where an informal greeting is followed by a formal term of address. A more extreme example is *Hey,* ↑ *Professor Smith,* ↓ *ain't ya'* ↑ *promulgating* ↓ *a gob of* ↑ *unwarranted presuppositions?*, which involves not only a shift in level of formality between greeting and term of address, but also in grammar and lexicon.

Unless it is being intentionally used for humorous purposes, such shifting is likely to be viewed negatively as 'style-slipping' by school teachers, particularly if it occurs in a written mode. In other languages, however, such intrasentential style-shifting may be quite appropriate. In Javanese (prior to World War II), for instance, there were at least three levels of 'status styles' encoded in both grammar and lexicon: *Krama*, the most formal and polite (H); *Madya*, intermediate (M); and *Ngoko*, informal (L). Since the choice of levels to be used depended not only on the relationship and relative status of speaker and hearer, but also on that of persons being referred to, a single sentence often contained words from different levels. If a speaker were using an H style to speak to a person of superior rank and said:

Dalem bade ↓ *kesah* ↑ *dateng* ↓ *gryanipun katja* ↑ *dalem*
H   H   M   H   M   M   H
(I am going to my friend's house.)

the forms referring to 'I go' and 'friend's house' would be shifted down to M. If he were using M style speaking to a friend and said:

Kula adjeng kesah teng ↑ *daleme pak guru.*
M   M   M   M   H   H   H
(I am going to my teacher's house.)

he would shift the forms referring to 'teacher's house' up to H (examples from Retmono 1967).

Some languages, such as Japanese, mark foreign words as such visually in their written form (using katakana rather than the usual hiragana symbols for Western borrowings, and kanji for Sino-Japanese), which adds another dimension to code-switching. Studies of code-switching have been limited almost entirely to the spoken channel of communication, but consideration should be given to written and nonverbal channels as well.

A number of linguists have suggested universal constraints on where within a sentence switching may occur (e.g. Berk-Seligson 1986; DiSciullo, Muysken, and Singh 1986; Sankoff and Poplack 1981; Woolford 1983). The fact that exceptions have been reported for almost all constraints yet posited (including examples of switching within a word, such as I have reported above) suggests that researchers who have focused exclusively on grammar may have been sociolinguistically naive in not taking the *contexts* of switching into account (cf. Lavandera 1980). Our emphasis here is on the variety of functions code-switching and style-shifting may have within a speech community: group identification, solidarity, distancing, and redefinition of a situation have already been mentioned. Additionally, switching languages may serve either to soften or strengthen a request or command, and saying something twice in different languages may serve either to intensify or to eliminate ambiguity. Jong A. Kiem reports that a superlative seems more powerful in Sranan than Dutch, for instance, and that a bilingual reduplication is used if something is really 'out of this world'. Morray provides the following examples for degrees of intensification in Sranan: *pikin* 'small'; *pikin-pikin* 'very small'; *pikin-tjoti* 'very, very small' ('small' in Sranan + 'small' in Hindi).

Switching may also be used for a humorous effect, or to indicate that a referentially derogatory comment is not to be taken seriously. It is also used for direct quotations, which may range from stereotypical imitative speech in joking to learned citations in Latin or Greek.

Switching may be used to make an ideological statement, as in the case of Mexican Americans referring to New Mexico as *Nuevo Mexico* [méhiko], or Texas as [téhas], in an otherwise English sentence. Not infrequently, such switching is employed by monolingual speakers of English or English-dominant bilinguals who wish to assert their Hispanic ancestry. A contrasting function was observed in Barcelona during a period of considerable tension between speakers of Castilian and Catalan (Woolard 1987). Code-switching by a popular entertainer there helped to ease group boundaries, serving for boundary-leveling rather than maintenance.

Switching may occur because of real lexical need, either if the speaker knows the desired expression only in one language, or if formulaic expressions in one language cannot be satisfactorily translated into the second. For this reason, native speakers of English who have learned some French, German, or Arabic continue to use such expressions as *savoir faire*, *macht's nichts*, and *inshallah*, respectively, in otherwise English sentences, and speakers of many other languages insert English *OK*.

One of the potentially useful functions of code-switching is to exclude other people within hearing if a comment is intended for only a limited audience, such as some of the children's insults I reported earlier. This may be considered rude, but it is not necessarily so. A Tanzanian professor residing in the United States, for instance, says that in the presence of guests in their home a husband and wife would employ code-switching for discussion concerning the comfort and needs of their guests. The exclusionary function was used by President and Mrs Herbert Hoover around the White House; they reportedly switched into Chinese when they did not wish to be understood by others. In such situations, the other language functions as a 'secret' language.

Code-switching is also used as an avoidance strategy, either if certain forms are incompletely learned in one of the languages, or if one language requires (usually because of pronominal selection) a social status distinction one does not wish to make. For this latter reason, many native speakers of Javanese find Bahasa Indonesian a useful post-independence, democratic alternative. For this reason, too, a speaker of a status-marking language such as Korean or Thai may switch to English with another speaker of that language when he or she prefers not to be deferential.

In some cases code-switching functions as a repair strategy, when the speakers realize they have been using an inappropriate code. This was a relatively frequent occurrence in Greece, during the period when liberal politicians trained in a rhetorical tradition which ranked Katharevousa over Demotike for formal speaking realized they were (ironically) using Katharevousa to advocate democratization of the national language. Shifting for repair is necessary when speakers realize they have begun an event, such as a telephone conversation, at an inappropriate stylistic level. The unitary nature of the telephone calling/answering routine is evident in the fact that such repair usually requires backing up to start over with a different greeting form, rather than switching or shifting in the middle of the routine.

Community attitudes toward switching and shifting are of interest for ethnographic description. These appear to be changing rapidly among English-speaking bilinguals in the United States, with the ability to code-switch becoming widely accepted as a symbol of ethnic viability and integrity. In the American Southwest poetry is being written, songs sung, plays performed, and formal speeches delivered in a Spanish-English mode. There are still diverse attitudes about the phenomenon, however, based on both age and political sentiment.

Whatever specific functions are served by code-switching within a community, it adds to the verbal strategies that speakers have at their command, and is to be recognized as a dimension of communicative competence.

CODE-MARKERS

The concept of code-markers is based on the distinction between *marked* and *unmarked* language forms first developed within the Prague School of linguistics. This distinction may be applied to all aspects of communicative behavior, and indeed has been adopted by ethnographers for more general descriptive and explanatory purposes. The basic assumption is that behavior can be distinguished as marked or unmarked according to certain component features, and that the unmarked is more neutral, more normal, or more expected.

In explaining the recognition and interpretation of different varieties of language within a speech community, it is necessary to assume that speakers have a concept of naturalness both for their language in general and in any specific context. Markedness on the more general level identifies language forms as belonging to a particular variety, such as regional dialect, register, or social category. Markedness in a specific context refers to usage which calls attention to itself, like an Australian variety of English being spoken in Canada, a formal register used in an intimate relationship, feminine gestures and interaction strategies used by a male, or adult language structures used by a young child.

Language forms must be perceptibly different in some systematic way to be recognized as distinct varieties. Variability in any aspect of a language may potentially serve a marking function, including vocabulary, pronunciation, grammar, paralinguistic elements, and visual appearance (in the case of written and manual forms). Variation in interactional strategies may also pattern along these dimensions. Different variables will be considered significant in each speech community, so no single set may be posited, and different aspects of language may mark different kinds of varieties within a single community. In American English, for instance, regional varieties are most marked by vocabulary and pronunciation features, but seldom by grammar; social class is most marked by grammatical features; ethnicity, sex, age, and personality most by pronunciation, paralinguistic features, and discourse strategies; and register most by vocabulary, grammatical complexity, and rhetorical organization.

It is possible that some kinds of linguistic features are inherently more suitable for signalling particular kinds of social meaning, but it remains a topic for empirical investigation. The lexical, syntactic, and rhetorical features marking register in English are more likely to be under conscious control than the phonological and paralinguistic features marking ethnicity, sex, age, and personality, and thus more likely to be available for manipulation. Since relative level of consciousness is related to both circumstances of acquisition and neurological factors, it is a possible universal.

Although some neurological factors are also involved in determining how much of a difference in language productions will be perceived by humans, no single degree of variability can be established as significant in all languages; very small differences in an absolute sense may carry a heavy load of social information, while major absolute differences may be socially meaningless. The difference between [s] and [š] is the shibboleth of Biblical days (Judges 12:4–6), which served a password function with mortal consequences, yet the same variation in Tonkawa (once indigenous to Texas) apparently carried no social weight, and may not have even been noticed, e.g. as in [maslak] versus [mašlak] 'white'.

The term *code-marker* as I am using it includes all variable features which are available to members of a speech community for distinguishing among the varieties in their communicative repertoire. It includes social markers (which mark such characteristics as social and educational status, occupation, and regional affiliation), physical markers (which mark such characteristics as age, sex, and physical condition), and psychological markers (which mark personality character- istics and affective states) (cf. Laver and Trudgill 1979).

In identifying and defining what a linguistic variable is, Labov (1972) distinguishes among three levels of these features, which he calls 'indicator', 'marker' (with a different meaning than that used here), and 'stereotype'. An 'indicator' is a variable which is not perceived at a highly conscious level in the speech community, although it does serve to mark varieties of language. The pronunciation of *caught* with the vowel [a] or [ɔ] for instance, is one regional marker in American English, but it does not carry much social significance. A 'marker' for Labov is a variable which has taken on social valuation, and is perceived at a conscious level. Voicing of the medial consonant in *greasy* is also a regional distinction in English, but one that has more social significance: the voiced variant generally carries a pejorative connotation toward the object being described for users of the [s]; the pronunciation is quite consciously perceived, and regional identity of the speaker inferred. The New York [r]-less variable described by Labov (1966) is also at this level, as is calling the evening meal *dinner* versus *supper*. Because this 'marker' level is conscious, such variables may be used for intentional metaphorical switching, while 'indicators' may not.

A 'stereotype' for Labov is the highest level of code-marking. It is likely to be commented on, and is used in characterizing groups when joking about them, but it need not conform to actual usage. Someone from Brooklyn (NY) may be characterized as saying *Toidy Toid (33rd) Street*, but that pronunciation is disappearing from actual use because of being heavily stigmatized. Similarly, French speakers when speaking English are stereotyped as saying *I sink (think)*, Texans as greeting everyone with *Howdy, pardner*, and Britishers as calling all men *chap*. Others in the speech community will recognize the group being referred to by such marking since this, too, is part of communicative competence, but it does not necessarily conform to linguistic reality.

Some code-markers are absolute, or *categorical* in their distribution, occuring only and always in a particular variety of language, but most are *gradient phenomena* which occur more or less in one variety than in another. It is not clear exactly how and to what extent native speakers interpret relative frequencies of market occurrence, but perception is undoubtedly conditioned by the relative importance of the social information its use conveys.

Determining the social meaning of code-markers is an important contribution of qualitative ethnographic research to variation theory, since 'Quantitative techniques can only sensibly be applied after a prior examination of the dependencies that a linguistic variable's significance has on other aspects of interaction structure and process' (Brown and Levinson 1979:333). An illustration of the contrastive meaning

which may be conveyed by alternating variables is found in
Huspek's (1986) analysis of *-ing* versus *-in'* in workers'
speech. Huspek found that *He went jogging* conveyed an
attitude of either respect or resentment toward the individual
being referred to, while *He went joggin'* conveyed lower social
status, but also ingroup identification. On the other hand, the
same linguistic variable may have different social meaning
depending on other features in the interaction situation, and
on other code-markers which may be present. The same
intonational variables which mark 'baby talk' signal warmth
and affection toward a young child, but may be interpreted as
mocking and demeaning if used with an older child or adult,
for instance, and the [r]-less variant which has negative
valuation when used by a working-class native of New York is
a marker of social prestige when it (along with the different
variants in vowel quality and lexicon) indicates the speaker is
an upper-class native of Boston.

Statistical analysis of frequencies and correlations may help
to verify or define certain tentatively identified relationships,
but in general the identification of hypotheses to be tested
regarding possible relationships should precede the application
of statistical techniques. Occasionally, however, quantitative
analysis will reveal previously unrecognized associations, or
will demonstrate regular patterns in data which seemed
amorphous.

The following sections of this chapter illustrate a number of
the social and cultural dimensions with which varieties of
language might be associated in a speech community, and the
range of communicative phenomena which might be marked.

VARIETIES ASSOCIATED WITH SETTING

Varieties of language which are more closely associated with
the setting or scene in which they are used than with the
people who are using them are usually included in the concept
of *register*, and distinguished from one another primarily on
the dimension of relative formality.

The physical setting of an event may call for the use of a

different variety of language even when the same general purpose is being served, and when the same participants are involved. English greeting forms may differ inside a building versus outside, for instance, or inside an office versus inside a church, as well as between participants at differing distances from one another. In this case, primary markers are voice level and nonverbal behaviors, but often also involve a choice of lexical and grammatical structures along a polite–casual, impersonal–personal, sacred–secular, or public–private dimension; all of these may be generally subsumed under formal–informal (Brown and Fraser 1979).

In question-and-answer exchanges between professor and students, appropriate language use is determined in large part by the setting, including the size of the room and the seating arrangement (e.g. chairs in fixed rows, in a circle, or around a conference table). In this case, different levels of formality are signalled primarily by whether or not students are expected to raise their hands and be formally recognized before speaking, and by whether or not strict turn-taking applies. Relative level of formality as determined by the setting will also affect how questions and answers are phrased, and what topics may be queried.

A formal greeting in a locker room would be considered a highly marked communicative event (especially if the partici-pants were not fully clothed), as would informal questions and interruptions by students in a large lecture hall. In these cases where level of formality in language use does not coincide with level of formality in the setting, language may serve to increase or decrease the distance between speakers. When physical distance cannot be maintained for some reason, such as in a crowded Japanese household where all four grandparents sometimes live with children and grand-children, very polite language (the highest form of *Keigo*) may be used to maintain social distance, even though a less formal variety of Japanese would normally be appropriate.

In some communities a particular setting is required for an event to take place: e.g. there may be a particular place in which it is appropriate to pray, or teach, or to tell stories, and these events are often concomitant with choice of different language varieties. Language restrictions or taboos are also often related to setting, such as constraints against talking about certain topics at the dining table, whistling in the house, or cursing in a place of worship.

VARIETIES ASSOCIATED WITH PURPOSE

Choice of language or variety of language according to purpose is included in the concept of diglossic speech communities as one aspect of the domain which determines appropriate selection but the marking of language according to the purpose for which it is being used is a much more inclusive phenomenon. Along a societal–institutional dimension, for instance, different varieties of language and patterns of language use serve religious, educational, and governmental purposes, as well as different occupations.

Language codes used primarily for religious purposes include Geez by Christians in Ethiopia, Latin by Catholics, Classical Arabic by Muslims, and Pali by Buddhists.

When a Japanese Buddhist priest in a California Buddhist church recites a *sutra* in Pali with his English-speaking congregation, this is a fine example of the spread of a particular language variety over enormous distances in space and time. When accounts of the Buddha and his sayings were collected and came to be accepted as the canon of Buddhist scripture, they were in a Middle Indo-Aryan language, Pali, whose exact provenience is not clear. When the Pali scriptures were used in worship in India and Ceylon, the language functioned as a special religious register in many speech communities where related Indo-Aryan languages were the worshippers' mother tongues. When Buddhism spread to areas such as Burma, Thailand, China, and Japan, the sacred scripture went along. Buddhist missionaries and scholars translated Pali and Sanskrit texts into other languages, but just about everywhere at least some uses of Pali were kept. In these new areas, the

Pali language, still functioning as a religious register, was no longer related at all to the language of the worshippers, but retained its aura of sacredness. (Ferguson 1978:3)

Brown and Levinson (1979) report that within the Arab world, distinctive dialects are used by different sects, e.g. Sunni and Shi'i followers in Bahrain speak different varieties of Arabic; and Hindus and Christians generally speak different dialects of Konkani in Western India (Ferguson 1978).

The use of glossolalia, or 'speaking in tongues', by certain charismatic Christian groups, also exemplifies language choice for religious purposes, although much of its meaning is conveyed through features other than verbal code (Goodman 1969). Certain language forms themselves are believed in some communities to be prescribed by a supernatural being and the only ones mortals may use for communication with that force, or they may be considered the medium through which the supernatural may speak to humans. In other cases the language forms themselves are considered embued with power, and they may be used to control the forces of nature.

When the same language is used in a community for both secular and religious purposes, the religious variety is often marked by more conservative forms: e.g. second person *thou*, *thee*, and *thy* in English. Other common markers are lexical (such as the use of different terms of address, or words used with unique meanings), morphological (often involving more deferential forms), paralinguistic (intoned speech, or different patterns of pitch, stress, and rhythm), and kinesic (head, hand, and body position and movement). Different channels of communication are often utilized, including bones, shells, horns, and drums, and receptive senses may be heightened or otherwise altered by drugs and trance states. Organization of discourse in religious events is frequently marked, including prescribed ritual openings and closings and the genre-specific 'one-many dialog, in which a speaker addresses the whole group and receives a unison response' (Ferguson 1986:209).

Some opponents of modernization of the English Bible believe that modernization ignores speakers' feelings that sacred beliefs are more appropriately expressed in a 'special' code rather than an everyday one, and that modernization thus reduces the capacity of English to serve aesthetic and religious purposes. Those who disagree often support Biblical language modernization on the grounds that religion should be accessible to each person without need for interpretation by others, and thus that its concepts are more appropriately expressed in the vernacular. Because the religious functions of language are not the same in all speech communities, any resolution of this controversy cannot necessarily be generalized to other societies.

A comparable issue in dispute is whether language used for such specialized purposes as curing, legal briefs, or contracts should be a 'special' variety, or 'plain' language. Specialized forms are required in many communities for curing rituals, including among the Rosebud Sioux, where a formal style of Lakota is used for such purposes.

> Labels for herbs, medicines and powers as well as prayers are uttered in the formal style because proper ritual prescriptions must be observed if the spirits are to respond as desired. Prayer is almost always spoken in formal speech, as supplication must be in the ritually prescribed form to be received. (Grobsmith 1979:357–8)

Sociolinguists studying doctor–patient communication in English (e.g. Pliskin 1987; Skopek 1975; Shuy 1974) document the misunderstanding which can result when technical medical terms are used, but many patients do not have faith in a doctor who 'doesn't talk like one'.

Specialized varieties of language are often used when the purpose is to be secretive, or to deceive. Argots have been created by criminals for secret communication among themselves since the days of the Roman underworld (Maurer 1940), and adolescents in many societies use a secret code comparable to Pig Latin in English, which involves permutation and addition of phonological segments. Most phonological changes intended to obscure various languages are quite simple. Of the secret varieties of Welsh which have been described, for instance, two involved merely inserting a vowel plus consonant in each sullable (Awbery 1984). These appear to have been quite widely used, while the distribution of one with a more complex structure seems to have been much more limited.

In a bar district of Addis Ababa, an Amharic argot which was created by school boys has reportedly been adopted by unattached young women for such purposes as 'concealing conversations and planning tricks at the customers' expense' (Demissee and Bender 1983:340). The pattern also primarily involves phonological substitution and duplication, but in this case there is in addition grammatical change, with occurrence of compound verbs in a form that does not occur in 'normal' Amharic.

Franklin (1977) describes three types of secret speech among the Kewa of New Guinea. *Ramula agaa* 'pandanus language' is used to protect people who travel in swamp forest areas where ghosts and wild dogs are present. People are instructed by their ancestors not to speak their 'normal' language, and to use a secret variety marked by special vocabulary. *Mumu ne agaa* 'whispering talk' is used whenever others within hearing of speech produced at normal volume are not supposed to know what is going on, as when the topic is trading, bespelling, or stealing something. *Kudiri ne agaa* refers to 'secret talk', or talk limited to insiders, such as cult initiates.

The first of these types is for external secrecy, known by all in the speech community and directed toward outsiders; the latter two are for internal secrecy, or inhibition of information flow within the community. Brandt (1977) describes these phenomena in Pueblo societies, where internal secrecy assures that no single member possesses all necessary information for the performance of rituals, and preserves the interdependence of subgroups in the social organization. Pueblo strategies for secrecy include: barring outsiders from performance of ceremonies in ritual spaces, such as kivas; constructing false and misleading information; evasion of questions; purging the language of Spanish and English loanwords in the presence of those who might understand them (sometimes requiring elaborate circumlocutions); use of special ritual varieties which contain archaic words, borrowings from other languages, and different semantic systems (i.e. different referents); and special styles of speaking, such as 'talking backwards'.

Secretive purposes may overlap with exclusionary ones for identification, as with teenage slang and 'CB (Citizens' Band radio) lingo'. The latter has been widely used by truck drivers in the United States for solidarity purposes, sharing information on road conditions, asking and giving directions, summoning help in case of emergency, and for trying to evade the common antagonist, the highway patrolman (called *Smokey the Bear*, and often seen driving a *plain blue wrapper*). Many drivers expressed considerable resentment during the mid-1970s when CB radio use became popular with thousands of 'outsiders', although they seem to have enjoyed the participation of the President's wife, Betty Ford, whose code name was *First Mama*.

Specialized language for governmental or academic purposes in most Western societies includes the extensive use of acronyms (often deliberately chosen for pronounceability) to designate administrative units: e.g. US *OBEMLA* 'Office of Bilingual Educational and Minority Language Affairs', British *CILT* 'Centre for Information on Language Teaching', Belgian *AIMAV* 'Association Internationale pour la Recherche et la Diffusion des Méthodes Audio-visuelles et Structuro Globales', Mexican *INI* 'Instituto Nacional Indigenista', Peruvian *CILA* 'Centro de Investigación en Linguística Applicada'. This pattern is generally tied to an alphabetic writing system: Chinese, in contrast, regularly selects elements for combination that are no smaller than what is represented by a single character, as in *Běi Dà* for *Běijīng Dàxué* 'Peking University'. In part, however, patterns are also related to political orientation. Since the communist revolution, the Russian pattern has been to use the first syllable of words rather than the initial letters; this pattern was used metaphorically by Orwell in *Nineteen Eighty-Four* for designating administrative units. The association of this linguistic pattern with a particular kind of political system is further illustrated by Cuba's change from an acronym to *Min Ed* 'Ministerio de

Educatión' with the rise of Castro to power. Further study of comparable patterns in other speech communities would be of interest, especially as they are related both to typological features of language structures and orthographic systems, and to sociocultural features of the society.

Specialized vocabulary and phrases must also be mastered in order to communicate about governmental functions and processes, as in US 'federalese': *zero-based budgeting, inhouse capabilities, RFP* (request for proposal), and *regs* (regulations). In one of the few quantitative studies on this topic, Chiu (1972) compared the frequency of words occurring in over 1,000 pieces of Canadian governmental correspondence with a number of word lists and found almost no overlap: e.g. the most common verbs in government writing were *make, attach, enclose, receive, require, appreciate* and *provide*, as opposed to Lorge's magazine count with *go, ask, say, come, make, know, get,* and *see*. All but one most common in government use are French/Latinate; Lorge's verbs are all Germanic. Grammatically, Chiu found administrative writing contains a much higher percentage of passives and modals than formal spoken English, and a much lower percentage of verbs in the simple present or progressive forms.

Lexical requirements are also quite specific to many occupational areas (including linguistics), which is one reason why training received through the medium of one language cannot be easily discussed in others. It is probably safe to estimate that no more than 3 per cent of the English lexicon can be considered immediately relevant to all of its speakers. Recognition of this has given strong impetus to development of programs and materials in ESP (English for Special Purposes) and Vocational English for non-English speaking adults who need to function immediately within a single occupational domain. These focus on developing competence in the narrow range of communicative activities which are most likely to be required (cf. Munby 1977; 1978; Widdowson 1973; Wilkins 1976; Bhatia 1987 (law); Maher 1986 (medicine)). Even within a single work place, however, there may be patterned lexical variation, as shown by Tway's (1975) study of language use within a pottery-making factory.

Different terms are likely to develop for the same object whenever there are spatial or social boundaries between types of work associated with it.

To paraphrase a point made earlier, while all languages may be inherently capable of serving all purposes which humans may ask of them, specific languages evolve differentially through processes of variation, adaptation, and selection. Speakers in different communities will have different purposes for using language, and a different hierarchy of purposes, and the way in which means of communication will be marked to serve these differential purposes is language specific. Study and description of one specialized use of language in a community must be related to the total means of communication if there is to be understanding of the patterning and interrelationship.

VARIETIES ASSOCIATED WITH REGION

Regional varieties of language develop as different norms arise in the usage of groups who are separated by some kind of geographic boundary. This is commonly in vocabulary, as when English speakers in New England carry water in a *pail* and those in Texas in a *bucket*, and in pronunciation, as when Navajo speakers call 'snow' *yas* versus *zas* on different sides of the Lukachukai mountain range. Grammatical markers associated with region are less common, but they do develop: e.g. English speakers in the south and south-eastern regions of the United States use such double modal constructions as *might could* and *might will*, which are rare or nonexistent elsewhere in the country.

As geographic boundaries increase in strength, so generally do the degrees of difference between speakers of the 'same' language. The very rugged terrain of the state of Oaxaca, Mexico, for instance, and the resultant difficulty in traveling from one village to another, is in large part responsible for the maintenance of 25 distinct languages in an area no larger than the US state of Indiana (*c.* 36,000 square miles). The major distinction in the colloquial Arabic spoken in Algeria is between sedentary and nomadic dialects, which although not a strict regional division, similarly reflects ecological influences in limiting interaction between subgroups.

Regional phonological and lexical markers have been studied in many languages as the result of research on dialect geography, but little attention has been paid to regional patterning in the other aspects of communication. One notable difference which has been studied in the United States is in naming practices, with southerners using double names (e.g. *Billy Joe, Billy Gene, Larry Leroy, Mary Fred*) and nicknames or diminutives, even in formal contexts (e.g. former First Lady *Lady Bird Johnson, Dr Billy Graham, President Jimmy Carter*); also *Bobby, Johnny,* and *Jimmy* are bisexual only in southern usage (Pyles 1959). Another regional difference is in terms of address: e.g. a southern man may call his wife or a female friend *ma'am* with no negative connotation intended, while a northern interpretation would be one of distancing, or implications that the woman is of a more advanced age.

Nonverbal behavior may also differ regionally, including facial expressions and the scope of body movements, but these patterns have received little attention as markers associated with regional varieties. Some nonverbal behaviors pattern regionally even across unrelated languages. The emblem for 'no' is a vertical head movement in Greece, Turkey, the Arabian Peninsula, and most of North Africa, for instance; Israel seems to be the one regional exception, using the horizontal head movement of the Northern European area. Other gestures which exhibit areal over genetic influence are those of greeting and farewell.

Although the development of mass communication and rapid transportation has done much to retard the forces of regional differentiation, local forces remain most powerful during the early years of language acquisition and hence are unlikely to be entirely offset. Furthermore, since these markers themselves serve a boundary function between a local group and 'outsiders', or provide a means of identifying people from 'home' when in another area, the differences may be accentuated (cf. Labov's 1963 report of linguistic change in Martha's Vineyard, which illustrates this process). The importance of this function differs from community to community, and is related to the value placed on being different or unique.

When several members of a group migrate to another area where the group is identified with higher or lower than average status, markers associated with their regional variety may become associated with social class. The stigmatized [r]-less variety of English used by lower-class Blacks in New York City as reported by Labov (1966), for instance, represents a subgroup immigration from the south, where that is a nonstigmatized regional pronunciation.

VARIETIES ASSOCIATED WITH ETHNICITY

A multiethnic speech community may pattern in several different ways with respect to language use: (1) subgroups in the community may use only their minority ethnic language(s); (2) minority group members may be bilingual in their ethnic language(s) and the dominant language; or (3) minority group members may be monolingual in the dominant language. In conditions (2) and (3), members of minority groups who identify themselves as such often speak a distinctive variety of the dominant language. These 'accents' are usually interpreted simply as arising from the influence of the ethnic language(s), and features indeed may be attributed to substratum varieties or to the mother tongue, but they may be maintained and cultivated (consciously or unconsciously) as linguistic markers of ethnic identity (Giles 1979).

In English, ethnicity markers are most likely to be at the levels of phonology, vocabulary, and overall style, since grammatical markers are more likely to be associated with social class and educational level on a standard-nonstandard dimension. One notable exception is the 'invariant *be*' of Black English, which is generally recognized as an ethnic marker (except by teachers in the schools, who misinterpret it as 'ungrammatical'); the use of a 'double negative' in English, on the other hand, is not considered a marker of Hispanic or

French ethnicity (although it is a grammatical feature in both mother tongues), but rather as nonstandard and uneducated usage.

Black English in the United States has been the best described ethnically marked speech, although linguists' attention has generally been limited to nonstandard varieties, and has failed to recognize the range of social levels within identifiably Black usage (Wright 1975; a notable exception is Baugh 1983). Black standard varieties differ from White varieties primarily in intonational features, and in the marked pronunciation of a few lexical items (including *particularly*, in which the penultimate syllable has secondary stress and an unreduced vowel). Other descriptions of ethnically marked speech include Indian English (Kachru 1976; 1983; Gumperz 1977), Gästarbeiterdeutsch (Dittmar 1977), Puerto Rican English (Wolfram 1973), and Chicano English (Ornstein-Galicia 1984). Ethnic markers also occur in American Sign Language, where Black signers in the south have developed some characteristics which are different from the signs used by Whites in the same region (Woodward 1976). Differences in signs are both lexical and phonological: Black signing has not shared with White signing the same changes with respect to centralization, symmetry, and morphological preservation.

Markers associated with ethnicity may include nonverbal features as well, including the side-to-side head movement of some speakers of Indian English, and the different eye contact patterns of American Whites and Blacks (cf. Harper, Wiens, and Matarazzo 1978).

Tannen (1981) discusses ethnic markers in conversational style, including differences in the use of questions, methods for getting and keeping the floor, topic cohesion, and the use of irony and humor. Dimensions of difference between New York Jewish and Los Angeles non-Jewish style in her study include relevant personal focus of topic; paralinguistic features of pitch, loudness, voice quality, and tone; pacing and timing with respect to other utterances; rate of spech; and choice of lexical items and syntactic forms. Analysis of narratives collected from different groups (e.g. Tannen 1980), provides additional interesting information on ethnic markers in patterns of language use.

Ethnic differences in style may be modified in accordance with the situation, of course, as may other variables. Baugh reports the perceptions of one of his Black constituents about an event which required consistent style-shifting when he addressed different participants:

> I'm in the middle cause I know them both. They are both my friends. . . . I have to talk to them [the whites] one way and then I have to turn back around and talk to them [the black girls] another way . . . and try to keep him [the white man] from feeling left out of this conversation, and the girls from feeling left out in the other conversation . . . so . . . it's kind of hard to sit in the middle of a situation like that. (1983:28)

Unlike using a foreign language, using an ethnically marked variety of language generally requires being born into group membership, unless the intent is to ridicule or joke (which indeed is often the case). One of the best sources of data on which ethnic markers are stigmatized and stereotyped is the imitative language markers used in telling ethnic jokes.

On the other hand, individual speakers born into the ethnic group – or the entire group membership – can generally succeed in eliminating all ethnic markers in their speech if they desire to fully assimilate to the dominant group, or they can develop both marked and unmarked varieties and shift between them depending on desired group identification in specific situations.

Changes which are occurring in Black varieties of both speech and sign provide good evidence for the types of social factors that are involved in ethnic marking. The speech of young Blacks appears to be diverging further from white speech than does the speech of Black adults. Bailey and Maynor (1987) attribute this increasing divergence to such social developments as migration to inner cities, economic stagnation, and residential segregation. Black youth are cultivating linguistic divergence as a vehicle for identification and solidarity. The sign language of young Blacks in the South, on the other hand, is converging with white forms.

Maxwell and Smith-Todd (1986) attribute this to the integration which has taken place in schools for the deaf; most deaf children learn sign language at school, rather than in home or community.

VARIETIES ASSOCIATED WITH SOCIAL CLASS, STATUS, AND ROLE

When describing patterns of language use in a speech community, determining what subgroups are accorded differential status and prestige, and understanding what criteria are used within the community for defining subgroup membership, must precede discovery of how the means of communication within the total linguistic repertoire may be differentially allocated according to social class, status, and role.

Social class may be defined primarily by wealth, or by circumstances of birth, or by occupation, or by other criteria specific to the group under investigation. If wealth is a criterion, this may be calculated in terms of money, or in terms of how many pigs, sheep, or blankets an individual or family possesses, or how much land they claim. Status is often largely determined by social class membership, but age or education may be more salient, or whether a person is married and has children. Role refers to the position(s) an individual holds which entails particular expectations rights, and reponsibilities vis-á-vis others in the society: e.g. chief, minister of education, head of family, friend.

In rigidly stratified communities social class membership is clearly defined, roles strictly compartmentalized, and associated varieties of language clearly differentiated. In such communities members of the lower strata have little opportunity to acquire 'higher' language forms. In more democratic communities individuals have a wider range of roles potentially open to them, and generally command a wider range of socially marked speech. Studies in the United States and Canada have shown that those who are upwardly mobile tend to adopt the variety of language spoken by the group just above them, often to the point of hypercorrection, although a social revolution may include the overthrow of prestige language forms as well as people who speak them.

The wider range of language available to higher social classes is exemplified by speakers of the East Godavari (India) dialect of Telugu (Sjoberg 1962). In this group only members of the upper class can use both formal and informal varieties, which are marked by two distinctive phonemic systems. This range relates directly to patterns of education, since the formal variety is learned only by those who attend school. For the same reaosn, written means of communication in many societies are available only to the upper class.

Most research on social class markers in language have focused on phonology and grammar, but other aspects of language may also be involved. There appears to be a social stratification in the use of color terms for women's fashion in English, for instance, with advertisements of clothes targeted for lower income groups using a limited set of color terms such as *blue*, *red*, *green*, *yellow*, and *purple*, perhaps together with the modifiers *light* and *dark*. Expensive clothes are advertised using a much greater variety of basic color terms: e.g. an advertisement from Saks Fifth Avenue included *rust*, *russet*, *camel*, *plum*, *wine*, *fuchsia*, *teal*, *sapphire*, *turquoise*, *emerald*, *seafoam*, *bone*, and *taupe*. A similar observation has been reported to me by native speakers of German, Spanish, and Arabic, although there is some disagreement over whether the diversity of color terms carries connotations of higher prestige or merely reflects the greater range of hues available in more expensive fabrics.

Individuals being trained to fill particular roles in a society may learn varieties that others do not: e.g. a Samoan 'talking chief' learns to use rhetorical forms limited to speakers in that role, and a boy who is expected to assume his father's role as curer, chief, or judge often learns the appropriate language forms in the process of informal observation, an opportunity which is not open to other children.

Roles are often marked by different pronouns or terms of address, and may require different levels of formality corresponding to different levels of prestige or deference which they are assigned. English-speaking rulers may refer to themselves with the 'imperial' *we*, for instance, and a French businessman was fined for addressing a policeman as *tu*. This was judged to be a 'rude' form of address to someone in that role (Eliason 1980). Such linguistic marking of a particular social role is to be distinguished from markers of the dyadic role-relationship of speakers, which will be discussed below.

Another linguistic characteristic of the rights and responsibilities inherent in some roles is the type of performative that can be uttered, and how others must respond. For example, *You're out* is felicitous only if spoken by someone in the role of baseball umpire, and *I hereby sentence you to . . .* only if spoken by someone in the role of judge (cf. Searle 1969).

Other markers of status and role include differential naming patterns for married versus unmarried women in many societies, and the Iranian practice of shaking hands with an unveiled woman, but not with one wearing a *chadour*. The function of clothing in signalling role or status is illustrated by all uniforms, whether nurse, police, or soldier (with auxiliary markings indicating exact rank). Complaints about nuns and priests abandoning religious garb generally reflect the uncertainty caused by the loss of signals of identity, which in turn help to structure appropriate interaction with them.

Change in status may be signalled linguistically, as with the change in name at marriage, or the change in the official term of reference for a person after he assumes high office and again after he steps down. Soon after Haile Selassie was deposed as emperor of Ethiopia, for instance, official references changed from 'king of kings' to merely 'king' (still used to distinguish him from other people with the same name). The choice of ways to refer to him constituted a conscious political statement at that time, as conservatives continued to refer to him with a respectful pronoun and the imperial title *janhoi*, radicals used an informal pronoun, and extremists used his former name *Teferi*.

The use of 'role-playing' techniques often allows a researcher to elicit informants' perceptions of the speech of people who are in the particular roles they pretend to assume. Children playing 'school' or 'house' often adopt the language markers they consider typical of teacher or parent roles, while adults asked to take the role of children use high voices and their perception of 'baby talk'.

A number of questions have been raised about the accuracy of judgements on social class and role which are based on linguistic markers alone, but several studies suggest they may in fact be quite reliable. Ellis (1967) for English found a correlation of 0.80 between the actual social class of speakers and the estimation of judges merely hearing them count from one to ten, and Shuy, Baratz, and Wolfram (1969) found considerable accuracy in social class identification of their Detroit sample based only on 30-second speech samples. Reviews of these and similar studies are available in Brown, Strong, and Rencher (1975) and in Robinson (1979); cross-cultural research is quite limited. Of interest is not only what markers are being perceived, but about beliefs people have in different speech communities about the relationship of language markers and social class and how these may affect both social organization and patterns of language use.

VARIETIES ASSOCIATED WITH ROLE-RELATIONSHIPS

While many aspects of language use consistently mark a particular role, the roles which individual speakers assume and the status they are accorded is generally dependent on their relationship to other participants in the communicative event. While the French court declared it 'rude' to call a man *tu* while he was in the role of policeman, for instance, it would be equally inappropriate for the same man to be addressed as *vous* if he were in the role of husband or friend. The relativity is clearly illustrated in Japanese, Javanese, Korean, Thai, and other languages which make extensive use of status-marking honorifics; the same speakers use different forms when speaking to someone in a superior versus someone in an inferior social position, even within the same conversation. These forms are not static markers of social class, but markers of the relative status of speakers in dyadic role-relationships.

In addition to choice of pronouns and use of honorific particles, which are well described in the literature (e.g. Brown and Gilman 1960; Tsujimura 1977), the relative status of speakers and their role-relationship may be marked in a variety of ways. Tyler's (1972) description of kinship terminology used by Koya speakers in India illustrates how choice of terms relates in a systematic way to both expectations and differences in contextual features; Nahuatl (Aztec) speakers in central Mexico use reflexive prefixes with causatives to imply respect for the person addressed or spoken of: e.g. 'he sleeps' is more politely expressed as 'he causes himself to sleep' (Sapir 1915); and Tzeltal speakers in Chiapas, Mexico use a sustained falsetto to express deference to the addressee (Brown and Levinson 1978).

Role-relationships may also be marked by the order in which participants speak, eye contact or avoidance, and body position. In a cyclic or interaction event with several people in sequence, such as greetings, introductions, or thanks, the order of address may mark relative deference or closeness. The cycle of Iranian families exchanging traditional New Year Greeting visits always begins with an early call of the youngest on the eldest relative, for instance, then the closest relative or friend, and then acquaintances, with the ordering considered an important sign of relative love and respect for each. The eldest in the family does not pay return visits until the third day or later in the celebration (Jafarpur).

Among the Sierra Popoluca (Mexico), women whisper to their husbands as a mark of deference, and children are expected to whisper when they are first learning to talk. This is an example of the 'powerless speech style' which women may adopt with men, children with adults, or ethnic minorities with majorities, and it marks a power relationship rather than the social categories of sex, age, or ethnicity (Giles, Scherer, and Taylor 1979). In conversation, subordinates more often pursue topics raised by those with superior status than the other way around, and superiors interrupt and touch more frequently (Zimmerman and West 1975). An example of similar status marking is reported by Goffman (1967), who notes that doctors touch other (lower) ranks as a means of showing support and comfort, but others consider it presumptuous to even return (let alone initiate) such contact with a doctor. The strategic selection of different linguistic forms for such functions as requesting or directing also indicates the nature of the role-relationship between speaker and addressee: i.e. pragmatic strategies are potential markers of social relationships (Brown and Levinson 1979).

In some speech communities particular role-relationships require that clearly distinct varieties of language be used, often involving avoidance or taboo in some respect. An aboriginal Guugu Yimidhirr man in Australia must use only a specialized vocabulary with his brother-in-law (Haviland 1979), for instance, and a Navajo man traditionally cannot speak directly to his mother-in-law, or even be in her presence. Furthermore, he cannot refer to her with the usual third person pronoun form, but employs a more remote fourth person to indicate deference and respect. Avoidance of personal names in some role-relationships is also found in several languages, for direct address and/or in reference. Subrahmanian (1978) reports this taboo is still observed in Indian villages, where women cannot mention their husband's name; this must be circumvented in census taking by asking neighbors.

Relative status in particular role-relationships often involves complex consideration of several factors and the relative importance of such characteristics as age, sex, occupation, kinship, and social class in the determination differs in different speech communities. Their relative salience is interesting not only for discovering patterns of language use in interaction, but as potential indicators of the communities' social organization and cultural values.

VARIETIES ASSOCIATED WITH SEX

A differential distribution of language resources by sex in a community is often associated with differential patterns of education and distribution of labor, including trade versus childrearing responsibilities. Males are more likely to be educated, and thus to control the formal and written varieties of a language. They are also more likely to be bilingual, both because of educational level, and because of mobility and contact in military encounters and trade. In Algeria, for instance, the only remaining monolingual speakers of Berber are women. Exceptions to this pattern occur in societies where women have equal opportunities for education, and possibilities for mobility without dependence on indigenous social structures (e.g. where there are no preferred cross-cousin marriages, or other family-arranged alliances), or in communities where women assume a primary marketing role (e.g. in Guatemala, where women take products to market and are most likely to be bilingual in Spanish and their native Mayan language).

In some communities, participation in certain kinds of events is restricted to a single sex, as where it is considered appropriate only for men to tell stories or preach; in others a particular mode of communication is restricted, as where only men whistle, or only women wail. The 'tuneful weeping' mode of northern India is used only by women, for instance (Tiwary 1975). Educated, urban women in that area are now refusing to accept this communicative role as one aspect of change in their social role in the community. A comparable shift among women in eastern Austria from German–Hungarian bilingualism to German-only is reported by Gal (1979) as a correlate of social change, including women's rejection of peasant life (and peasant husbands).

Some type of sexual differentiation in patterns of speech is likely, perhaps universal, whenever there is social differentiation between male and female roles. Linguistic markers associated with sex often include phonology: e.g. English-speaking women tend to use more socially prestigious speech forms than men (Labov 1966; Trudgill 1975), as well as higher pitch and more variable intonation patterns (Smith 1979); Boas (1911) found that female speakers of some Eskimo dialects used voiced nasals [n, n, ng, ng,] in final position, which corresponded to male stops [p, t, k, q]; and Sapir (1915) found Yana women unvoicing final vowels.

Morphological markers include different first person inflections used by men and women in the North American language Koasati (Haas 1944; cf. Saville-Troike 1988), reduplication for emphasis of a verb by Thai women versus the addition of *mak* by Thai men, and the sentence-final particle *ne* in Japanese used almost exclusively by female speakers (Smith 1979). Morphology may also be marked for the sex of the listener, as with the second person inflections of Hebrew, or the different terms for 'they' in the North American language Tunica depending on whether a man or woman is being addressed (Haas 1941). Based on data collected for the Linguistic Atlases of the Upper Midwest and the North Central States, Van Riper (1979) reports women at all levels of education use significantly more of the past tense forms prescribed as 'correct' in English usage handbooks than do men, although there is less difference between male and female speakers who have more formal education. Grammatical markers associated with sex in Japanese include affirmative and nonaffirmative usage of the copula, and differential use of interjections at the beginning and end of utterances; syntactically, women are more likely to use subject inversion and topic-comment constructions.

Lexical markers may also be associated with the sex of either speaker or listener: e.g. a Hopi woman would use a different term if expressing the concept 'That's a beautiful area' to a man than she would to a woman, and swear words in many languages differ not only with the sex of the speaker, but also with whether a member of the opposite sex is within hearing. Some English words, such as *adorable* and *lovely*, are associated more with women speakers, and *beautiful* and *handsome* more appropriately used in reference to females and males respectively.

Topics considered appropriate for discussion may also differ for men and women, as may form or content of insults or other speech acts. In a study of the topics of teachers' conversations in a US faculty room, for instance, Kipers (1987) found females most likely to talk about social issues such as child abuse and women's rights, and males about recreational and work-related activities. At the University of Illinois, in one department female graduate students lodged a formal protest that they were excluded from the opportunity for interaction with male faculty equal to that accorded male graduate students, because the principal topic of conversation was usually sports, with which they were less familiar than the males. Tiwary (1975) reports males in Northern India may insult each other by threatening the chastity of mother, sister, or daughter, while women assert the other's sexual activities with father, brother, or son, and curse each other with barrenness or widowhood. In English, a man is traditionally congratulated on the occasion of engagement or marriage, while a women is offered 'best wishes'.

Nonverbal marking associated with sex includes traditional male hat-doffing and handshaking in English, with handshaking between women or between men and women still generally interpreted as a statement of 'women's liberation', providing another example of sex differentiation in communicative patterns declining with the lessening of division in social roles. In Mali, where role distinctions are more strictly maintained. Bambara men also shake hands in greeting, but women never do; a female may kneel down when greeting a man, which is never done by males, and she may use only limited eye contact. Clothing markers associated with sex may be relevant to interpreting patterns of communication, including whether or not one or more participants are veiled. (Although this is usually associated with women, men are also veiled in the nomadic Atobak tribe of southern Algeria, and can show their faces to no one except their wives.) Whether women wear dresses or trousers may also be significant, as may whether members of a non-Western society wear traditional or Western garb.

The maintenance of clearly distinct male–female roles is also illustrated by the rules of speech such as those followed by Tamil couples, at least in rural areas of central Tamil Nadu: the husband can address his wife by her name, but the wife is expected to use a non-specific respect term; the husband uses a familiar verb inflection with his wife, while the wife uses the more respectful second person plural ending in return; and the wife is expected to give the 'right of way' to her husband in conversation with other adults (Britto).

Either men or women are often considered to be more polite or indirect than the other in their style of speech. For example, Keenan (1975) reports only men in Malagasy possess the valued skills of using metaphor and proverb, with women perceived as informal and direct, and Strathern (1975) finds Melpa women excluded from taking part in public verbal display because they cannot use 'veiled talk' and are always direct; on the other hand Laver and Trudgill (1979) report men use a higher percentage of direct imperative constructions in English when 'giving suggestions', while women use a higher percentage of more indirect interrogatives and tag questions. Some of the stylistic differences attributed to men versus women have not been corroborated in observational studies of actual usage, or yield contradictory evidence (cf. Smith 1979 for a review of studies on English), although the attitudes and expectations revealed even by unsupported stereotypes within a community are of considerable ethnographic interest, as are their social implications.

Also of interest are perceptions and attitudes regarding apparent violations, such as female markers used by males and vice versa. A Japanese female who uses less polite forms is considered 'rough', for instance, while a Japanese male who is too polite is 'effeminate', as is a Tunisian male who speaks a Parisian variety of French. Male speech considered imitative of women's is called 'sweet-talking' by Black Americans, on the other hand, and is quite appropriate for use in a courting situation without threatening male identity (Abrahams 1973).

Switching to a style of speech in which stereotyped features considered characteristic of the opposite sex are exaggerated may function as a marker of homosexual identity, or may be used in teasing or mocking the addressee by suggesting sexual deviance. The mocking signs used to refer to deaf homosexuals are touching the middle finger to the nose and flinging it back with a limp wrist, for instance, or by touching it to the tongue and then flattening the eyebrow (Rudner and Butowsky 1980). A general characteristic of American Sign Language which may also be interpreted as reflecting sex stereotypes is that signs associated with males are made on the forehead (as are those referring to intellect and decision-making), while those associated with females are made near the mouth (as are those for words of emotion and feeling, or for personal appearance).

Sex differences in language forms and patterns of interaction cannot be understood apart from situation and social factors. In all speech communities they are interrelated with setting, age, social class, education, occupation, and (perhaps most importantly) with the role-relationship of participants in the communicative event. Some aspects of the potential complexity are illustrated in the rules observed by a Mixe-Zoque family walking to market in Oaxaca, Mexico, as reported by O'Neill:

Women will walk three steps behind their husbands, or an elderly relative, as a sign of respect. If the head of the household is the eldest son (occasionally the child will be only six or eight years old), the mother will still walk about two steps behind the son. Grandmothers and elderly aunts are an exception to this rule. They are permitted to walk in front of the male head of a daughter's/niece's household. This deference is based on her age status, but the same grandmother must still walk the required number of steps behind her own husband.

A woman walking beside her daughter indicates her position has been elevated from childhood to adulthood. Usually, this occurs at the age of ten to twelve years.

The smallest male child will walk beside the grandfather in order to hear stories about the town and its people. The grandfather will also use this time to instruct the youngest child how to judge different character types – 'who is an honest man'.

The younger children frequently imitate the adults by arranging themselves in line so that the young male children will be in front of their sisters. The older sisters will usually push the smaller brothers back in line, and inform them that they should lead because they are older.

In this case it is proxemics, or social space, which serves to mark categories of sex, age, role, and status.

VARIETIES ASSOCIATED WITH AGE

In most speech communities, age is a major dimension for social categorization. Three kinds of markers associated with age should be distinguished: those which yield information about the speaker, those which yield information about the receiver, and those which yield information about the role-relationships between the two which are influenced by their relative age. Markers associated with young children as speakers, for instance, generally relate to developmental stages and processes in language acquisition. 'Baby talk' is associated with young children as receivers; it is characterized by the linguistic modifications which adults make when addressing young children, rather than direct imitation of child language forms. The use of baby talk is often associated with a caretaker role-relationship, and marks this relationship even if participants are not adult and young child: e.g. a young child (who does not speak baby talk with adults or peers) may use baby talk with a doll or infant sibling, or an adult may use baby talk with a small pet. Use of baby talk between adults may mark an affectionate relationship or be interpreted as insulting, depending on the context.

Baby talk is not part of the linguistic repertoire in all speech communities, but where it is, similar modification of adult language forms are to be found. In his characterization of baby talk in fifteen languages, Ferguson (1964) lists these shared features: processes of reduction (especially in phonology), substitution, assimilation, and generalization; repetition of words, phrases, and sentences; exaggerated intonational contours and deliberate articulations; diminutive affixes; and high pitch. A few alternative modifications have been reported for other languages, including using a relatively fixed word order and whispering in Quiché, a Mayan language of Guatemala (Pye 1986).

The actual effect of such modifications on child language

development is not clear, although there is some evidence children may attend better to baby talk (Snow 1972), and that its prosodic features may facilitate the acquisition of segmentation (Garnica 1977).

Beliefs about the appropriateness of baby talk and its relation to child language acquisition are of considerable interest. Among English speakers, baby talk is generally considered appropriate for females to use with children from birth to age three or four. The use of baby talk with a child approaching school age is considered potentially damaging to his or her emotional and linguistic development, both by parents and teachers. Children who use baby talk when they enroll in kindergarten or first grade are the subject of peer ridicule, and they almost immediately switch to more mature linguistic forms. Some English-speaking males use baby talk with young children, but father's language does not usually indicate the same caretaking relationship as does 'motherese' (cf. Gleason 1975; Gleason *et al.* 1977; Gleason and Weintraub 1978). This difference may diminish with the middle-class trend to share childrearing responsibilities; Gleason (1976), for instance, does not find significant differences in the speech of male and female day care attendants, although she reports that English-speaking children taking the role of father when playing with dolls typically do not use baby talk, but use a 'gruffer' voice quality and a greater percentage of threats and imperatives than when they play 'mother'.

In addition to linguistic forms, communicative phenomena associated with young children include beliefs about the appropriateness of children listening to or participating in coversations among adults, beliefs about what topics should be discussed by them or in front of them, different terms of address used by them and for them, and expectations regarding their nonverbal behavior.

The elderly in a society may be accorded higher status and greater deference, or they may be considered less competent. General ways in which deference for age may be marked are listed by Silverman and Maxwell (1978): spatial (special seats), victual (given choice foods), linguistic (addressed in honorifics), presentational (special posture assumed in their presence), service (housekeeping performed for them), presentative (given gifts, or having the right to sing certain songs), and celebrative (ceremonies held in their honor).

The view that they are less competent may be conveyed by others talking to old people in a loud voice and at a very slow rate, assuming they are hard of hearing and losing mental faculties (Helfrich 1979), or the elderly may be recipients of demeaning caretaker behavior similar to that used with children: e.g. a son or daughter may order meals for them in a restaurant, or speak about them in the third person when they are present.

Some of the speech markers associated with age relate to physiological change, but many more are stylistic in nature, or reflect the different status or roles of speakers which relate to age. Some markers may also be the result of language and culture change, but we cannot assume that age-grade differences in a speech community indicate diachronic processes until their relation to the life cycle has been explored. An American's age may be marked by saying *ice box* rather than *refrigerator*, for instance, or *Negro* rather than *Black*, reflecting actual shifts in usage. However, in some languages it may be the case that a different term is appropriate for an older person to use, and that the young person who uses one term today will change to the other at age fifty or so.

One very interesting age marker has been reported by Gardner, who says the Paliyans of south India 'communicate very little at all times and become almost silent by the age of 40' (1966:398). There has been speculation that elderly speakers of English employ different strategies for topic switching than younger speakers, and that they pause longer in narratives or conversations without giving up the floor. Helfrich (1979) reports age differences in a speaker's preference for action-oriented style (verbs dominating) or qualitative style (adjectives and nouns dominating), but few studies have yet been done which identify markers associated with speaker age other than those dealing with child language development.

VARIETIES ASSOCIATED WITH PERSONALITY
STATES AND 'ABNORMAL' SPEECH

Markers associated with personality states include some that
are physiological in nature, as well as some that are socially
determined. Even among the former, however, there may be
culture-specific constraints and interpretations that are of
interest for the ethnography of communication.

The most extreme examples are probably markers associated
with psychotic states, such as schizophrenia. Language is
considered by some psychologists to be such a reliable
indicator of this disease that purely verbal measures have
been said to prove valid in diagnosis and judgements of
severity (Gottschalk and Gleser 1969). The content of a
doctor–patient interview is analyzed in terms of (1) theme
(unfriendly, hostile, avoidance), (2) inaudible or unintelligible
remarks or words, (3) illogical or bizarre statements, (4)
repetition of phrases or clauses, and (5) questions directed to
the interviewer. Linguistic analysis can also be used to
distinguish false and genuine suicide notes. Gottschalk and
Gleser report that in genuine notes, the percentage of
references to others is less than 14 per cent, and the
percentage of references to inanimate objects is greater than 1
per cent. This procedure predicts 94 per cent of the genuine
notes and misidentifies only 15 per cent of the false ones, as
judged by whether the writer of the note actually attempts
suicide. Other themes are also related to personality disorders.
We consider depressed people laconic; they talk about self-
deprecatory and morose topics. Manic people are verbose,
and talk about achievements and frequent superficial contacts
with people.

Although comparable features may be found in other
languages, the resulting diagnosis/interpretation cannot be
generalized. Mental illness is culturally defined, and behavior
a person may be institutionalized for in one society may be
considered 'normal' in a second, and valued as supernaturally
determined in a third.

Children may be characterized as 'good' or 'bad' at least

partly in terms of their language use, not only in terms of the employment of politeness rules and 'proper' vocabulary, but even in features of pronunciation: e.g. English-speaking children who pronounce *coming* as [kəmɪn] are judged less well behaved or intelligent than those who say [kəmɪŋ] (Fischer 1958). Frender, Brown, and Lambert (1970) elicited judgements based on the langauge use of French-Canadian third grade boys of the same nonverbal IQ and social class, but with different grade averages; the boys with higher grades had greater variance in intonation, and were judged to sound more 'appropriate', more confident, and to have higher pitch. Brown, Strong, and Rencher (1975) speculate lower pitch at this age could reflect strong identification with tough, masculine models and less with the values of the educational system.

Several studies show that the same features of speech are interpreted as markers of different personality characteristics in males and females within the same speech community, but few have compared perceptions and interpretations in different cultures. Scherer (1979) reports correlations between certainty–uncertainty markers in American speech with self-rating of aggressiveness and dominance, and with ratings by American judges, but not by German-speaking judges. Scherer also suggests there are subcultural differences, such as loudness of voice indicating friendliness and sociability for lower class people, and boorishness and aggressiveness for upper class.

Speakers of English have stereotypic perceptions of personality differences between Americans, British, and Australians, and it would be interesting to know what specific differences are serving as markers for the groups, and how and why the personality attributions are derived. Similar studies might be conducted across languages to determine what markers are associated with personality traits considered 'typical' of particular ethnic groups, and the extent to which similar markers are used by members of one speech community to type all 'others'. Such verbal behavior as repeated interruptions and dominating a conversation may be characteristic of a particular personality type, but these may also be strategies which have been learned in a particular speech community as conversational rules for asserting power or solidarity, and thus may be markers of role-relationship more than of personality.

Finally, speech may be intentionally marked to indicate personality traits or emotions in someone else. Sapir (1915) reported that in Nootka, 'Cowards may be satirized by "making one's voice small" in referring to or addressing them, in other words by speaking in a thin piping voice that suggests timidity.' Hymes (1979a) analyzes [s] and [ł] prefixes inserted in the speech of bear and coyote in Takelma folklore as having a similar metaphorical function: the [s] conveys 'diminutive meanings that have to do with condescension, sympathy, even affection on the part of an audience, and closeness between actors', while the [ł] conveys greater emotional distance, 'depreciation, disdain for coarseness and stupidity, and . . . distance between actors.'

Speech markers may also be used to imply physical characteristics. In Nootka this speech-mockery was done by suffixed participles and by inserting or altering consonants:

> The physical classes indicated by these methods are children, unusually fat or heavy people, unusually short adults, those suffering from some defect of the eye, hunchbacks, those that are lame, left-handed persons, and circumcised males. (Sapir 1915:180–1)

Sapir reported that speech-mockery in Nootka was also used in reference or address with people who have speech defects. Those recognized in the community are: (1) involuntary nasalization of all vowels and continuants (a 'nasal twang'), (2) 'hole in palate' (cleft palate?), (3) palatalization of all [s] and [ts] to [š] (speakers are thought to be keeping their teeth open), (4) 'to talk as one with missing teeth' (lisping), and (5) stuttering. Speech-mockery takes the form of imitation of the defect.

Like mental illness, what is considered pathological speech is culturally determined. Discovering what is considered 'abnormal' provides an enlightening dimension in revealing the perceptions and attitudes of a group, and in defining 'normal'; it deserves more attention than it has thus far been accorded in sociolinguistics.

NON-NATIVE VARIETIES

Three very different types of language varieties are included in this category: (1) the marked forms and patterns used by speakers in a foreign or second language; (2) the lingua francas or international language codes; and (3) the languages which have developed with official or auxiliary but 'transplanted' status in societies where there are not indigenous speakers.

Within the first category there is a major distinction to be made between foreign and second languages in terms of function and the relationship of their speakers to a speech community. The former are generally used for learning about another culture or for intercultural communication, and may enable speakers to participate more or less successfully in that speech community without becoming members of it; sometimes they are used for one-way knowledge transfer, and many are content to acquire only reading skills, and do not become 'speakers'. Second languages are used within a speech community for many of the same functions they serve for native speakers, and their speakers must usually be considered members of the community in its sociological/anthropological sense even when the linguistic forms and rules are as yet quite imperfectly acquired. Both kinds of varieties are most commonly marked by an 'accent' which identifies speakers' native language identity, intralingual developmental phenomena, and ways of speaking and writing which are inappropriately translated into the target language.

English has replaced French as the most common international language, and the variety generally used for international communication is characterized by minimal use of metaphorical and idiomatic expressions, and neutralization of regional differences. Suprapto calls this 'Standard English for Foreigners', and reports from her obseravations:

Even the native speakers of English strive to minimize their type of English in pronunciation and syntax. Thus, for example, an Englishman would try not to sound too British, nor an American too American.

This variety functions as a lingua franca at the World Bank and many other international agencies, and at meetings and conferences where there is a forum for the exchange of information in various academic or political domains. It is an elaborated code which makes minimal assumptions about shared cultural experiences among its speakers, other than that they all have a high level of formal education.

The essential difference in the nature and functions of non-native official/auxiliary languages from those of the other varieties has been argued most extensively with respect to 'Indian English' by Kachru (e.g. 1976; 1980; 1983), who extends the distinctions to the Englishes of the Philippines, the Caribbean, and West Africa as well. He is primarily concerned with a situation

in which *Indian* English is used as a language of interaction, for maintaining *Indian* patterns of administration, education, and legal system, and also for creating a pan-Indian (Indian English) literature which forms part of the world writing in English. (1976:223; emphasis his)

In other words, 'The medium is non-native, but the message is not' (Kachru 1986:12).

It is interesting that this role for English has developed while efforts to promote a more artificial international language, such as Esperanto, Novial, Occidental, Interlingua, and Volapük have had only limited success. This may be because of language attitudes, or because a natural language is more adequate as a medium for communication.

The range of varieties used for auxiliary national purposes even within a single country, such as India, runs from pidginized English on the one extreme, through regionally marked varieties (e.g. Punjabi English, Kashmiri English), to 'educated Indian English', and finally to varieties which very closely approximate British or American norms.

Such varieties are part of the communicative repertoire in India, West Africa, South Asia, and the West Indies, with important functions in each of the national contexts. Kachru (1983) lists these as: (1) instrumental, especially for education; (2) regulative, in legal systems and administration; (3) interpersonal, as a 'link language' between speakers of different languages and a symbol of prestige and modernity; and (4) imaginative/innovative. The use of a non-native language in creative contexts, as a medium for literature and drama, indicates that it is being more deeply embedded in the culture of its speakers and undergoing nativization. Subvarieties developed as part of this process, as variables in the transplanted language begin to serve as markers in the society.

The development and creative use of non-native varieties of language provides further evidence for the point made earlier that there is no intrinsic reason that the structures and vocabulary of one language cannot be used in many domains of communication within other speech communities to express the cultures of those communities, and in ways in keeping with their rules of appropriate behavior.

4

The Analysis of Communicative Events

In undertaking an ethnography of communication in a particular locale, the first task is to define at least tentatively the speech community to be studied, attempt to gain some understanding of its social organization and other salient aspects of the culture, and formulate possible hypotheses concerning the diverse ways these sociocultural phenomena might relate to patterns of communication (as discussed in Chapters 2 and 3). It is crucial that the ethnographic description of other groups be approached not in terms of preconceived categories and processes, but with openness to discovery of the way native speakers perceive and structure their communicative experiences; in the case of ethnographers working in their own speech communities, the development of objectivity and relativity is essential, and at the same time difficult.

Some early steps in description and analysis of patterns of communication include identifying recurrent events, recognizing their salient components, and discovering the relationship among components and between the event and other apsects of society. The ethnographer is also interested in attitudes toward the event (Chapter 5), and how both relevant communicative skills and attitudes are acquired (Chapter 6). The ultimate criterion for descriptive adequacy is whether someone not acquainted with the speech community might understand how to communicate appropriately in a particular situation; beyond that, we wish to know why those behaviors are more appropriate than alternative possibilities.

Observed behavior is now recognized as a manifestation of a deeper set of codes and rules, and the task of ethnography is seen as the discovery and explication of the rules for contextually appropriate behavior in a community or group; in other words, what the individual needs to know to be a functional member of the community.

RELATIONSHIP OF ETHNOGRAPHER AND SPEECH COMMUNITY

In part because anthropology until recently has been concerned primarily with non-Western cultures, and has relegated the study of Western cultures to sociology, psychology and the other social sciences, the techniques of ethnography have been little applied in our own society except occasionally in caricature. It has been observed that this division of effort has not been accidental, and that anthropology has reflected Western ethnocentric distinctions between conquered colonial (or internal neo-colonial) groups and their conquerors. The outside observer, foreign to the society and unfamiliar with the culture, could innocently collect and report any information, confident that the group would allow indulgence for breaches of etiquette, and that protection was provided by the fact that involvement in the society could be terminated at any point by returning home.

In recent years the awareness has grown that the researcher can develop a deeper understanding of the culture under study by adopting a functional role and becoming a participant. This may in fact be necessary at times if the lack of a defined status and role would cause problems of acceptance by the community (Williams 1967; Spradley 1979). Some kind of rationale may be required for the observer's presence, particularly in studies within his or her own society. When the observer knows the rules of the culture, and the members of the community know that he or she knows the rules of the culture, they expect the observer to behave like a member of the society. Thus, they are likely to find it aberrant for observers to inquire about or record behavior which they are assumed to know, and little tolerance will be shown for violations of rules. There is considerable awkwardness, severe constraints are involved, and problems of ethics emerge. In addition, observers, taking for granted large aspects of the culture because they are already known 'out of awareness', may find it difficult and less intellectually rewarding to attempt to discover and explicate the seemingly obvious, the 'unmarked' case.

Nevertheless ethnographers, precisely because of this knowledge of a broad range of the world's cultures, are able to bring a comparative perspective to work even within their own society. And by keeping a mental distance from the objects of observation, and by treating subcultures such as that of the school or the factory as 'exotic', they can maintain some of the detached objectivity for which anthropology is noted.

One of the advantages of studying one's own culture, and attempting to make explicit the systems of understanding which are implicit, is that ethnographers are able to use themselves as sources of information and interpretation. Chomsky's view of the native speaker of a language as knowing the grammar of the language opened the way to introspection by native speakers as an analytical procedure, and recognized that the vastness of this knowledge extended far beyond what had been revealed in most linguistic descriptions by non-native speakers. The extension of this perspective to the study of culture acknowledges the member of the society as the repository of cultural knowledge, and recognizes that the ethnographer who already possesses this knowledge can tap it introspectively to validate, enrich, and expedite the task of ethnographic description.

A further advantage to ethnographers working within their own culture is that some of the major questions regarding validity and reliability raised by the quantitatively oriented social sciences can be at least partially resolved. While there may be no one to gainsay claims concerning cultural practices in a remote New Guinea village, any description of activities in the observer's own society becomes essentially self-correcting, both through feedback from the community described and through reactions by readers who are themselves members of the same society.

At the same time, the emphasis in recent ethnographic work on an existential/phenomenological explication of cultural meaning further justifies the value of ethnographers working within their own culture. Combining observation and self-knowledge, the ethnographer can plumb the depths and explore the subtle interconnections of meaning in ways that the outsider could attain only with great difficulty, if at all. In the same way then, with the ethnographer able to function as both observer and informant, some of the problems of verification can be overcome, and a corrective to unbridled speculation provided.

When ethonographers choose to work in other cultures, the need for extensive background study of the community is critical, and a variety of field methods must be employed to minimize imposition of their own cultural categories and perceptions on recording the interpretation of another system. In some cases 'outsiders' may notice behaviors that are not readily apparent to natives of the community, for whom they may be unconscious, but conversely no outsider can really understand the meaning of interaction of various types within the community without eliciting the intuitions of its members. Garfinkel noted:

> The discovery of common culture consists of the discovery *from within* the society by social scientists of the existence of common sense knowledge of social structures. (1967:76–7; emphasis his)

It is likely that only a researcher who shares, or comes to share, the intuitions of the speech community under study will be able to accurately describe the socially shared base which accounts in large part for the dynamics of communicative interaction. The value of combining perspectives of both insider and outsider as field workers is illustrated by Milroy (1980).

A second issue is that of community access. Milroy provides good illustrations of how this may be negotiated in her discussion of the methodology used by Blom and Gumperz in Norway and of her own in Belfast:

I introduced myself initially in each community not in my formal capacity as a researcher, but as a 'friend of a friend' . . . so that I acquired some of the rights as well as some of the obligations of an insider. (1987b:66)

Obtaining access to minority communities which may have a history of exploitation poses ethical as well as practical problems. In the United States, most research on minority communities has traditionally been conducted by members of the majority group or by foreigners (e.g. the work of Madsen, Rubel, and Holtzman and Diaz-Guerrero on Mexican Americans, or Hannerz and Ogbu on Black Americans). A member of the group under study who is also a researcher will already have personal contacts which should contribute to assuring acceptance, although taking such a role can result in the (sometimes justified) perception that a group member has 'sold out' to the dominant establishment.

The realization of the historical colonialist associations of anthropology has made the science suspect in some communities, and created barriers to access by fieldworkers. One extreme example reportedly occurred in a Pueblo community in New Mexico, where it is said the informant for an anthropologist was killed some years ago after the anthropologist published his study and the community found out how much the informant had divulged.

It is necessary to recognize that sensitivities exist in certain quarters, and that the question of the use to which ethnographic research is to be put has been raised as an ethical issue in the profession. There are many potential applications of data on patterns of communication, ranging from improving education and the delivery of social services (e.g. law and medicine) to contributing to the effectiveness of advertising or propaganda, and it is the ethnographers' responsibility not to exploit the communities in which they work. Often access can be negotiated to the benefit of all by including relevant feedback into the community in a form it may use for its own purposes. Positive examples can be found in the work of a number of anthropological linguists working with Indian groups in the United States. These include Ossie

Werner (Northwestern University), whose research on Navajo anatomical terminology and their beliefs about the causes and cures of disease is providing input to improvements in the delivery of health care, and William Leap (American University), whose research on Isletan Tiwa has yielded a written form of the language and bilingual reading materials. These materials were developed in response to community fears that the language is in a state of decline, and to their desire to maintain it.

There are some data that should go unreported if they are likely to be damaging to individuals or the group. Whenever the subjects of research are human beings, there are ethical limits on scientific responsibility for completeness and objectivity which are not only justified but mandated. Furthermore, information which is given confidentially must be kept in confidence. The two linguists whose work with communities was cited above also provide positive examples of this dimension of professional integrity: some of the information about Navajo health beliefs and practices should be disseminated only within the Navajo community, and although the complete data base is being reported by Werner, this portion will remain untranslated into English. Leap made no attempt even to elicit stories which had religious significance for the Tiwa (and thus were secret in nature), while his selection and content for the bilingual readers were submitted to a Parents' Advisory Board for approval prior to publication.

A third issue, partly contained within the second, is that of interviewer race or ethnicity. In the past, when studies were carried out in foreign environments or in minority communities by members of the majority group, the myth of the observer as a detached, neutral figure obscured the social fact that whether a conscious participant or not, the observer was inescapably part of the social setting and affected the behavior of other participants, as well as being influenced and sometimes even manipulated by them. The lack of familiarity of researchers with the culture, the language, and the community often made them vulnerable to such influence, the more so since it was unperceived.

The effect of the observer's presence on other participants – the *observer's paradox*, so called because the observer cannot observe what would have happened if he or she had not been present – has been studied in certain situations, and appears to be variable. Labov (1970) discovered that replicating the interview procedures of Bereiter and Engelmann (1966), using a White interviewer with Black children in a threatening environment, produced a very low amount of verbalization compared with using a Black interviewer in a familiar (home) environment, but Galvan and Smith (Smith 1973), both White, were successful in eliciting fluent speech from Black children in Texas schools. The bilingual situation is more complex, at least as it affects the study of language behavior, but the effect on the study of other cultural features is less certain. The MELP (Measure of English Language Proficiency) study conducted by the Center for Applied Linguistics in 1975 found no significant effect from interviewer ethnicity on the quality of data collected (controlled assignment of interviewers was carried out at three sites), and the Institute of Social Research at the University of Michigan has found that non-matched interviewers conducting social survey research secure better and more reliable data than do ethnically matched interviewers using the respondents' language.

At the outset researchers must know the general framework, institutions, and values which guide cultural behavior in the community and be able to behave appropriately, both linguistically and culturally, within any given situation, if their participation is to be genuinely accepted. Similarly, researchers must be able to establish a common basis of shared understandings and rules for behavior if interviews or interactions are to be productive.

Hymes (1978) has distinguished three types of ethnography: *general*, *topic focused*, and *hypothesis testing*. All are important, and each type is in many respects dependent on the one before. The linguistic and cultural knowledge of the ethnographer can greatly speed the progress of research to the third level, and aid in the generation of hypotheses for testing and further study.

TYPES OF DATA

While not all types of data are necessarily relevant for every study conducted, at least the following should be considered for any ethnographic research on communication:

1   Background Information

Any attempt to understand communication patterns in a community must begin with data on the historical background of the community, including settlement history, sources of population, history of contact with other groups, and notable events affecting language issue or ethnic relations. A general description is also generally relevant, including topographical features, location of important landmarks, population distribution and density, patterns of movement, sources and places of employment, patterns of religious affiliation, and enrollment in educational institutions. Published sources of information should be utilized as background preparation whenever they are available, and a search should be made of MA and PhD theses to avoid duplication of research effort. Relatively current data may be available from national, state, regional, or local levels of government, or through embassy representatives.

2   Material Artifacts

Many of the physical objects which are present in a community are also relevant to understanding patterns of communication, including architecture, signs, and such instruments of communication as telephones, radios, books, television sets, and drums. Data collection begins with observation and may include interviewing with such questions as 'What is that used for?' and 'What do you use to . . .?' The classification and labeling of objects using ethnosemantic procedures is an early stage in discovering how a speech community organizes experience in relation to language.

3   Social Organization

Relevant data may include a listing of community institutions, identities of leaders and office holders, the composition of the business and professional sectors, sources of power and influence, formal and informal organizations, ethnic and class relations, social stratification, and distribution and association patterns. Information may be available in newspapers and official records of various types, and collected through systematic observation in a sample of settings and interviews conducted with a cross section of people in the community. A network analysis may also be conducted, determining which people interact with which others, in what role-relationships, and for what purposes. The procedure may also be used to identify subgroup boundaries within a heterogeneous community and discover their relative strength.

4   Legal Information

Laws and court decisions which make reference to language are also relevant: e.g. what constitutes 'slander', what 'obscenity', and what is the nature and value of 'freedom of speech', or how is it restricted. It is of interest, for instance, that a West German court acquitted two former SS members of murder charges in part because 'all the evidence presented was verbal, with not one piece of evidence in writing' (Associated Press 1980). Laws may also prescribe language choice in official contexts, as those enacted in Quebec and Belgium, or as in the Voting Rights Act in the United States, which required ballots to be printed in any language spoken by over 5 per cent of the voting-age citizens in any state or political subdivision. In communities where such information is formally codified, much is available in law books and court records, and in all communities it is accessible through interviews with participants in 'legal' events of various kinds, and observation of their procedures and outcomes.

5   Artistic Data

Literary sources (written or oral) may be valuable for the descriptions they contain, as well as for the attitudes and values about language they reveal. Additionally, the communicative patterns which occur in literature presumably embody some kind of normative idealization, and portray types of people (e.g. according to social class) in terms of stereotypic use of language. Relevant artistic data also include song lyrics, drama and other genres of verbal performance, and calligraphy.

6   Common Knowledge

Assumptions which underlie the use and interpretation of language are difficult to identify when they are in the form of unstated presuppositions, but some of them surface after such formulas as 'Everyone knows . . .', and 'As they say . . .', or in the form of proverbs and aphorisms. These are 'facts' for which evidence is not considered necessary, the 'rules of thumb', and the maxims which govern various kinds of communicative behavior. Some of the data can be elicited with questions about why something is said the way it is in a particular situation instead of in an alternative way, and even more by studying the formal and informal processes in children's acquisition of communicative competence (discussed in Chapter 6). Ethnoscience and ethnomethodology are most directly concerned with discovery of this type of data (discussed under Data Collection Procedures below).

7   Beliefs about Language Use

This type of data has long been of interest to ethnographers, and includes taboos and their consequences. Also included are beliefs about who or what is capable of speech, and who or what may be communicated with (e.g. God, animals, plants, the dead). Closely related are data on attitudes and values with respect to language, including the positive or negative value assigned to volubility versus taciturnity.

8   Data on the Linguistic Code

Although it is a basic tenet in this field that a perspective which views language only as static units of lexicon, phonology, and grammar is totally inadequate, these do constitute a very important type of data within the broader domain. These, along with paralinguistic and nonverbal features in communication, are included in the model for the analysis of speech events as part of the 'Instrumentality' component (discussed below). Preparation to work within any speech community, particularly if the language used is not native to the ethnographer, should include study of existing dictionaries and grammars. Skills in ethnography of communication are probably best added to skills in linguistic analysis in its narrower sense in order to assure that this component is not neglected or misinterpreted.

SURVEY OF DATA COLLECTION PROCEDURES

There is no single best method of collecting information on the patterns of language use within a speech community. Appropriate procedures depend on the relationship of the ethnographer and the speech community, the type of data being collected, and the particular situation in which fieldwork is being conducted. The essential defining characteristics of ethnographic field procedures are that they are designed to get around the recorders' biased perceptions, and that they are grounded in the investigation of communication in natural contexts.

Ethnographers should thus command a repertoire of field methods from which to select according to the occasion. Although an ethnographic approach is quite different from an experimental one, quantitative methods may prove useful (even essential) in some aspects of data collection, especially when variable features of language use are being explored. Quantitative methods are essentially techniques for measuring degree of consistency in behavior, and the amount and nature of variation under different circumstances. The ethnographer may profitably collaborate with the sociologist, psychologist, or sociolinguist interested in quantitative analysis, but if quantitative methods are to be used, they must first be developed and validated by qualitative procedures. Quantitative procedures may in turn serve to determine the reliability of qualitative observation, which is apt to be casual and uncontrolled, and the validity of generalizations which may be made on the basis of a very limited sample.

The criterion for descriptive adequacy which will be kept in mind is that enough information should be provided to enable someone from outside the speech community under investigation to fully understand the event, and to participate appropriately in it.

1   Introspection

Introspection is a means for data collection only about one's own speech community, but it is an important skill to develop for that purpose. This is important not only for data collection per se, but for establishing the fact that everyone has a culture, and that questions about various aspects of language and culture require answers from the perspective of researchers' own speech communities as well as those of their subjects. Ethnographers who are themselves bicultural need to differentiate between beliefs, values, and behaviors which were part of their enculturation (first culture learning) and acculturation (second culture learning or adptation), and this exercise in itself will provide valuable information and insights on the group and on individuals.

The most productive means for developing this skill in a training program is to ask individuals to formulate very specific answers from their own experience to various questions about communication, such as those listed in the section below on Components of Communication. A second step is to recognize the significance of differences between answers which reflect cultural 'ideals' or norms, and the 'real', or what actually occurs. This distinction between the *ideal* and the *real* – long familiar to anthropologists – is not a matter of truth and falsehood, and should not be put in a negative light.

Rather it is a recognition of specific behaviors. A useful analogy may be drawn with the question of what drivers do when they encounter a stop sign: the 'ideal' answer is that they always stop; the 'real' specific behaviors show that slowing (but not completely stopping) is a common response, and sometimes drivers fail to stop at all. Distinguishing between 'ideal' and 'real' behaviors is an important stage in viewing culture objectively. Responses to questions about language and culture will usually be in categorical 'ideal' terms, and learning the 'ideal' answers is an important part of the formal education of group members. 'Real' behaviors, which exist on a continuum, are more often acquired by informal modeling, and are more likely to occur 'out of awareness' where they may be difficult for individuals to consciously recognize. Thus there is no inherent contradiction if someone asserts that he or she never fails to stop at a stop sign, and then proceeds to do so. The actual behavior may be quite honestly denied even if it is pointed out, or dismissed as an aberration which does not affect the validity of the general categorical statement.

Thus, even when researchers are sure they 'know' about patterns of language use in their own speech community, it is important to check hypotheses developed on the basis of their own perceptions with the perceptions of others, and against objective data collected in systematic observation.

2   Participant-Observation

The most common method of collecting ethnographic data in any domain of culture is participant-observation. The researcher who is a member of the speech community was born into that role, and anthropologists have found it possible to perceive and understand patterned cultural behaviors in another society if they are immersed in the community for a year or more. The key to successful participant-observation is freeing oneself as much as humanly possible from the filter of one's own cultural experience. This requires cultural relativism, knowledge about possible cultural differences, and sensitivity and objectivity in perceiving others.

Malinowski was responsible for leading a revolution in fieldwork about 1920, and is credited with the establishment of this approach. Prior to that date, ethnographers described other cultures on the basis of travelers' reports, or at best lived apart from the group under investigation (often in the more comfortable housing of colonial administrators), merely visiting on a regular basis to observe and take notes.

One of the most important benefits of participation is being able to test hypotheses about rules for communication, sometimes by breaking them and observing or eliciting reactions. Participation in group activities over a period of time is often necessary for much important information to emerge, and for necessary trusting relationships to develop. The role of the outside ethnographer in a community remains problematic, but if at all possible it should be one which contributes to the welfare of the host group in a way they recognize and desire. Whether this is as teacher or construction worker cannot be determined out of context, but the ethnographer should not be 'taking' data without returning something of immediate usefulness to the community.

Potential problems for 'outsider' ethnographers include not only what role to assume, but what information to provide about themselves before knowing the meaning of such information in the community. Furthermore, it is very difficult to behave 'appropriately' (even when one knows what to do) when one is ill, or when appropriate behaviors violate one's own values and mores. Ethnographers must first of all understand their own culture, and the effects it has on their own behavior, if they are to succeed in participant-observation in another.

It should be clear that for a participant-observation approach, a high level of linguistic as well as cultural competence is a *sine qua non* for successful fieldwork, particularly if it is to take place within a delimited time frame. The investigator, to be able to enter into various speech events relatively unobtrusively as a participant-observer, and one with whom other participants can feel comfortable, should share as closely as possible the same linguistic background and competence as the members of the community under observation. Nevertheless, some naturalistic experimental variation of conditions or interaction will be desirable in order to evoke or test for the occurrence of different response patterns.

Collecting data in situations in which they themselves are taking part requires ethnographers to include data on their own behaviors in relation to others, and an analysis of their role in the interaction as well as those of others.

3 Observation

Observation without participation is seldom adequate, but there are times when it is appropriate data collection procedure. Some sites are explicitly constructed to allow unobtrusive observation, such as laboratory classrooms with one-way mirrors, or others which allow the researcher to be visible but observe quite passively without being disruptive to the situation. Also, in observing group dynamics in a meeting or other gathering, it is generally better for a marginally accepted observer to refrain from taking active part in the proceedings. Observation from a balcony or porch is usually less disruptive to the patterns of children's interaction when their play is under observation than any attempt at participation.

Observation of communicative behavior which has been videotaped is a potentially useful adjunct to the participant-observation and interview, particularly because of the convenience of replaying for micro-analysis, but it is always limited in focus and scope to the cameraman's perception, and can only be adequately understood in a more holistic context. Furthermore, ethnographers should always remember that the acceptability of taping, photographing, and even note-taking depends on the community and situations being observed. When filming or videotaping is feasible in a relatively fixed context, it is best to use a stationary wide-angle studio camera for 'contextual' footage as well as a mobile camera to focus on particular aspects of the situation. To obtain a visual record of interactional events in which participants are more mobile (such as children playing together out-of-doors, or scenes in a hunting or fishing expedition), a hand-held and battery-operated 8 mm, video camcorder is most suitable. In such situations a small radio microphone may be attached to a single focal participant, with a receiver on the camera which records the sound directly on film. Most radio microphones will pick up not only what the focal participant says, but anything said by a speaker within at least three or four feet. When a wider range of audio coverage is needed, a second radio microphone and receiver tuned to a different frequency can provide input to an auxiliary tape recorder. Multiple input from different frequencies directly to the camera audio track requires additional equipment which greatly reduces portability. (For a discussion of videotaping in linguistic fieldwork, see Troike and Saville-Troike 1988; Jackson 1987 includes an extensive discussion of different types of recording equipment.)

Whiting and Whiting advise ethnographers 'not to embark on systematic observation which is laborious and time-consuming unless they are convinced that informants cannot report their own behavior or the behavior of others reliably' (1975:312). According to them, the reasons why an informant might not be able to do this are: he might not perceive the regularities in behavior and therefore could not generalize about categories; he will be unaware of his behavior in certain domains; he could not report acts he did not perform; his perception would be distorted because of conflict between the ideal and reality; and he might not remember relevant past events.

Since the potential range of settings for observation is enormous, priority must be determined by the focus or primary purpose of investigation. If the focus is on children in an educational situation, for instance, these include most obviously school itself, but also the playground, home, and the social environs most frequented by the child or which appear to have the greatest affective and linguistic effect on the child, such as perhaps the church. The work plan should be sufficiently flexible and open ended so that important settings which emerge in the course of ethnographic and linguistic research can be added or substituted, as appropriate.

It would not be adequate in this education example to limit observation to the classroom setting without taking into account the larger social context of communication.

Persons first developing skill in this method should just report observable behaviors without imposing value judgements or drawing conclusions; more advanced steps involve making inferences about such unobservable aspects of culture as beliefs and values, from the behaviors or things which are observed. The key to successful observation and inference is, again, freeing oneself from one's own cultural filter.

4   Interviewing

Interviewing may contribute a wide range of cultural information, and may include collection of kinship schedules, information on important religious and community events, and elicitation of folktales, historical narratives, songs, exposition of 'how to' in relation to various aspects of technical knowledge, and descriptions of encounters among members of the community in different contexts. While an interview setting is often formal and contrived, it need not be, and the procedure is an efficient – perhaps necessary – supplement to observation and participation. Types of questions and interviewing styles may be so different that few overall generalizations can be made.

The most common ethnographic interview is composed of questions which do not have predetermined response alternatives. These are appropriate for collecting data on virtually every aspect of communication: what regional varieties are recognized, and what features distinguish them from one another (e.g. Do the people who live on Red Mountain/in Green Valley, etc., talk in a different way from you? Can you understand them? What are some examples?); attitudes toward varieties of language (e.g. Who talks the 'best'? Who talks 'funny'? Why do you think they talk that way?); identification of different kinds of speech events (e.g. What are they doing [with reference to people interacting in various ways]? What kind of talk is that?); social markers in speech (e.g. How do you greet someone who is older than you?

Younger? A man? A woman? A servant? Your employer?).

Where possible, it is probably best to impose as little structure as possible on an interview, and to insert questions at natural points in the flow rather than having a rigid schedule of questions to follow.

The essence of the ethnographic interview is that it is open ended, and carries as few preconceptions with it as possible, or at least constantly attempts to discover possible sources of bias and minimize their effect. The ethnographer must be open to new ideas, information, and patterns which may emerge in the course of interviewing, and to differences between 'ideal' and 'real' culture as reflected in statements of belief or values and in actions, respectively.

Closed-ended questions which are precoded for statistical analysis may also be used, but only after the probable range of answers and possible interpretations have been established. Even so, in precoding there is danger of violating the principle of being open to new meanings and unforeseen patterns of behavior, and continuous qualitative validation is required.

Answers to the 'simplest' of survey questions are culture specific. Responses regarding age and number of children, for instance, cannot be interpreted without first knowing on what basis age is calculated within a particular speech community, or if 'how many children' means only living children, or only male children, or only children of the same sex as the respondent. In interviewing Tanzanian nationals living in the United States, Jalbert discovered it is inappropriate to ask how many children are in a family because, he was told, 'We don't count children'. The desired information can be elicited by asking 'How many of your children were born in Tanzania and how many were born here?' Especially when interviewing members of a minority group in a society, family membership and house occupants may be considered sensitive topics if dominant marriage customs are not being followed, and they may be very threatening if undocumented aliens are present in the home.

The meaning of terms typically used in the closed-ended survey questions must often be explained, even when administered to native speakers of the same language. When I have asked about 'marital status', for instance, a common answer has been 'yes', and questions on the 'ordinal rank' of a child have often been answered with identification of religious affiliation.

Questions which utilize scaled responses, such as a semantic differential, may also be used in some situations, but only if they are preceded and followed with open-ended questions to allow valid interpretation. The importance of probing scaled responses was illustrated when I asked students from several different countries to rate characteristics like ambitious, competitive, dominating, sympathetic, and tactful according to whether they are more typical of men or women in their own speech community. Responses were then used as a basis for elicitation of how these characteristics are reflected differentially in the ways males and females speak. While almost all students rated men as more 'dominating', some said this was reflected in their talking more, while others said the same characteristic was reflected in their greater taciturnity. Similarly, when students rated members of speech communities other than their own on such traits as friendliness, subsequent discussion on what constitutes 'friendly' verbal behavior revealed substantial differences: the same questions about school and family background which Japanese perceived as 'friendly', for instance, were considered 'unfriendly' by Americans, who thought they were an attempt to rank addressees socially; and the quantity of small talk considered 'friendly' by speakers of Spanish was considered 'unfriendly' by Japanese, who in general feel a great quantity of talk indicates social distance rather than friendliness. As one Japanese student exclaimed, 'If you are friends with someone you know them, and thus have no need to talk much.'

Such group interviews of members of several different speech communities can be very useful for developing concepts of relativity during the training process; while all of the students participating in this discussion agreed that 'friendly' behavior is a good thing, it became clear that communicative behaviors that will be interpreted as being 'friendly' are language and culture specific. The ethnographer can never assume that the same labels used in close-ended or scaled responses refer to similar patterns of language use, even if they have been translated into the respondents' language; that remains to be determined by open-ended interview and observation-participation procedures.

Possible effects of interviewer race and ethnicity have been discussed above, but sex and age are factors which must also be considered. Females are considered less threatening than males in many communities, and are thus more readily accepted as interviewers, but in other communities it is considered entirely inappropriate for women to behave in such a manner. Further, there are often limitations on what kinds of questions an interviewer of one sex may ask an interviewee of the other. Wolfram trained his young son (Wolfram and Wolfram 1977) as an interviewer to help collect information on how people respond differentially to questions asked by adults and children, yielding data an adult would have had great difficulty collecting, and young interviewers from children's magazines have scooped their adult rivals (including reporting the identity of Carter's 1976 vice-presidential running mate), at least in part because adults in this society seem to find it more difficult not to answer children's questions.

Eliciting information from child informants involves additional considerations, both because their perspective on the world is different from adults' (even within the same speech community), and because an adult–child interview is likely to embody an unequal power relationship in which children cannot communicate freely. Special precautions must be taken to avoid 'adult-centrism' in interpreting responses (Tammivaara and Enright 1986), and to convey complete openness to a child's knowledge and piont of view.

Differences in children's world-views are illustrated by research which has explored the nature of their concepts of astronomy, including the shape and size of the earth (Vosniadou and Brewer, in press). When they were interviewed about this subject, almost all children by the age of six said that the earth is 'a circle' or 'round'. Interpretations of what this answer *really* meant, however, required such follow-up activities as having children draw or construct clay models of the earth, and answer probing questions about where people live, why they don't fall off the bottom, and whether if you walk far enough you will get to the edge. These supplementary procedures revealed that for many of the children 'round' meant circular but flat (i.e. a disk), and others believed people live *inside* a sphere (not *on* it), or that there are really two earths (a flat one we live on and a round one in the sky). Interesting cultural differences included Indian children's perceiving the earth as a flat disc floating on water, and Samoan children's forming a ring-like shape when asked to make a model of the earth with clay (Brewer, Hendrich, and Vosniadou, in press).

When children's responses are carefully probed, it becomes apparent that they have their own well-developed notions about the world around them, including the language(s) they hear and speak, and how people learn them. This topic will be discussed further in Chapter 6.

Among the critical issues in any kind of interviewing are:

(a) Selecting reliable informants. Often the people who make themselves most readily available to an outsider are those who are marginal to the community, and may thus convey inaccurate or incomplete information and interfere with the acceptance of the researcher by other members of the group.

(b) Formulating culturally appropriate questions. This includes knowing what is appropriate or inappropriate to ask about, why, and in what way.

(c) Developing sensitivity to signs of acceptance, discomfort, resentment, or sarcasm. Such sensitivity relates to the first two issues by contributing information on informant reliability and the appropriateness of questions, and on when an interview should be terminated.

(d) Procedures for data transcription, arrangement, and analysis. These will differ to some extent with the kind of information that is being collected and often with the theoretical orientation of the researcher; whenever the interview is conducted in a language not native to the researcher, however, transcription requires skill in using another orthographic system or a phonetic alphabet (even if a tape recorder is in use).

These issues are discussed at length in Spradley (1979), Taylor and Bogdan (1984), and Williams (1967), while Brislin, Lonner, and Thorndike (1973) provide a useful list of potential communication problems between interviewer and respondent which may affect the validity of the findings. The special problems which arise in interviewing young children are considered in Tammivaara and Enright (1986). The potential biases they describe include cultural differences in respondents' feelings of ability to answer questions. People in the US, for instance, often feel they must answer any question that is put to them, but this may or may not reflect real knowledge of the subject. Some respondents will answer questions in the way they feel will most please the interviewer (the 'courtesy bias'), while others consider it great sport to 'put on' outsiders (the 'sucker bias'). Williams (1967) reports that while he was doing a census among the Dasun in Nothern Borneo, he was told in each household that he must drink two cups of strong wine or his mother-in-law would become blind (a joke which created great problems for him in completing his fieldwork). In some speech communities, respondents are concerned about possible 'after effects' of talking (either social or supernatural), and these must be given particularly serious consideration. It must also be remembered that an interview itself is a communicative event which will have culture-specific rules for conduct and interpretation. Indeed, an 'interview' may not be an appropriate mode at all for getting information. Briggs (1984; 1986) discusses how metacommunicative competence in native events which function to elicit information may increase the 'cooperativeness' of collaborators, and similar insights are reported by Stoller (1986) regarding his work among the Songhay. The following exchange was with an elder in the community who was willing to advise Stoller after he found out that he had not been getting truthful responses to his questionnaire:

'You will never learn about us,' he told me, 'if you go into people's compounds, ask personal questions, and write down the answers. Even if you remain here one year or two years and ask us questions in this manner, we would still lie to you.'

'Then what am I to do?'

'You must learn to sit with people,' he told me. 'You must learn to sit and listen. As we say in Songhay: "One kills something thin only to discover that it is fat".' (Stoller 1986:53)

Many problems can be avoided by doing a pretest before attempting a large-scale data collection, including an exploration of who can be interviewed, how people within the community exchange information, and what forms of questions are appropriate (Hymes 1970).

The reliability of information can best be judged by asking similar questions of several people in the community and comparing their answers, and by relating information collected through interviews to observations. These should be required steps in all interview procedures.

5   Ethnosemantics (Ethnoscience)

Ethnosemantics is concerned primarily with discovering how experience is categorized by eliciting terms in the informants' language at various levels of abstraction and analyzing their semantic organization, usually in the form of a taxonomy or componential analysis. Because an adequate ethnography of communication must include the categories and contexts which are culturally significant within the speech community under investigation, including how they group language use into kinds of communicative events (as described in Chapter 2), the perspective and methods of ethnosemantics are highly relevant.

A possible initial step in data collection is selecting a domain or genre, and then asking (recursively), 'What kind of —s are there?' One might ask 'What kind of insults are there?', for instance; if the response were 'Friendly insults and unfriendly insults', the next question would be 'What kind of friendly insults are there?' in order to elicit subcategories and examples, and then 'What kind of unfriendly insults are there?', etc. This step is usually followed by questions which elicit the dimensions which the speaker is using for comparison and contrast: e.g. 'In what way are these two things/acts/events different?' 'How are they the same?' 'Of these three, which two are more alike and in what way?' 'How does the third differ from them?' The first type of questioning strategy yields information primarily about hierarchically structured categories, and the latter primarily about feature sets. Possibilities for applying microcomputer technology to these data collection procedures are discussed in Werner and Schoepfle (1987).

An extension of this method might be called ethnopragmatics, or the discovery of why members of a speech community say they do things as opposed to why ethnographers say they do them: e.g. why people say what they do when someone sneezes.

The ultimate goal of ethnographic description is an *emic* account of the data, in terms of the categories which are meaningful to members of the speech community under study; an *etic* account in terms of a priori categories is a useful preliminary grid for reference and for comparison purposes, but is usually not the ultimate goal of description.

6   Ethnomethodology and Interaction Analysis

As developed by Harold Garfinkel (1967; 1972), ethnomethodology is concerned primarily with discovering the underlying processes which speakers of a language utilize to produce and interpret communicative experiences, including the unstated assumptions which are shared cultural knowledge and understandings. According to Gumperz (1977; 1984), this is the first tradition to deal with conversations as cooperative endeavors, and to focus on sociological analysis of verbal interaction. To Garfinkel, social knowledge is revealed in the process of interaction itself, and the format required for description of communication is dynamic rather than static.

There are general (perhaps universal) processes through which meaning is conveyed in the process of conversational interaction (Gumperz 1977):

(a) Meaning and intelligibility of ways of speaking are at least partially determined by the situation, and the prior experience of speakers.
(b) Meaning is negotiated during the process of interaction, and is dependent on the intent and interpretation of previous utterances.
(c) A participant in conversation is always committed to some kind of interpretation.
(d) An interpretation of what happens now is always reversible in the light of what happens later.

A clearly emerging concept is that of the extent to which speakers must share experience to successfully develop conversational exchanges of any depth and duration.

Gumperz builds on this in proposing the outline of a theory of how social knowledge is stored in the mind, retrieved from memory, and integrated with grammatical knowledge in the act of conversing. Conversational inference is 'the "situated" ' or context-bound process of interpretation, by means of which participants in a conversation assess others' intentions, and on which they base their responses' (Gumperz 1977:191).

Because of its cultural base, the 'meaning' that emerges in a conversation is likely to be different for different participants if they are not members of the same speech community. Examples of cross-cultural (mis)communicative events serve to highlight the importance of such factors as the information or presuppositions the communicants bring to the task, the extralinguistic context, and nonverbal cues. For example, I observed the following exchange in a kindergarten classroom on the Navajo Reservation:

A Navajo man opened the door to the classroom and stood silently, looking at the floor. The Anglo-American teacher said 'Good morning' and waited expectantly, but the man did not respond. The teacher then said 'My name is Mrs. Jones', and again waited for a response. There was none.

In the meantime, a child in the room put away his

crayons and got his coat from the rack. The teacher, noting this, said to the man, 'Oh, are you taking Billy now?' He said, 'Yes.'

The teacher continued to talk to the man while Billy got ready to leave, saying, 'Billy is such a good boy', 'I'm so happy to have him in class', etc.

Billy walked towards the man (his father), stopping to turn around and wave at the teacher on his way out and saying, 'Bye-bye.' The teacher responded, 'Bye-bye.' The man remained silent as he left.

From a Navajo perspective, the man's silence was appropriate and respectful. The teacher, on the other hand, expected not only to have the man return her greeting, but to have him identify himself and state his reason for being there. Although such an expectation is quite reasonable and appropriate from an Anglo-American perspective, it would have required the man to break not only Navajo rules of politeness but also a traditional religious taboo that prohibits individuals from saying their own name. The teacher interpreted the contextual cues correctly in answer to her own question ('Are you taking Billy?') and then engaged in small talk in an attempt to be friendly and to cover her own discomfort in the situation. The man continued to maintain appropriate silence. Billy, who was more acculturated than his father to Anglo-American ways, broke the Navajo rule to follow the Anglo-American one in leave-taking.

This encounter undoubtedly reinforced the teacher's stereotype that Navajos are 'impolite' and 'unresponsive', and the man's stereotype that Anglo-Americans are 'impolite' and 'talk too much'.

Describing and analyzing the negotiation of meaning requires discovering what aspects of speech signal role and status relations, and serve as a metalanguage for transmitting information about them. The researcher then infers changes in assumptions about the relationships as a conversation progresses.

Potential problems arise in applying these methods to research in other speech communities because speakers' inferences must usually in turn be inferred by the researchers, and this secondary level of inference may be based on quite different assumptions. The widely used system developed by Flanders (1970) for coding classroom interaction is fatally flawed for use in multicultural education contexts, for instance, because such categories as 'positive response' of teacher to student are predetermined by an ethnocentric process of inference. The meanings of situations which are described in terms of such precoded categories 'are totally dependent on the outsider's frame of reference – they make no concessions to the immediate cultural milieu' (Walker and Adelman 1975:75). For example, the interpretation of such behaviors as using students' names, smiling, and touching as being 'positive' is entirely dependent on the culture of those who have done the precoding. These same behaviors may be perceived as offensive or even as quite negative control measures by students from different cultural backgrounds.

While the foci and procedures of traditional ethnography and various models of interaction analysis differ, they are in a necessary complementary relationship to one another if an understanding of communication is to be reached. Ethnographic models of observation and interview are most useful for a macro-description of community structure, and for determining the nature and significance of contextual features and the patterns and functions of language in the society; interactional micro-analyses build on this input information, and feed back into an ethnography of communication clearer understandings of the processes by which members of a speech community actually use and interpret language, especially in everyday interaction – a vital aspect of their communicative competence.

7   Philology

The interpretation and explanation of texts or *hermeneutics* (cf. Soeffner 1985; Tyler 1978), has traditionally been a science or art applied to writing, rather than speech, and especially to Biblical texts. (The Greek term for 'to interpret' derives from *Hermes*, the messenger of the gods.) In addition to the referential meaning of the texts themselves, a variety of written sources may yield information on patterns of use in the language, and on the culture of the people who read and write it.

As discussed under Types of Data above, much of the necessary background information on a community may be found in written sources, including theses and dissertations, governmental publications, old diaries and correspondence, and archival sources. Newspapers and census records may also be used as clues to the social organization of the community, law books and court records to language-related legal information, and literature to idealized patterns of language use, and to attitudes and values about language.

For information on contemporary language usage, one good source is the advice columns published in most US newspapers (e.g. 'Ann Landers', 'Miss Manners', and 'Dear Abby'). These contain letters from people asking advice or giving opinions, with replies from the columnists. They regularly include questions and comments on appropriate forms of address, appropriate responses to compliments, etc. These might be compared with the older advice columns and books written by Emily Post, in order to document changing ideals of usage. An example of the use of this type of data source comes from Kempf (1985), who demonstrates how use of pronouns and terms of address in a newspaper, *Neues Deutschland*, can be used to study language variation in relation to social class, political party membership, and other social factors. Although generalization from written text to other channels must be used with caution, direct investigation of spoken usage in this case would have posed severe political and practical limitations.

Obituary notices in newspapers may provide information on social organization and values by allowing inferences as to who is given special treatment when they die (e.g. is the notice on the front page or near the classified section, and of what length), what accomplishments are mentioned (e.g. for women, the husband's occupation is mentioned; the reverse is almost never the case), and what is taboo or requires euphemisms. Classified advertising sections are an index to goods and occupations that are available, and their organization indicates salient categories and labels in the community.

For communities with a literate tradition, written sources may be used to document language shifts over time: e.g. historical reconstruction for English speech communities has long included contrasting the forms used in letters versus plays, and secular versus religious writings, and has been used to document changes in such aspects of the language as the use of second person pronouns, and the relation of such changes to the sociocultural context of time. Changes in the status and functions of languages can be inferred in the shift of language choice for the same genre: e.g. Latin versus English, French versus English.

Old travelers' accounts, texts, dictionaries, and grammars are the only evidence now available from which we may reconstruct cultural information about many groups who have been exterminated or who have fully assimilated to another culture, including many American Indian tribes. A combination of techniques from ethnomethodology and literary analysis has been applied by Hymes (1980; 1981) and others to the oral texts recorded as prose by linguists and anthropologists, uncovering internal poetic structure and coherence, verbal patterns of openings, closings, and transitions, and assumptions about characters and their appropriate behaviors and fates – the 'common knowledge' we seek to understand.

IDENTIFICATION OF COMMUNICATIVE EVENTS

Communication in societies tends to be categorized into different kinds of events rather than an undifferentiated string of discourse, with more or less well defined boundaries between each, and different behavioral norms (often including different varieties of language) appropriate for each kind. Descriptive tasks include enumerating the kinds of events which are recognized or can be inferred in a community, the nature of boundary markers which signal their beginning and end, and the features which distinguish one type from another.

Since a communicative event is a bounded entity of some kind, recognizing what the boundaries are is essential for their identification. A telephone conversation is a communicative event bounded by a ring of the telephone as a 'summons' and hanging up the receiver as a 'close'. Event boundaries may be signaled by ritual phrases, such as *Did you hear this one?* and then laughter to bound a joke; *Once upon a time* and *They lived happily ever after* to bound a story; or *Let us pray* and *Amen* to bound a prayer. Instead of these, or in addition, there may be changes in facial expression, tone of voice, or bodily position between one communicative event and the next, or a period of silence. Erickson and Schultz (1979) also report changes in gaze direction, change of participants' position in relation to one another, and change of rhythm of speech and body movements. Perhaps the surest sign of a change of events is code alternation, or the change from relatively consistent use of one language or variety to another. Boundaries are also likely to coincide with change of participants, change in topical focus, or change in the general purpose of communication. Major junctures in communication are signalled by a combination of verbal and nonverbal cues.

Consecutive events may be distinguished in a single situation. In a trial, for instance, the opening event begins when the bailiff cries *Hear ye, hear ye* and ends when the judge enters the courtroom and sits down on the bench, and all others are seated. Within the same situation, direct and cross examination of witnesses or the defendent may be identified as separate events because participants are in a different role-relationship, and there is a change in manner of questioning and responding: i.e. different rules for interaction. These events may be bounded by the change in participants, and perhaps by a verbal routine such as *I call — to the stand* to open and *You may stand down* or *Your witness* to close. If a recess is called before a boundary is reached, the interaction can be considered a single discontinuous speech event, even if continued on another day.

Formal ritual events in a speech community have more

clearly defined boundaries than informal ones because there is a high degree of predictability in both verbal and nonverbal content of routines on each occasion, and they are frequently set off from events which precede and follow by changes in vocal rhythm, pitch, and intonation. Brief interactions between people almost always consist of routines, such as greetings and leavetakings, and the boundaries of longer and most informal communicative events, such as conversations, can be determined because they are preceded and followed by them (Goffman 1971).

Since the discovery of communicative norms is often most obvious in their breach, examples of boundary violations may highlight what the appropriate boundary behavior is. Some people are annoyed with what they consider to be premature applause by others at the end of an opera, for instance, which indicates differences in what 'the end' of the event is perceived to be: the end of the singing or the end of all music. Still others may whisper through the overture, since for them the event has not yet begun. Christina Paulston (personal communication) reports the occurrence of a serious misunderstanding between Jewish and Christian parents attending an ecumenical service because the Jewish parents continued conversing after entering the place of worship, while the Christians considered this inappropriate behavior once the physical boundary into the sanctuary was crossed.

Micro-analysis of boundary signals in less formal situations commonly requires filming a communicative situation, and then asking participants to view the film themselves and to indicate when 'something new is happening'. The researcher then elicits characterizations of the event, and expectations of what may happen next (and what may *not* happen next), in order to determine the nature of the boundary signals, and how the context has changed from the point of view of the participants.

The communicative events selected initially for description and analysis for one learning to use this approach should be brief self-contained sequences which have readily identifiable beginnings and endings. Further, they should be events which recur in similar form and with some frequency, so that regular patterns will be more easily discernible: e.g., greetings, leavetakings, prayers, condolences, jokes, insults, compliments, ordering meals in restaurants. More complex and less regular events yield themselves to analysis more readily after patterns of use and norms of interpretation have already been discovered in relation to simpler and more regular communicative events.

COMPONENTS OF COMMUNICATION

Analysis of a communicative event begins with a description of the components which are likely to be salient (cf. Hymes 1967; 1972; Friedrich 1972):

1   The *genre*, or type of event (e.g. joke, story, lecture, greeting, conversation).
2   The *topic*, or referential focus.
3   The *purpose* or *function*, both of the event in general and in terms of the interaction goals of individual participants.
4   The *setting*, including location, time of day, season of year, and physical aspects of the situation (e.g. size of room, arrangement of furniture).
5   The *key*, or emotional tone of the event (e.g. serious, sarcastic, jocular).
6   The *participants*, including their age, sex, ethnicity, social status, or other relevant categories, and their relationship to one another.
7   The *message form*, including both vocal and nonvocal channels, and the nature of the code which is used (e.g. which language, and which variety).
8   The *message content*, or surface level denotive references; what is communicated about.
9   The *act sequence*, or ordering of communicative/speech acts, including turn taking and overlap phenomena.
10 The *rules for interaction*, or what proprieties should be observed.
11 The *norms of interpretation*, including the common knowledge, the relevant cultural presuppositions, or

shared understandings, which allow particular inferences to be drawn about what is to be taken literally, what discounted, etc.

All of these will be discussed in turn below.

Scene (Genre, Topic, Purpose/Function, Setting)

The first four components comprise the *scene*, or extra-personal *context* of the event. Of these, only the setting may be directly observed, although even for this component researchers might not notice an aspect of the setting which is not salient in their own culture: e.g. the relative elevation of chairs may be very important for understanding the meaning of the event (as in Japanese), and whether chairs in a classroom are arranged in straight rows or a circle may signal the appropriate level of formality (as in English).

The time of day, day of the week, or season of the year often affects choice of language form. This may include whole genres of events designated only for particular times; e.g. in Navajo one cannot talk about hibernating animals except during winter months, so that traditional stories about them may only be told at certain times of the year, and Orthodox Jews are constrained from discussing secular topics on the Sabbath. Routines such as *Merry Christmas*, *Happy New Year*, and *April Fool* can only be interpreted as joking or sarcastic out of their appropriate temporal or cultural context.

Place and time may affect the meaning of greetings. It is not appropriate for a speaker of the Abbey language to greet everyone in just any location, for instance, Hepié reports on his own usage:

Suppose I go back to my country [Ivory Coast] and run into a relative in the street. I won't greet him, but quickly let him know that I am on my way to his home to greet him. [This is because] the greeting in such cases shows you care about such people. Therefore it has to be at home, where the relative can at his ease get the news from you.

Nwoye reports that for Igbo, morning greetings are the most significant,

> since the morning is the beginning of the day and it is believed that the sort of person you first encounter in the morning determines your fortune for that day. . . . Therefore people consciously refrain from speaking to those who they know or suspect can bring ill luck and ruin their entire day.

Descriptive questions to be answered regarding the scene are:

- What kind of communicative event is it?
- What is it about?
- Why is it happening?
- Where and when does it occur?
- What does the setting look like?

Additional questions which may prove relevant to understanding the significance of a setting include:

- How do individuals organize themselves spatially in groups for various purposes (e.g. in rows, circles, around tables, on the floor, in the middle of the room, around its circumference)?
- What geospatial concepts, understandings, and beliefs exist in the group or are known to individuals?
- What is the knowledge and significance of cardinal directions (North, South, East, West)?
- What significance is associated with different directions or places (e.g. heaven is up, people are buried with heads to the west, the host at a meal should sit facing the door)?
- What beliefs or values are associated with concepts of time of day or season, and are there particular behavioral prescriptions or taboos associated with them (e.g. not singing certain songs in the summertime lest a snake bite, not telling stories until the sun has set)?

The organization of time and space is of enormous significance in most cultures, and one of the most frequent areas for cross-cultural conflict or misunderstanding, in large part because it is so often unconscious. In particular, ethnographers cannot assume that many of the concepts and attitudes regarding time and space (including personal space) held in their culture will hold for others.

Other components of the scene are not directly observable. The *genre*, or type of event, should be categorized according to indigenous perceptions and diversions (cf. Chapter 2). Relevant background questions for both *genre* and *purpose* might include:

- What is considered sacred and what secular?
- What beliefs and practices are associated with natural phenomena (e.g. eclipses and phases of the moon, comets, stars), and who or what is responsible for rain, lightening, thunder, earthquakes, and floods?
- Are particular behavioral prescriptions or taboos associated with natural phenomena?
- What holidays and celebrations are observed by the group and individuals?
- What is their purpose (e.g. political, seasonal, religious, didactic)?
- What range of behaviors is considered 'work' and what 'play'?
- What clothing is 'typical'? What is worn for special occasions?
- Are there any external signs of participation in any ritual events (e.g. ashes, dress, marking of skin)?

Key

According to Hymes, 'Key is introduced to provide for the tone, manner, or spirit in which the act is done' (1972:62). In labeling this component in English, we may think in terms of contrasts: e.g. teasing vs serious, sincere vs sarcastic, friendly vs hostile, sympathetic vs threatening, perfunctory vs pain-staking. Key is often redundantly ascribed to genre (e.g. jokes are jocular, condolences are sympathetic), but this is not a necessary relationship. In some cases jokes may be made in a sarcastic key, or condolences may be threatening. A particular key may also be associated primarily with a particular function of language use, role-relationship between participants, or message form and content.

The importance of this component in the description and analysis of communicative events lies in the fact that while redundancy is common, key may be independently variable with respect to any other component of a communicative event. When there is an apparent conflict between components, the key generally overrides other elements. For example, if a compliment is made in a sarcastic key, the sarcasm overrides the form and literal content of the message, and signals a different relationship between participants than would be the case if the compliment were sincere.

Key may be signalled by choice of language or variety, by nonverbal signals (e.g. wink or posture), by paralinguistic features (e.g. degree of aspiration), or by a combination of elements. In the sample analyses below, for instance, the sorrowful key of the formal condoling event among the Abbey is dependent on men's not standing fully erect during the ceremony, and the friendly and casual key of the Chinese dinner invitation event is signalled primarily by the frequency of interjections used in the message form and the extent of rising and falling intonation.

As with other components of communication, interpretation of key is culture-specific and must be determined according to indigenous perceptions. Because of its overriding importance to the meaning of an event, accounting for key is a crucial aspect of analysis.

Participants

The basic descriptive question to answer about *participants* is:

● Who is taking part in the event?

An adequate description of the participants includes not only observable traits, but background information on the composition and role-relationship within the family and other social institutions, distinguishing features in the life cycle, and differentiation within the group according to sex and social status. Answers to such questions as the following may prove relevant:

- Who is in a 'family'? Who among these (or others) lives in one house?
- What is the hierarchy of authority in the family?
- What are the rights and responsibilities of each family member?
- What are the functions and obligations of the family in the larger social unit?
- What are criteria for the definition of stages, periods, or transitions in life?
- What are attitudes, expectations, and behaviors toward individuals at different stages in the life cycle? What stage of life is most valued? What stage of life is most 'difficult'?
- Who has authority over whom: To what extent can one person's will be imposed on another? By what means?
- Do means of social control vary with recognized stages in the life cycle, membership in various social categories, or according to setting or offense?
- What roles within the group are available to whom, and how are they acquired?
- Do particular roles have positive or malevolent characteristics?

Among the questions relating participants to language and culture which will be answered in the process of ethnographic description and analysis are:

- How is language related to the life cycle?
- Is language use important in the definition or social marking of roles?
- What forms of address are used between people in various role-relationships?
- How is deference shown? How are insults expressed?
- Who may disagree with whom? Under what circumstances?
- How do the characteristics of 'speaking well' relate to age, sex, or other social factors?

- How does speaking ability, literacy, or writing ability relate to achievement of status in the society?
- What roles, attitudes, or personality traits are associated with particular ways of speaking?
- Who may talk to whom? When? Where? About what?
- What is the role of language in social control? What variety is used? In multilingual contexts, what is the significance of using the first versus the second language?

The dress of participants may also be relevant to the interpretation of their communicative behavior, and thus require description: e.g. Arab males may stand closer to females when talking if the woman is wearing a veil.

Belief about who may participate in communicative events is culture-specific, and is often not limited to humans. In the sample analyses below, for instance, Abbey speakers consider the drum and the invisible people who are invoked by the drum participants in condoling events, and the spirit of the deceased is an important participant for Igbo speakers; speakers of English and other European languages often believe they can communicate with pets.

Message Form

In studying the various social, cultural, and situational constraints on communicative behavior, both verbal and nonverbal codes are significant in the *message form, message content,* and *act sequence* components of communicative events, and each type of code as transmitted by both vocal and nonvocal channels. This four-way distinction on the dimensions of verbal–nonverbal and vocal–nonvocal is shown in figure 4.1. Where there are varieties recognized on any dimension (e.g. register or regional dialect), this is also considered part of message form.

Descriptions of verbal codes are generally limited to spoken and written language, but other modes of verbal communication are quite widespread. Communicative systems based on instrumental sounds (such as whistles and drum beats) are found in several parts of the world, for instance, and codes

CHANNEL

		Vocal	Nonvocal
CODE	Verbal	Spoken language	Written language (Deaf) Sign language Whistle/drum languages Morse code
	Nonverbal	Paralinguistic and prosodic features Laughter	Silence Kinesics Proxemics Eye behavior Pictures and cartoons

Figure 4.1

have been developed for electronic and telegraphic transmission, communication between ships, and other specialized purposes. Whistle or drum codes may involve a signal mode where short texts are repeated over and over, or they may involve a 'speech' mode in which a much wider range of texts is transmitted. The latter type of verbal code is referred to as *surrogate language* (described by Nketia 1972).

A more common example of verbal/nonvocal communication is the occurrence of well developed systems of manual sign language in communities which include individuals who are deaf or hearing impaired. Even though sign language may not be accompanied by any vocalization, it shares all other features of verbal communication with speech. In signing, a range of visual behaviors in addition to hand movements (which would be considered nonverbal in speech) operate on the verbal dimension. These include some facial expressions, which may even function at a syntactic level in this code. The nonverbal dimension of sign language includes the silence deliberately induced by closing the eyes or averting eye gaze.

Within linguistics, silence has traditionally been ignored except for its boundary-marking function, delimiting the beginning and end of utterances. The tradition has been to define it negatively – as merely the absence of speech. I will focus on it here in the discussion of message form to emphasize that adequate description and interpretation of communication requires that we understand the role of such phenomena as silence, as well as of speech.

In considering silence, a basic distinction must be made between silences which carry meaning, but not propositional content, and silent communicative acts which are entirely dependent on adjacent vocalizations for interpretation, and which carry their own illocutionary force. The former include the pauses and hesitations that occur within and between turns of talking – the prosodic dimension of silence. Such nonpropositional silences may be volitional or nonvolitional, and may convey a wide variety of meanings. The meanings carried by pauses and hesitations are generally affective in nature, and connotative rather than denotative. Their meanings are nonetheless symbolic and conventional, as is seen in the various patterns of use and norms of interpretation in different speech communities (see examples in Tannen and Saville-Troike 1985).

Silent communicative acts conveying propositional content may include gestures, but may also consist of silence unaccompanied by any visual cues. Even in a telephone conversation where no visual signals are possible, silence in response to a greeting, query, or request which anticipates verbal response is fraught with propositional meaning in its own right. Just as 'One can utter words without saying anything' (Searle 1969:24), one can say something without uttering words. Silence as part of communicative interaction can be one of the forms a 'speech' act may take – filling many of the same functions and discourse slots – and should be considered along with the production of sentence tokens as a basic formational unit of linguistic communication.

Analyzing the structure of silent communication might best be approached by considering how silence which carries grammatical and lexical meaning may replace different elements within discourse. One form of the WH- question typically used by teachers, for instance, is a fill-in-the-blank structure, e.g., 'This is a —?' (often said with lengthened or tensed *a* and nonterminal intonation), meaning 'What is this?' This form may also occur in conversational contexts when one speaker asks someone he or she has just met, 'And your name is —?' Utterances are also commonly completed in silence when the topic is a particularly delicate one or the word which would be used is taboo, or when the situation is emotionally loaded and the speaker is 'at a loss' for words. The Japanese term *haragei*, 'wordless communication', captures the essence of this latter type of silence. There is a belief in Japanese that as soon as an experience is expressed in words (oral or written), the real essence disappears.

Complete 'utterances' may also be composed of silence, as illustrated in the following conversational exchange:

P1   We've received word that four Tanzanian acquaintances from out of town will be arriving tommorrow. But, with our large family, we have no room to accommodate them. (Implied request: 'Would you help us out?')

P2   [Silence; not accompanied by any distinctive gesture or facial expression] (Denial: 'I don't want to' or 'I don't have any room either.')

P1   What do you think?

P2   Yes, that is a problem. Were you able to finish that report we were working on this morning?

The negative response by the second participant (P2) in the cultural milieu in which this took place violated P1's expectation that guests would be welcomed, and frustrated his goal in initiating the conversation (reported by Jalbert). Communicative events which include silent 'utterances' are also included in the sample analyses below.

Silence is often used over even longer segments of communication to convey a more generalized meaning, as in the 'stylized sulking' by young American Blacks that Gilmore observed in classrooms. This was intended to call attention to the 'speaker' and express disapproval of others' behavior. The following excerpts are from her description of this phenomenon:

Girls will frequently pose with their chins up, closing their eyelids for elongated periods and casting downward side glances, and often markedly turning their heads sidewards as well as upwards. . . . Striking or getting into the pose is usually with an abrupt movement that will sometimes be marked with a sound like the elbow striking the desk or a verbal marker like 'humpf'.

Boys usually display somewhat differently. Their 'stylized sulking' is usually characterized by head downward, arms crossed on the chest, legs spread wide and usually desk pushed away. Often they will mark the silence by knocking over a chair or pushing loudly on their desk, assuring that others hear and see the performance. (1985:149)

Entire communicative events without sound are also common. Especially in ritual contexts, silence may be conventionally mandated as the only form which could achieve the event's communicative goals. Thus the invocation in Christian ritual: 'The Lord is in His holy temple; let all the earth keep silence before Him.'

Methodologically, in the description of an unfamiliar (or even a familiar) culture, silence is often not documented because it does not attract attention in the same way that audible or visible behavior does. Because linguists typically define silence negatively as the *absence* of other features, Whorf's ghost stalks the pages of field notes and tape transcripts which omit potentially meaningful occurrences of silence. A special meta-awareness is needed to attend to the range of possible silences, and particular care is required in seeking their proper interpretation.

A similar case might be made for the importance of including occurrences of 'backchannel' signals and laughter in the description of communicative events. The 'backchannel' in an interaction is composed of the responses of participants who are being addressed (cf. Schegloff 1982). In English conversations, for instance, these include such nonverbal vocalizations as *mm hm* and *uh huh*, verbal *yeah* and *I see*, or nonvocal head nods and postural shifts. These may function merely as passive acknowledgement, actively encourage continuation, or indicate that change of topic or speaker turn is called for. Similar phenomena in other genres include responses of *Amen* by Christian congregation members during a preacher's sermon, or audience feedback to performers during an entertainment event. Although laughter is seldom even transcribed, it too is socially organized and thus patterns in relation to type of event, topic, key, and other components of communication (see Jefferson, 1984; discussion in Heritage 1985).

One problem which must be faced in recording communicative behavior other than spoken and written language codes is the complexity it adds to transcription. In describing such nonverbal/nonvocal behavior as kinesics and facial expression, for instance, it is important to identify: (1) the part of the body (i.e. what is moving or in a marked position), (2) the directionality of the movement, or how it differs from an unmarked state, and (3) the scope of movement, if any. Several systems for transcribing nonverbal behaviors have been developed (e.g. Birdwhistell 1952; Hall 1963; and Ekman, Friesen, and Tomkins 1971) especially for use when this channel is the primary focus of analysis. It is particularly important to correlate verbal and nonverbal behavior with an indication of their relationship to the verbal act sequence.

In most communicative events the message is carried by both verbal and nonverbal codes simultaneously, albeit only one or the other may be involved. Although such forms are universal, the specific value and meanings of each are relevant only in terms of individuals or particular groups.

Selection rules govern the use of particular message forms when a choice is made between possible alternatives. An example is provided by the selection of kinship terminology: while ethnographers may collect a single set of static reference terms for people in a particular genealogical relationship, in actual use speakers may select from a great variety of alternatives for the same individual in order to express nuances of feeling, or because of differences in other components in the event.

Once a selection has been made there are restrictions on what other alternative forms may co-occur. The usual distinction is between *paradigmatic constraints* and *syntagmatic constraints* (cf. Ervin-Tripp 1969; 1972): paradigmatic constraints govern selection of a form from among a possible set of items which might fill the same slot, and syntagmatic constraints govern the sequential selection within the same speech act.

Message Content

Message form and message content are closely interrelated, and the two components often cannot be separated in description and analysis. Message content refers to what communicative acts are about, and to what meaning is being conveyed. Hymes (1972:60) suggests that one context for distinguishing form and content would be: 'He prayed, saying ". . ."' (quoting message form [which also includes content]) versus 'He prayed that he would get well' (reporting content only). In the conversational exchange reported in the previous section, both the direct quotation of speech and the silent response exemplify message form, while their interpretation as a request for help in providing room for guests and a denial of help, respectively, exemplify message content which is not included in what was actually said.

In face-to-face communication meaning is derived not only from verbal and nonverbal message form and its content, but also from extralinguistic context, and from the information and expectations which participants bring to the communicative event. Because the various elements are processed simultaneously, it is difficult in most instances to isolate any subset for analysis. In order to examine the role of nonlinguistic factors in communication, I have chosen to study interaction between speakers of mutually unintelligible languages who lack knowledge of the language being spoken by the other participant – a phenomenon I call 'dilingual discourse' (Saville-Troike 1987).

The following examples illustrate the extent to which negotiation of meaning can be successful even without the availability of a common linguistic code. These exchanges involved a young Chinese-speaking child (P1) who had just arrived in the US and an English-speaking nursery school teacher (P2) who did not understand any Chinese:

1 P1 *Wode xie dai diao le.*
    (My shoelace is loose.)
    P2 *Here you go.* [She ties it.]

2 [P1 holds up a broken balloon.]
    P1 *Kan. Kan. Wo zhei mei le. Kan. Kan.*
    (Look. Look. Mine is gone. Look. Look.)
    P2 *Oh, it popped, didn't it? All gone.*

3 [P1 is looking at water standing in the sink.]
    P1 *Zenme zheige shui dou bu hui liu a?*
    (How come the water doesn't drain out?)
    P2 *It fills up, uh huh. It doesn't drain out very fast, does it?*

In each of these examples, agreement on the topic of interaction is achieved because there was an object or an unusual condition upon which mutual attention could be focused, and which was needing repair or was otherwise worthy of mention. P2 responded appropriately to what P1 had said both because of the physical context, and because her experience had given her the skill to expect what a child would likely comment on in that context (an inexperienced teacher was far less successful at this).

The importance of expectations is highlighted in the next example, where semantic coherence was not achieved. In this dialogue, the teacher had just shown some children a picture of a dog, and she expected that any comments they made would be about the dog in their own experience. She thus interpreted P1's Chinese utterances to be about a dog he had, and his gestures to be indicating the dog's size. Instead, P1 was informing her about dinosaurs, and his horizontal hand movements were illustrating geological formations. The teacher could not infer the message content in this case because it was outside of her 'structures of expectations' (Tannen 1979b) for what a child in nursery school would be talking about, as well as for the setting.

4   P1 *Konglong hao jiu hao jiu. Konglong xian zai dou yi jing bian cheng mei huang le.*
(Dinosaurs long time ago, long time ago. Dinosaurs now all already become coal mine.)

P2 *Do you have a dog with you?*

P1 *Hen shen o. Yi bo yi bo yi bo. Benlai di zai zhe bian. Di shi zhe yang chi lai. Gao dao zhe bian.*
(Very deep. One layer after another. Originally it was on the ground. The ground rose up like this. The ground is here.)

[P1 uses his hands in horizontal gestures to show what the ground looked like.]

P1 *Konglong zai zhe bian.*
(Dinosaurs are here.)

P2 *Oh. Growing big.*

Correctly conveying and interpreting message content is central to the establisment of even a minimal level of what is to be considered 'successful communication', although that concept may best be dealt with in terms of degree rather than absolutes. The first three examples of dilingual discourse related above can be considered successful at least to the extent that there was a shared topic for reference and understanding of speaker intent. While these illustrate that message content can be conveyed in some (highly predictable) situations even in the absence of a common linguistic code, abundant examples could also be cited of misunderstandings of message content when participants are speaking the same language, but do not share the same intralinguistic knowledge and expectations. To ignore any of these elements in the analysis of communicative interaction is to limit understanding of the processes involved.

Act Sequence

The *act sequence* component includes information about the ordering of communicative acts within an event.

We deal with the sequencing of action in which the move of one participant is followed by that of another, the first move establishing the environment for the second and the second confirming the meaning of the first. (Goffman 1971:149)

Ordering is usually very rigid in ritual events, such as greeting, leavetaking, complimenting, and condoling, and less so in conversation.

In describing a sequence, communicative acts may be characterized in terms of their function, with a typical example of the message form and content often also listed. Although description is usually at a level of abstraction which accounts for regular patterns in recurring events, verbatim examples are useful as illustrations. In analyzing opening sequences in Japanese door-to-door sales encounters, for instance, Tsuda (1984) bases her generalizations on 23 which she observed and recorded, but includes a verbatim transcript of only one which she considers 'typical'. Her data might be arranged in the following manner:

1   P1 (Salesperson): Greeting.
       Gomen kudasai.
       (Excuse me.)
2   P2 (Housewife): Acknowledgement
       Hai.
       (Yes)
3   P1: Identification
       Shitsurei shimasu. J degozai masu. Hai, J de gozaismasu.
       (Excuse me, I'm from J [company's name].
       Yes, J [company].)
4   P2: Question about purpose
       Nande shō?
       (What do you want of me?)

5   P1: Information about purpose

> *Anō, Okusan terebi de senden shite orimasu de sho? Anō, atsumono demo usumono demo nueru to yū.*
>
> (Do you know, *Okusan* [meaning housewife] about television commercial? The one we can sew even very thick ones or even very thin ones. . . .)

6   P2: Expression of disinterest/interest

> *Un, anō, mishin uchi ni aru wa.*
>
> (Well, a sewing machine. We have one at home.)

This level of abstraction not only allows regular patterns to be displayed, but cross-cultural comparisons to be made. In this case, the act sequence is found to be the same in openings of 'typical' door-to-door sales encounters in the United States, although there are significant differences in the form and content: e.g. American salespeople usually identify themselves first by name rather than by company affiliation, as in Japan.

Rules for Interaction

The *rules for interaction* component includes an explanation of the rules for the use of speech which are applicable to the communicative event. By 'rules' in this context, I am referring to prescriptive statements of behavior, of how people 'should' act, which are tied to the shared values of the speech community. They may additionally be descriptive of typical behavior, but this is not a necessary criterion for inclusion in this component. How, and the degree to which, this 'ideal' is indeed 'real' is part of the information to be collected and analyzed, along with positive and negative sanctions which are applied to their observance or violation.

The rules may already by codified in the form of aphorisms, proverbs, or even laws, or they may be held unconsciously and require more indirect elicitation and identification. Rules for interaction are often discoverable in reactions to their violation by others, and feelings that contrary behavior is 'impolite' or 'odd' in some respect.

One example is turn-taking rules in conversation: in English, if one speaker utters a compliment, request, or invitation, politeness usually requires the addressee to make an appropriate response on the next turn; in describing communicative patterns of speakers who live on the Warm Springs Indian reservation, Philips (1976) reports politeness would not require any response, or the response might be given at a later date.

In the sample analyses below, rules for interaction in a Bambura village meeting require turn-taking based on order of influence or importance in the group, and that each prospective speaker first request permission to speak from the chief. Rules may also prescribe nonverbal behavior, as in the examples of Abbey condolences, a Japanese marriage proposal, and a Newari prospective bride interview. They may even prescribe silence, as in the Igbo condolence when there had been a 'premature' death.

Norms of Interpretation

The *norms of interpretation* component should provide all of the other information about the speech community and its culture which is needed to understand the communicative event. Even the most detailed surface level description is inadequate to allow interpretation of the meaning conveyed. In the sample analyses below, for instance, a Bambara speaker in a village meeting must know that direct speech is used to defend a point, while riddles or parables are to be interpreted as opposition; an Igbo speaker condoling family members must know that an early death cannot be by natural causes, and that someone who causes another's death cannot stand before the spirit of the deceased without incurring immediate retaliation.

I am calling these 'norms' of interpretation because they constitute a standard shared by members of the speech community, they may also be related to rules of use in the prescriptive sense (cf. Shimanoff 1980), but the positive or negative valuation and sanctions on use which characterize rules are not a necessary condition for inclusion in this component.

RELATIONSHIP AMONG COMPONENTS

In addition to identifying the components of a communicative event, it is important to ask questions which relate each component to all of the others. For instance:

● How do the genre and topic influence one another?

There is probably a limited range of subjects which can be prayed about, joked about, or gossiped about. Conversely, it may be appropriate to mention a particular topic only in a religious genre, or perhaps only in a joke.

● What is the relationship between genre and purpose?

The primary purpose of myths might be to entertain, to transmit cultural knowledge, or to influence the supernatural; jokes might serve primarily to entertain, or might be a means of social control, or a testing ground for determining hierarchical relationships between speakers in the social structure.

● How are genre or topic and setting related?

Prayers might be said in a particular place, perhaps with altar and specified religious paraphernalia, and at certain times of the day or week; particular prayers might be appropriate only for certain holidays or seasons. Topics for stories might be limited by location, with different ones appropriate at the dinner table or in a classroom from those appropriate in a clubroom or a camp in the woods. Often topics are limited by season, as illustrated above.

● What is the relationship between genre, topic, setting, participants, and message form?

Some genres will require a more formal variety of language than others, or a different language entirely. In two events of the same genre, such as a greeting, the form might differ depending on season, time of day, whether indoors or outside, or other features in the setting. A lecture on the same topic might be more or less formal depending on the size of the room, the arrangement of furniture, and the number (or identity) of persons in the audience. The genre may also influence word order: Kululi speakers prefer Object–Subject–Verb for requests and teasing, for instance, but Subject–Object–Verb for narratives and stories (Duranti 1985).

The interrelationships of components may be very complex, as when the message form of a greeting is influenced not only by the season, time of day, and physical location, but the age, sex, and role-relationship of the participants, and the purpose of the encounter. While not all components will be salient in each event, nor even necessarily in each speech community, they provide one type of *frame* (Bateson 1955) within which meaningful differences can be discovered and described. The interpretation by the addressee of the utterance 'It's cold in here' as an informative statement, complaint, request, or command depends on the scene, participant role-relationships, what precedes and follows in the sequence of communicative acts, and such paralinguistic and prosodic features of speech as pitch, intonation, rhythm, and amplitude. These signal what kind of speech event participants are engaged in: i.e. their metacommunicative frame (cf. Gumperz 1977; Tannen 1979a).

ELICITATION WITHIN A FRAME

Part of the task of analysis is discovering which components are relevant within the particular speech community under investigation. At an early stage in description it is generally useful to consider the *frame*, a somewhat static entity which may be manipulated in the data collection process to allow elicitation of what differences in and among the components are meaningful from the perspective of native speakers.

In its simplest form the use of the frame is not unlike the 'minimal pair' technique of structural linguistics. In investigating possible differences in a greeting event, for instance, the ethnographer may observe and record several greetings, noting any differences in message form, content, participant, key, and scene. Participants may then be interviewed to discover if they perceive any difference in meaning among varieties of greeting which have been observed. The ethnographer may probe further by holding the frame constant except for minimal changes and elicit information about what differences these would make in communicative behavior or its interpretation. Questions might include: What if one participant were older than the other? What if one were male and one female? Would it make a difference whether or not the woman wore a veil? What if it were evening instead of morning, or on the street instead of in a building? And so on.

A more complex discovery procedure discussed earlier calls for role-playing on the part of informants, where they are asked to pretend to be in a particular situation so the ethnographer can observe what they believe appropriate behavior would be. Role-playing often yields idealized or stereotypic behavior which cannot be accepted as actual usage unless validated by more naturalistic observation, but in itself provides interesting insights into the perceptions of native speakers in the event.

A creative extension of this technique of elicitation within a frame was used by Laughlin to collect data on communicative situations in the Zinacantán (Mayan) community in Chiapas, Mexico, which he was not permitted to directly observe.

> Amorous intrigues and daredevil elopements are the spice of daily gossip; but so vigilant is the watch upon the trails and waterholes that it has always seemed to me a nearly superhuman feat to exchange a word with a girl without the knowledge and chastisement of the town. Piqued by curiosity, but despairing over the prospects of ever becoming a participant observer, I finally handed Romin Teratol [his informant] three titles and asked him to provide the scenarios and script for the melodramas that follow. These fictional accounts present what Romin believes to be typical exchanges of conversations between a man and his prospective girlfriend. (1980:140)

Laughlin is thus able to include in his ethnographic texts 'Fictitious Seduction of Girl', 'Fictitious Seduction of Widow by a Married Man', and Fictitious Seduction of Girl by a Drunk'.

ANALYSIS OF INTERACTION

Adequate analysis must go beyond a static concept of frame to the consideration of frame in an interactive model, as dynamic 'schemata' or 'structures of expectation' (as discussed under *Message Content* above). This approach requires us to recognize that:

> people approach the world not as naive, blank-slate receptacles who take in stimuli as they exist in some independent and objective way, but rather as experienced and sophisticated veterans of perception who have stored their prior experiences as 'an organized mass', and who see events and objects in the world in relation to each other and in relation to their prior experience. This prior experience or organized knowledge then takes the form of expectations about the world, and in the vast majority of cases, the world, being a systematic place, confirms these expectations, saving the individual the trouble of figuring things out anew all the time. (Tannen 1979b:144)

Understanding what the speakers' frames are, what processes they are using to relate these expectations to the production and interpretation of language, and how the schemata and interaction processes relate to their shared cultural experiences, is the ultimate goal in explaining communicative competence; but developing methods for collecting and analyzing such information is a formidable challenge.

A project directed by Wallace Chafe has involved showing a film to subjects in ten different countries, and then eliciting narratives describing its content (the Pear Stories, briefly mentioned above). Speakers' culturally determined structures of expectation were then inferred from the way objects and events were organized and changed in the retelling (Chafe 1980; Tannen 1981). Films (or even still photos) of various communicative situations within the community may also be used in eliciting subsequent explanations from participants about what was going on at the time the picture was taken, from their own perspective. Since the film maker must select and focus on particular features in the total context, another potentially useful technique in collecting ethnographic data is to have one or more members of the group being studied control the camera themselves, collecting examples of different types of speech events (cf. Worth and Adair 1975). Where culturally appropriate and acceptable, this is likely to yield data not only on the classification of events and their salient components, but also on their temporal and spatial boundaries, and on the 'point' of the interaction.

Another model for dynamic analysis is provided by the work of Gumperz in the analysis of cross-cultural conversation events. In one interview session between a British counselor and a Pakistani mathematics teacher, for instance, Gumperz (1979) illustrates how the different sociocultural rules for appropriate language use each participant brings to the encounter yield different intepretative frames. The types of rules highlighted there include those in the 'structures of expectation' as they emerge in the process of *conversational inferencing* (Gumperz 1977). This analytic procedure makes an important contribution to the description of speech events by yielding not only abstract communicative frames, but by accounting for the dynamic interaction processes which occur within those frames – the construction and negotiation of meaning.

Other methods which have proved useful in inferring the principles being used by speakers in their dynamic use of language include *playback* (Fanshel and Moss 1971; Labov and Fanshel 1977), in which participants are interviewed in depth about the meaning of their own utterances in the process of microanalysis, and the study of institutionalized speakers who are judged by psychiatrists to exhibit communicative behavior which is 'inappropriate in the situation' (Goffman 1963). Such procedures may be profitably integrated with more traditional ethnographic methods to assist in discovering patterns of communication.

SAMPLE ANALYSES OF COMMUNICATIVE EVENTS

The following are examples of communicative events based on descriptions by former graduate students at Georgetown University and the University of Illinois who are native speakers of the languages involved: Bambara, Abbey, Japanese, Thai, Igbo, Cebuano (Bukadon/Philippines), Newari, and Chinese. In these events the message form, content, and act sequence are generalized as 'typical', and are reported here without verbatim examples. They are intended to illustrate the type of information perceived as relevant in the components that are identified by these speakers, and one possible model for the arrangement of data.

1   Issiaka Ly describes a traditional village meeting among Bambara speakers in Mali.

TOPIC: How animals should be kept away from farms

FUNCTION/PURPOSE: Making a decision that will regulate the village life

SETTING:
    If mid-afternoon with a hot sun overhead, under trees
    If in the late afternoon or during evening hours, in the village common place

KEY: Serious

PARTICIPANTS:
    All of the male inhabitants of the village:
    P1 – Chief
    P2 – Herald
    P3 – Active inhabitants (age 45+)
    P4 – Semi-active inhabitants (age 21–45)
    P5 – Passive inhabitants (age 14–20)

MESSAGE FORM:
    Spoken Bambara
    P2 uses loud voice; others use soft voices

ACT SEQUENCE:
    P1 recites agenda
    P2 transmits agenda to assembly

P3 (one) asks for floor
P2 transmits request to P1
P1 grants consent or rejects request
P2 transmits consent or rejection to speaker P3
P3 gives opinion (if P1 consents)
P2 transmits opinion to P1 and assembly
[Acts 3–8 are repeated as active members (P3s) take turns giving their opinions]
P1 summarizes the debate and makes a proposal
P2 transmits the summary and proposal to the assembly

RULES FOR INTERACTION:
Only active members (age 45+) may ask to speak
Semi-active members (21–45) may be asked their opinion, but not volunteer it
Each speaker must request permission to speak from the chief
The chief and other participants should not talk directly to one another; the herald always transmits speech from the chief to the assembly, or from any individual speaker to chief and assembly
Active inhabitants should take turns speaking in order of influence or importance

NORMS OF INTERPRETATION:
Direct speech (laconic and clear) means the speaker is defending a point
Indirect speech (e.g. riddles and parables) means the speaker is opposing a point
The people in the assembly are serious
The Herald is not necessarily being serious.

2   Marcellen Hepié describes a greeting event between Abbey speakers in the Ivory Coast to illustrate the concept of 'variation in a frame' with respect to the sex and age of participants. His focus is on differences this makes in the act sequence. The setting of the greeting also makes a difference in the content and sequence, but that component is held constant in this example:

FUNCTION/PURPOSE: Reaffirming the good relationship between participants at the beginning of a visit

SETTING: A private home

KEY: Friendly

PARTICIPANTS:
   P1 – Resident of home
   P2 – Visitor
   Variable conditions
      A   P1 and P2 are both adult males, or P1 is male and P2 female
      B   P1 is female, P2 male
      C   P1 is child, P2 adult
      D   More than one visitor comes at the same time

ACT SEQUENCE:
Condition A
   Phase One – 'greeting and response'
      P2 Greeting
      P1 Acceptance of greeting
         P1 looks for chair for P2 (if none is immediately available, this may involve a long pause in the greeting sequence)
   Phase Two – 'having a seat'
      P1 offers P2 a seat
      P2 returns greeting
   Phase Three – 'asking the news'
      P1 and P2 sit down
      P1 asks P2 of the news
      P2 gives standard, formulaic response
Condition B
   Phase One and Phase Two are the same
   P2 then rushes to seek nearest man to complete greeting sequence
   If she does not find any, she breaks the rules, apologizes, and completes the greeting herself by 'asking the news'
Condition C
   If P1 is a young child, no greeting takes place
   P2 asks P1 to call parents
   If P1 is older child, Phase One and Phase Two may be completed before seeking an adult
Condition D
   The youngest visitor who is considered an adult is the one who carries out the news

For Phase Three, P1 talks directly to the one who has been appointed by the group to give the news; the person must consult the group before responding

RULES FOR INTERACTION:
A child beyond age ten has a 'right' to be greeted
Between friends, the order of greeting may be relaxed, but 'a woman who always greets first would not be well-judged'

NORMS OF INTEPRETATION:
If Phase Two or Phase Three is omitted, or there is any change in order, it indicates there is something amiss in the relationship between P1 and P2
'Asking the news' is part of the greeting and not considered the point of the visit
After conventional responses regarding the 'news', P2 will bring up the actual reason for the visit (beginning another speech event).

3   Hepié illustrates variation within another genre of Abbey communication as he contrasts formal (A) and informal (B) condoling events.

PURPOSE/FUNCTION:
A   The goal of formal condolence is more than simple sympathy to the family of the deceased. It is a proof of solidarity and unity within a village, and between villages, because outsiders come to condole the afflicted village.
B   The goal of informal condolence is to provide moral support for the bereaved, plus material assistance.

SETTING:
A   Takes place on a street nearest to the bereaved family's residence.
    The time is in the evening after dark, within 24 hours of death; it is prior to the burial ceremony.
    Two lines of seats are up – one for receivers (on the right side), the one facing it for visitors.
B   Takes place at the bereaved's home, usually under a shelter in the courtyard. (A shelter is normally built for any dead person, except perhaps a baby.)
    It may take place a week or more after death, and after burial.

KEY: Sorrowful

PARTICIPANTS:

    P1 – Males from the village which receives condolences

    P2 – Principals who come to condole, both male and female

    P3 – Spectators, including women, children, and men who are not directly involved (and will not occupy seats)

    P4 – The drum, a sacred instrument only used in formal situations for communicating with the invisible word and transmitting bad news to neighboring villages

    P5 – Invisible people invoked by the drum

B   P1 – Men and women in two separate groups, usually members of the family (children are normally kept away from a place where a dead body is exposed)

    P2 – Outsiders, men and women who come to condole, whether they are from the same village or not

MESSAGE FORM AND SEQUENCE; RULES FOR INTERACTION:

A   Condolences are nonverbal. Participants offering condolence gesture with their right hand, one after another. A participant in such an event is expected to walk appropriately. A condoling person should not be standing fully erect during the ceremony. Also, he should bow when he arrives in front of an important person. Women in the condoling visitors line do not make any gesture, but just walk normally and usually go to the end of the line.

    P4 transmits the bad news

    P2 arrive, announced by three guns firing

    P4 spreads the news of the arrival of P2

    P1 already in place, seated in chairs, are waiting to be condoled

    P3 get closer to the scene to watch

    P2 are joined by some people of the host village who guide them to act appropriately

    P2 condole P1 in a line, from right to left – nonverbal, as described above

    P1 watch condoling gestures seriously

B   P2 can cry loudly while approaching the scene. Crying is the women's duty. Men, whether P1 or P2, are not expected to cry except for a very short time (less than one minute)

    P2 women are crying

    P2 men walk straight and verbally condole P1 men

    P1 women then take a seat among the P1 men

P2 women keep on crying until P1 women demand that they stop, then P2 women verbally condole P1 men
P2 women take seats among P1 women
(Men usually sit in chairs, women on the ground)

NORMS OF INTERPRETATION:
Formal condoling is required in situations such as where a woman from one village marries a man in another. If she dies, she will be buried in her village of origin (except where there is strong opposition). People from her village of origin go to the village of residence to condole not only her relatives there, but the whole village as well; i.e. those being condoled include affinal kin, those condoling include consanguinal kin.

4 Harumi Williams describes a Japanese marriage proposal, a communicative event which consists of only one verbal utterance.

FUNCTION/PURPOSE:
To declare intention to marry
To establish or develop an appropriate role-relationship

KEY: Serious

PARTICIPANTS:
P1 – Male; young adult
P2 – Female; young adult
(Their occupation and status is not relevant)

MESSAGE FORM:
Verbal – spoken Japanese; silence
Nonverbal – kinesics; eye gaze

MESSAGE CONTENT AND SEQUENCE:
P1 Holds P2's hand (optional)
Looks at P2
Says 'Please marry me'
P2 Stands with head down
Silence

RULES FOR INTERACTION:
A man must propose to a woman
At an emotional climax, there should be silence
The woman's head should hang down, and the direction of her eye gaze should be lower than the man's

NORMS OF INTERPRETATION:

The head of the household is to be the man, and therefore he has to take the initiative in the decision of marriage. This custom has its roots in an early Japanese myth when Ezanami (female god) and Izanagi (male god) married. First Ezanami proposed marriage to Izanagi and they married, but they could produce only evil creatures like worms, so they had to have the marriage ceremony again. This time Izanagi proposed, and the marriage was a success, producing a country called 'Japan'. This custom continues until the present day and the commonly held view is that the rule should not be violated.

There is also a belief that as soon as an experience is expressed in words (oral or written), the real essence disappears. When parents die, when the son passes the entrance examination to a university, and when we see something extremely beautiful, there should be silence. There is a well-known poem which starts 'Oh, Matsushima (name of an island in Japan) . . .', but because the poet was so impressed by its beauty he could not continue; this poem is considered one of his masterpieces.

Marriage is a climax in a girl's life, its main goal. The proposal is therefore such an important event, the only appropriate response can be silence. The hanging head and lowered gaze imply modesty, a highly prized virtue in a girl.

This response is what the young man expects, and it confirms that this is indeed the girl he wants for his wife; their future life will be quiet, and one with him as head of the household. He was not really asking her a question and expecting an answer, but declaring his decision to marry her.

5 Suphatcharee Ekasingh describes an introduction among Thai speakers.

PURPOSE/FUNCTION:

To establish participants' relationship

SETTING:

An informal social gathering

KEY: Friendly and polite

PARTICIPANTS:
  P1 – Thai female in early 40's
  P2 – Thai male student in mid 20's
  P3 – Thai female in late 40's
  P1 and P2 know each other very well; P1 is a very close friend
        of P2's parents and she considers P2 to be a relative
  P1 and P3 are acquaintances; both have lived in the same
        neighbourhood for more than ten years

MESSAGE FORM:
  Spoken Thai, central dialect, polite register
        The polite register includes the tone of the utterances and
        the use of appropriate pronouns according to age, sex, and
        social status
  Hand gestures and body position
        The *wai* is a gesture made by putting the palms of the hands
        together and then raising them in front of the face while
        bending down the head and bowing the body

MESSAGE CONTENT AND SEQUENCE:
  P1   Introduces P2 to P3, using their first names
  P2   Greets P3, using male polite particle
        Simultaneously performs the *wai*
  P3   Accepts greeting, using female polite particle
        Simultaneously performs the *wai*
  P1   Provides P3 with more information about P2
  P3   Then continues conversation with P2, asking primarily about
        his studies

RULES FOR INTERACTION:
  In an informal setting like this where differences in social status
        are not salient, P2 and P3 should be introduced by
        first name. Once the relationship has been established,
        nicknames may be used.
  The younger P should be introduced to the older P.
  The polite register must be used.

NORMS OF INTERPRETATION:
  Age plays a significant role in this genre; it is believed that if
        the older does the *wai* first, they will have short lives.
  The height of the *wai* indicates the degree of respect.
  Asking personal questions is part of getting to know another

and not considered impolite, although questions about income or age may be offensive.

6   A communicative event may take place with no speech at all, as illustrated by Gregory Nwoye in this description of a condoling event among Igbo speakers in Nigeria on the occasion of a 'premature' death.

PURPOSE/FUNCTION:
To express sympathy, and to prove innocence of being responsible for the death

SETTING:
Inside the home of the bereaved family
Approximately four days following the death
Seats are around the room for mourners

KEY: Sympathetic

PARTICIPANTS:
P1 – Sympathizer/mourner; adult male
P2 – Family members
P3 – Spirit of the deceased
P4 – Other mourners; adult males

MESSAGE FORM:
Silence and proxemics

ACT SEQUENCE:
P2 is standing inside the house
P3 is hovering nearby
P1 a) enters
    b) stands before P2 and P3
    c) sits silently among P4
    d) again presents himself to P2 and P3
    e) leaves

RULES FOR INTERACTION:
The bereaved family should be avoided for several days after the death
Mourners should present themselves in the home of the bereaved while the spirit of the deceased is still present (before final burial rites)
Mourners should not speak

NORMS OF INTERPRETATION:
> Death is a normal part of the life cycle and should occur only at a ripe age – premature death causes profound grief, and must have been caused by malevolent forces
> Verbal reference to death increases grief
> Physical presence indicates sympathy with the bereaved
> Someone who causes another's death cannot stand before the spirit of the deceased without incurring immediate retaliation

7 Genoveva M. Ablanque describes a ritual response to lightning among the Bukidons of the southern Philippines.

FUNCTION/PURPOSE:
> To avoid punishment for doing something unnatural

SETTING:
> Inside a house during a severe thunderstorm, usually in afternoon
> Lightning and thunder often accompanied by impending rain and strong wind
> Air sometimes dark and heavy

KEY: Foreboding

PARTICIPANTS:
> P1 – Evil spirits
> P2 – All persons in the house
> P3 – Member of household who accepts responsibility for ritual acts

MESSAGE FORM:
> Silence
> Cutting and burning of locks of hair

ACT SEQUENCE:
> P1   Arrival signalled by lightning and thunder
> P2   Cease speech and all other activity
> P3   Builds a fire, if there is not one
> Gets scissors and cuts a lock of hair from each P2 (including self)
> Carries locks to stove and burns them

RULES FOR INTERACTION:

The individual who performs the ritual cutting and burning of hair (P3) self-selects, but it should be a mature adult (usually the mother).

There must be absolute silence during the ritual.

The smell of burning hair should be strong enough to dominate the air.

NORMS OF INTERPRETATION:

After someone does something unnatural, evil spirits are present.

'Unnatural' acts include marrying a relative, causing animals of some different species to fight, talking to an animal, and laughing while playing with worms, picking lice, or watching dogs copulate.

Lightning is sent as punishment from the spirit who presides over destiny; if a person is struck by lightning, it would be presumed that the individual was guilty.

The belief is traced to a legend that a girl and her suitor were struck by lightning after she talked to her pet dog; the rain fell so hard that the place became Pinamaloy ('punishment') Lake.

Children are most likely to be guilty since they may not know how to discern what is considered 'unnatural', but they are still vulnerable to the punishment.

8 Jyoti Tuladhar describes a typical event among Newari speakers in Nepal in which a prospective bride is being interviewed by a member of the suitor's family.

PURPOSE/FUNCTION:

To determine the suitability of the bride by initial superficial examination

SETTING:

The prospective bride's home, in the evening

The participants are seated close to one another

KEY: Judgmental

PARTICIPANTS:

P1 – Suitor's aunt

P2 – Prospective bride's aunt

P3 – Prospective bride

MESSAGE FORM:
> The Kaltimandu dialect of the Newari language as used in traditional households, interspersed with no foreign loan words except *school* and *college*

The women's bodies are relaxed, but still

CONTENT AND SEQUENCE:
> P1 Such a pretty girl, your niece. Where do you go to school, child?
> P3 At Kirtipur.
> P2 She'll be graduating in April.
> P1 Wonderful! I here you're very smart?
> P3 (Smile) (Silence)
> P2 She's never stood second in her class.
> P1 My nephew broke the record in his college, too. Did you hear about that?
> P3 (Nod) (Silence)

RULES FOR INTERACTION:
> Genteel women do not make 'gross' hand gestures. The position of the body should be relaxed and still.
> Young girls should be shy, silent, and accept compliments with a smile.
> Direct remarks like 'such a pretty girl' in the presence of the subject can be made only by an elderly person to a young girl, and only in such situations as this interview. It is not the general practice among Newars to compliment someone on her beauty directly in social interchanges. A girl may even be offended by such a remark on other occasions.
> Genteel young girls stay silent in the presence of unfamiliar elderly women (even more so with men), unless addressed with direct questions. Their replies should be short or even monosyllabic. If they choose not to reply at all, this is not considered rude or impolite.
> A verbal response to the final question might have been considered arrogant; its intent was to place her in a difficult situation as a test of her manners.

NORMS OF INTERPRETATION:
> In a situation such as this, the girl's family would already have decided that the suitor was a suitable match for their daughter, and would have agreed to the encounter so

that his family could decide if she was appropriate for him. The girl would generally be unaware of the purpose of the visit.

Even though the suitor's aunt asks the girl a number of questions she is not interested in the answers so much as the manner of response. She had obtained all necessary information from the girl's aunt prior to this meeting. The girl's performance in this case would be considered quite satisfactory.

9   As a final example, Hong-Gang Jin describes an informal dinner invitation between Chinese graduate students who are temporarily residing in the US.

FUNCTION/PURPOSE:
  To enhance personal relationships
  To express gratitude for help which others have offered

SETTING:
  P2's office at a US university, 5 p.m.

KEY: Friendly and casual

PARTICIPANTS:
  P1 – Chinese graduate student, male
  P2 – Chinese graduate student, male
  P1 and P2 are from the same city in China, and got to know
      one another through relatives there
  P2 recently returned to China for a short visit, and brought
      back some things for P1 from P1's parents

MESSAGE FORM:
  Spoken standard Chinese, Beijing dialect
      Casual register, including many interjections during dis-
      course; rising and dropping intonation
  Head movement (nodding, shaking); facial expression

CONTENT AND SEQUENCE (organized into phases):
  Phase one: Opening
      P1   Greeting
      P2   Accepts greeting
            Offers a seat
            Returns greeting

Phase Two: Invitation

P1   Hints that he will ask P2 to do something
     Pauses to look for P2's reaction (observes facial expression)
     Offers the invitation to dinner at his home
P2   Refuses the invitation (surprised expression, then frown)
P1   Insists on acceptance
P2   Accepts indirectly (facial expression indicates he has no alternative)
P1   Reassures P2 of sincerity of invitation; sets definite time
P2   Agrees on time; expresses thanks
P1   Reassures P2 it will be informal

Phase Three: Closing

P1   Confirms the time
     Makes an excuse for leave-taking
P2   Thanks P1 again
     Closing salutation
P1   Closing salutation

RULES FOR INTERACTION:

The host should insist at least two or three times, but control his insistence according to the reaction of the person being invited.

The invitation should be refused two or three times before it can be accepted:

First decline modestly, then accept indirectly.

Show through facial expressions that one is reluctant to accept the invitation, and accepts it because there is no other alternative.

NORMS OF INTERPRETATION:

In China, inviting someone to a dinner is seen as an important social activity which fulfills basically two functions: (a) to enhance social relationships, and (b) to express appreciation for something another has done for the host, or sometimes to express a need for someone to offer help.

The host's degree of insistence varies according to his reading of the guest's face and the wording and tone of his answer.

If the guest's face shows hesitance or indifference, or if the answer is directly 'no' or a good excuse, the host will not insist further.

The way of accepting an invitation reflects a person's manners and self-discipline: modestly declining and then accepting indirectly and with thoughtfulness is considered courteous, good-mannered, and considerate; the opposite will be considered discourteous or ill-mannered.

ARRANGEMENT OF DATA

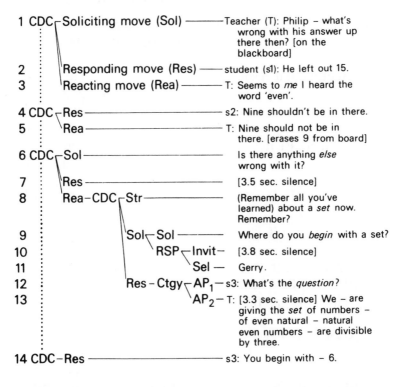

CDC = Classroom discourse cycle
Str = Structuring move
RSP = Respondent selection process
Invit = Invitation for a volunteer

Sel = Selection
Ctgy = Contingency sequ
AP = Adjacency pair

Figure 4.2

Other models for the arrangement of data may be more appropriate for focusing on different aspects of an event. In her description of classroom discourse cycles (CDCs), for example, Johnson (1972) graphically presents the structure of an act sequence and the relation of acts to one another by using the format shown in figure 4.2. Given the amount of embedding present in this cycle, it is easy to understand why s3 (act 12) has lost track of the question.

Formalization of the act sequence using features which are salient in the event may allow variable conditions to be expressed. The Abbey greeting described above might be partially accounted for with the following ordered rules:

Greeting sequence → Greeting and response + Having a seat + Asking the news

(1) Greeting and response →

$$
\text{P2 greets P1 if} \quad \text{P2} = \begin{bmatrix} + \begin{bmatrix} \text{male} \\ \text{adult} \\ \text{friendly} \end{bmatrix} \\ \alpha \ [\text{female}] \\ - \begin{Bmatrix} \text{child} \\ \text{unfriendly} \end{Bmatrix} \end{bmatrix}
$$

$$
\text{P1 responds if} \quad \text{P1} = \begin{bmatrix} + \begin{bmatrix} \text{adult} \\ \text{friendly} \end{bmatrix} \\ \alpha \ [\text{older child}] \\ - \ [\text{unfriendly}] \end{bmatrix}
$$

(2) Having a seat →
P1 offers P2 a seat
P1 returns greeting

(3) Asking the news →

$$
\text{P1 asks P2 the news if} \quad \text{P1} = \begin{bmatrix} + \begin{bmatrix} \text{adult} \\ \text{male} \end{bmatrix} \\ \alpha \ [\text{female}] \\ - \ [\text{child}] \end{bmatrix}
$$

P2 gives formulaic response

This would read as:

(1) P2 utters a greeting if P2 is a friendly, adult male; P2 may greet if a female, but this is less likely; P2 will not greet if unfriendly or a child. P1 will accept greeting if a friendly adult (male or female); P1 may accept if an older child; P1 will not accept if unfriendly.
(2) If a greeting has been given and accepted, P1 (male or female of any age) will offer P2 a seat and return the greeting.
(3) P1 will ask the news if an adult male; a female may ask news, but is less likely to do so; even an older child who has accepted greetings cannot ask news.

These rules are ordered in the sense that the remainder of the rules are blocked from application if one fails to apply: i.e. if a female P2 does not greet P1, P1 cannot respond, offer P2 a seat, nor ask P2 the news. Features are marked $(+)$ if the rule always applies if they are present, (α) if it applies variably, and $(-)$ if it does not apply at all.

Larger units of communication may also be described with rules or diagrams. The opening sequence in the Japanese door-to-door sales event listed earlier is part of a longer encounter, and Tsuda (1984) uses the flow chart shown in figure 4.3 to summarize its optional and obligatory components and their ordering.

The ethnography of communication, like the blend of scientific and humanistic approaches which it is, seeks always to discover the general from the particular, and to understand the particular in terms of the general, to see the unique event and the recurrent pattern both from the pespective of their native participants and the vantage point afforded by cross-cultural knowledge and comparison. There are many roads to understanding, and many approaches to the integrative insights sought by the investigator. Mechanical arrangements of data are not in themselves an equivalent of understanding, nor a substitute for careful observation, patient inquiry, or meticulous recording of data. But while the classification and

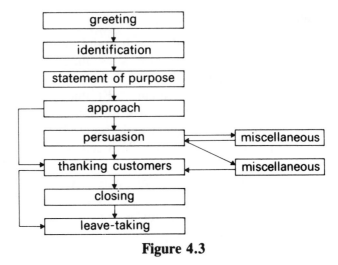

Figure 4.3

organization of data in various formats or displays is never the end of analysis, it can be a valuable procedure in bringing to light conditions or constraints which might otherwise have escaped notice, and in revealing patterns of interrelationships and features which had resisted more direct efforts at discovery. In addition, such organization of data can be useful in presenting findings in ways that make them more intelligible and coherent than an extended prose treatment might do.

Since the ethnography of communication is a relatively new field, much remains to be explored in developing methods and models for analysis and presentation. The examples of descriptive treatments given above are meant to be illustrative of some of those now in use, but many other possibilities are emerging as the field grows and develops. General ethnographies on ways of speaking are still very limited in number despite the general recognition of their theoretical and methodological importance. One of the notable exceptions remains the work of Ethel Albert with the Burundi of Central Africa from 1955 to 1957, which was actually conducted before the concept of the ethnography of communication was enunciated by Hymes (Albert 1972). She relates situation-specific 'rules for speaking' to Burundi cultural views and social structure, relates both to personal strategies, and discusses some of the problems encountered in cross-cultural communication and fieldwork.

Other important holistic models are provided by such work as that of Blom and Gumperz (e.g. 1972), who account for the interrelationship of social constraints, cultural values, and language rules in Norway; Barth's ([1964a] 1972) study of social processes and language boundaries in Pakistan; Abrahams' (1983) analysis of Afro-American speaking behavior; the Scollons' (1979) analysis of linguistic convergence at Fort Chipewyan, Alberta; Philips' (1983b) description of the Warm Springs Indian Reservation in Oregon; and Sherzer's (1983) extensive study of the ways of speaking among the Kuna population of San Blas, Panama. One major outcome has been a fuller understanding of how the social organization of a community is related to language use, and conversely, how language use signals social role.

Most other holistic research has focused on a single subculture within a society, such as those defined by religion (Bauman 1974; 1983; Enninger and Raith 1982; Schiffrin 1984), or by race or ethnicity (e.g. Blacks in a neighborhood in Washington, DC (Hannerz 1969) or a bar in Philadelphia (Bell 1983), or a Puerto Rican neighborhood in New York City (Attinasi, Pedraza, and Poplack et al. 1982). Some of these have been referred to earlier in Chapters 2 and 3.

Many descriptions and analyses of individual communicative events in diverse communities have appeared, some of the best in collections by Gumperz and Hymes (1986), Bauman and Sherzer (1974), and Baugh and Sherzer (1984). Most of these focus on ritual events rather than on everyday encounters, in part because such events by their nature are most likely to recur in regularized form, and in part because their meaning is most clearly dependent on shared beliefs and values of the speech community. (Philipsen and Carbaugh (1986) have compiled a bibliography of over 200 studies conducted within their paradigm to that date.)

A final caveat is in order in this discussion of methodology. Even as we attempt to be faithful to the realities of behavior as it is enacted, we must not ignore the broader context within which the actions we observe are situated. We must constantly seek for both the antecedents and the contingencies which give meaning to the scenes we witness. At the same time, we must continually test our perceptions and under-standings against those of the participants, if our 'objective' account of their communicative competence is to adequately reflect the experienced reality of their own subjective world.

5

Attitudes toward Communicative Performance

Attitudes toward language and its use have been of major interest to researchers in recent years, and have been elicited and analyzed from a variety of disciplinary perspectives. Of particular relevance for ethnographers are questions of how culture-specific criteria for 'speaking well' function in the definition of marking of social roles, how attitudes toward different languages and varieties of language reflect perceptions of people in different social categories, and how such perceptions influence interaction within and across the boundaries of a speech community. In addition to their value in adding to our understanding of functions and patterns of language use, answers to such questions are relevant to the explanation of language maintenance and shift, and to applied concerns in the fields of cross-cultural communication, language planning, and education. Some of these issues have been briefly addressed in the discussion of language varieties, but all warrant further attention.

Language attitude studies may be characterized as: (1) those which explore general attitudes toward language and language skills (e.g. which languages or varieties are better than others, to what extent literacy is valued, etc.); (2) those which explore stereotyped impressions toward language, their speakers, and their functions; and (3) those which focus on applied concerns (e.g. language choice and usage, and language learning). Underlying each are questions of the nature of language attitudes, their causes, and their effects.

One reason language attitudes are of particular interest to ethnographers is that individuals can seldom choose what attitudes to have toward a language or variety. Attitudes are acquired as a factor of group membership, as part of the process of enculturation in a particular speech community, and thus basic to its characterization.

It is because attitudes toward communicative performance are generally culturally determined that they are so strongly influenced by the social structure of the community in question. This may be considered a Whorfian notion in its mirror image, as has been articulated by Hymes (1966b). While Whorf said that the structure of language may influence social structure, interaction, and thinking. Hymes suggests that the social structure may influence our attitudes toward particular kinds of language. In other words, the social differences are there to begin with, and we can then use concomitant linguistic differences to symbolize them. At that point, we may use language to discriminate and to control, because we may use it to categorize people, to put or keep them in their place.

METHODOLOGY

It is perhaps appropriate that in this area of communication research there is the greatest division in professional attitudes toward methodology. Qualitative research is considered unreliable by many, on the one hand, because of limited samples, possible subjective biases, and lack of explanatory power. The validity of experimental research is questioned from an ethnographic perspective, on the other hand, because of the unnaturalness of the situation and means by which data are elicited, and equally possible subjective biases, both in research design and interpretation of findings.

A large number of quantitative studies which relate attitudinal–motivational factors to various kinds of academic achievement have been conducted, including many of second-language proficiency. There are also a large number of studies on stereotypic attitudes which are held by one language group toward speakers of other languages or other language varieties. One common elicitation technique used is the 'matched-guise' procedure, in which subjects listen to recorded samples of speech which are purported to be from different speakers. To determine attitudes toward speakers of different languages, bilingual speakers have actually been used, speaking once in one language and once in the other (e.g. Lambert, Hodgson, Gardner and Fillenbaum 1960). Subjects rate each speaker on a series of attitudes, and an analysis is made of differential ratings of the same speaker when using different languages. These attributes often include judgements on intelligence, personality, and suitability for particular occupations. One of the most interesting findings has been the readiness of so many subjects to judge others on the basis of only limited speech samples.

A word of caution must be added about the use of quantitative measures with people from different cultural backgrounds, as it was earlier for the study of variable social markers. While they may be quite reliable, the validity of such studies can be established in these situations only through qualitative research. Judging occupational suitability, for instance, presumes a hierarchy in terms of prestige, and what this is must be determined anew for each culture being investigated. One widely accepted study of the relationship of attitudes to academic achievement among American Indians concludes Indian students have the lowest self-concept of all minority groups tested, but deduces this largely from students' feelings that they have little or no control over their environment. Most American Indian groups do not believe that actively controlling natural forces is desirable, or even reasonable, so the conclusion that they have a low self-concept based on an ethnocentric interpretation of the data, is accordingly invalid.

Macaulay (1975) raises similar questions regarding the validity of many attitude studies, including Labov's (1966) tests of 'linguistic insecurity' in New York City, d'Anglejan and Tucker's (1973) forced choice responses in Montreal, and Macaulay and Trevelyan's (1973) use of interviews in Glasgow.

Probably the weakness in all three approaches lies in the attempt to investigate such a complex question as linguistic attitudes from the outside on the basis of a single hit-or-miss trial. What is missing in all three studies discussed above is corroboration from members of the speech community that the investigators' conclusions are consistent with perceptions of the situation within the community itself. (Macaulay 1975:160)

On the other hand, the use of quantitative measures may allow the discovery of patterning in situations which might otherwise merely be seen as random variation. Especially in attitude research, an integration of both qualitative and quantitative procedures is clearly desirable.

ATTITUDES TOWARD LANGUAGE AND LANGUAGE SKILLS

Attitudes toward language in general, its nature, and its functions, may be captured by some of the expressions a speech community has that include reference to language. In many languages, for instance, the 'heart' of language is perceived to be the tongue. English speakers say *She has a sharp tongue*, *He has a loose tongue*, *He speaks with two tongues* (or) *with a forked tongue*, and *She spoke tongue in cheek*. Other parts of the anatomy less often relate to language, but we also use such expressions as *Button your lip* and *He put his foot in his mouth*. The person who has a sharp tongue in English has a 'hot tongue' in Dari, and 'a pointed tongue' in Pashto, but 'hairs on his teeth' in German.

There are abundant examples of proverbs from different speech communities which attest to the value of silence. For example: *Silence is golden* (English), *If you talk [you'll get] a small sum of money; if you remain silent, a lot of gold* (Thai), *Because of the mouth the fish dies* (Spanish), *The way your eyes look can say more than your mouth* (Japanese), and *Man becomes wise through the ear* (Farsi). A counter-sentiment is expressed in the Serbo-Croatian proverb *(Who) asks does not wander* and the English *The squeaky wheel gets the grease*.

How language is used in various communities to categorize people according to the way they speak is also relevant, as are perceptions of how these categories should be ranked in value. Speakers of English may be labeled *braggart*, *gossip*, *big-mouth*, *liar*, *eloquent*, *pedantic*, *loquacious*, *quiet*, or *tactful*. According to Albert (1972), male speakers of Rundi would value being eloquent and loquacious most highly, tactful least; being a gossip or braggart would be more highly valued in that speech community than being discrete or quiet. Speakers of Navajo would conversely value quiet and tactful, and strongly disvalue a braggart. In contrast, in the Old English poem *Beowulf*, the hero is approvingly described as 'eager for praise'.

Within a single speech community attitudes may vary concerning what constitutes 'speaking well' for males versus females, or for members of different social classes. While eloquent and loquacious are valued categories for Burundi males, for instance, females are trained for evasiveness, careful listening, and 'artful silence' (Albert 1972). Conversely, Americans traditionally value a male who is the 'strong and silent' type, while a female exhibiting the same communicative behaviors is likely to be negatively valued as shy, aloof, or unfriendly.

Attitudes about the nature of language and its functions may be inferred from derogatory comments which are made about it, or restrictions placed on its use. The role of language as an agent for socialization was clearly recognized in the 1880s by the US Commissioner of Indian Affairs, as can be judged from his statement on language and educational policy:

> The first step to be taken toward civilization, toward teaching the Indian the mischief and folly of continuing in their barbarous practices, is to teach him the English language . . . we must remove the stumbling-blocks of hereditary customs and manners, and of those language is one of the most important. (Atkins 1887)

The potentially sacred nature and functions of language are illustrated in a religious edict issued in Saudi Arabia early in 1986. This edict made it an offense to discard Arabic language newspapers in trashcans, since they usually contain Mohammed's sayings and verses of the Koran (*World Press Review*, February 1987:47).

Derogatory comments about language change, or what Roger Shuy calls 'the-world-is-going-to-hell-in-a-basket-and-language-is-leading-the-way syndrome', may also be enlightening, in that complaints about what is changing usually reveal attitudes about what has been valued as it was. In the United States these are abundant in magazine and newspaper articles, letters to the press, and reports on the state of language and education. Comparable attitudes are also expressed elsewhere in the world. In Japan, for example, educated adults express concern about young people's declining language skills, especially writing, blaming such media as TV, radios, and comic magazines for tempting them not to read the 'good' material which would transmit such ability.

The expression of concern about writing in particular in this example also indicates more value being placed on written versus oral language skills. While widespread, this attitude is far from universal. Oratory is highly cultivated as an art form in many speech communities, and concepts of 'good' and 'bad' speech are not dependent on standardization of a language or a tradition of literacy (Bloomfield 1927), although primary valuation of oracy may accompany literacy, as shown in the following example:

[In the Foreword to *Mein Kampf*], Hitler is most apologetic about giving his Nazi elite a *written* manual. He tells us that he knows that men are moved by the spoken, not the written, word and that every great movement owed its growth to great orators, not to great writers. (Duncan 1962:236)

An inverted recognition of the social importance of literacy, on the other hand, may be inferred in situations where there has been denial of literacy to certain portions of the population. This practice was justified during the slavery period in the US by the claim that literacy made slaves more likely to revolt, and rendered them 'unfit for their place in society' (Bullock 1970:75).

Technological changes may result in changed attitudes toward speaking styles, as was illustrated during the 1980 US presidential campaign. The television camera has shifted the valued political style from traditional ringing oration at a distance to the illusion of intimate encounter. John F. Kennedy's early campaign style was perceived as 'bombastic' by many TV viewers, and Ronald Reagan's as 'warm' and 'sincere'. Reagan's speech accepting the Republican nomination was very obviously and effectively directed to the camera and to the millions of people in the unseen audience rather than to the thousands actually present in the convention hall, a strategy which probably contributed to his eventual election.

The most highly regarded language skill in other societies may be knowing how to use speech levels well, or the ability to use similies, metaphors, proverbs, and rhymes in appropriate contexts; the same skills are suppressed when members of such societies are studying in English-medium universities, where 'directness' is the valued style and 'clichés' are penalized.

Other general areas where there may be culturally based differences in general attitudes toward language include the possible after-effects of speaking, and the degree to which one person may speak for another or for the group. Such information is important for the elicitation and interpretation of all data collected from members of a particular speech community.

ATTITUDES TOWARD LANGUAGES AND
VARIETIES

The range of dimensions along which linguistic codes may be judged is captured by Kachru (1982) in his listing of the dichotomous attitude marking terms which are used to describe them. These include aesthetic/unaesthetic, correct/incorrect, cultivated/uncultivated, developed/undeveloped, educated/uneducated, effective/ineffecive, proper/improper, religious/non-religious, and vigorous/non-vigorous. These dimensions refer to both formal and functional aspects of codes, and judgements apply to both multiple languages and varieties of a single language.

One interesting source of attitudinal data is the labels referring to language which may be used to characterize particular groups, whether selves or others, exemplifying the inclusive and exclusive functions of language diversity. Self-reference terms of American Indian tribes are usually equivalent to 'the people', and reference to other groups 'the strangers' or 'the enemies', but identification may make reference to language: e.g. the name of the *Popoloca* tribe of Oaxaca means in Nahuatl (Aztec) 'the people who babble'. Identification may also be in terms of ways of speaking: e.g. Hopkins (1977) reports that any speaker of Tzeltal or Tzotzil refers to the speech of any other Tzeltal or Tzotzil as *baç'il k'op* 'true (proper) speech', and among Bambara speakers in Mali, the prestigious Segu-Kaw group refers to the Beledugu-Kaw as *nya-ni-nyele*, a phrase which includes common female names. The implication is that they look down on the Beledugu-Kaw as being women; talking 'like women', whether male or female, is disvalued (Ly). Chinese speakers in Beijing give nicknames to people from other regions in accordance with how they are perceived to speak. People from Taijin are called *mie zui zi* 'Tianjin mouth' because the dialect sounds 'talkative'; people from Shanxi *shanxi lao xir* 'old west people' because the dialect sounds rough, like the land in the west; and people from Henan *henan kua zi* 'Henan bumpkins' because the dialect sounds like 'country folks'.

Another potentially useful source of attitudinal data is the use of language features in joking (mentioned in the earlier discussion of ethnic varieties), which typically highlights stigmatized forms. This source is particularly fruitful in languages like Farsi, where use of dialect features when joking about a subgroup is considered virtually mandatory. Joking usually involves mimicking marked phonological and lexical features, but may be extended to more complex stylistic factors, as in the Apaches' joking imitation of 'the Whiteman' as described by Basso:

a style characterized by stock phrases, specific lexical items, recurrent sentence types, and patterned modification in pitch, volume, tempo, and voice quality – that signals to those familiar with it that a particular form of joking has begun. (1979:9)

Jokes which make fun of syntactic differences are less common. One comes from China, where speakers of southern dialects make more extensive use of the preverbal aspect particle *you* than do northerners (including Beijing). When teasing someone or joking about the south, Beijing speakers parody this usage with constructions such as *We you zhi mei you dao*, roughly 'I don't know', with *you* inserted between the bound morphemes of *zhi-dao* 'know' (an impossible form in Beijing dialect). This seems comparable to northern US speakers parodying southern speech by inserting *you-all* in inappropriate places and producing utterances which would be ungrammatical to a Southerner. Such exaggerated usage is typical (at least in English) of any effort to parody another language variety (and perhaps of parody in general as a 'literary' device).

Using stereotyped features for one's own ethnic group may also be valued in joking performances, although this is even more likely to be only an in-group phenomenon: e.g. English speakers of Irish ancestry may be adept at shifting to a 'brogue', and Australians may effectively use broad 'Strine'.

Examples abound from speech communities where personality or social characteristics are attributed to speakers of different varieties of a language. Iranian informants listed the following regional varieties of Farsi and the traits they associated with speakers of each. [NB: these attitudes were expressed prior to the 1979 revolution, or by Iranian students who have not resided in Iran since that event.]

Tehrani – industrious, sociable, pleasure-loving
Rashti – simple, stupid, dishonorable (with reference to sexual behavior)
Ishfahani – clever, skillful, witty
Shirazi – hospitable, lazy, pleasure-loving, good-sounding

Mashadi – stubborn, obstinate, closed
Yazdi – honest, industrious, stingy, religious

When speakers are from the same area in Iran, if one does not use that regional variety, he is perceived as not wanting to be identified with that group, and so is valued negatively. A non-group member may intentionally speak another variety for instrumental purposes: e.g. 'a Tehrani in Isfahan would try to speak Isfahani rather than Tehrani so as not to be cheated.'

Japan is a very complex speech community, in which the Tokyo dialect is considered standard and all others again nonstandard, and in this case there are also quite different personality traits associated with different nonstandard varieties. Speakers of Zuzu Ben (in eastern Japan) are perceived as somewhat harsh and disagreeable, for instance, while speakers of the Osaka variety (in western Japan) are perceived as friendly and gentle.

Another illustration is from the Kathmandu Valley of Nepal, where varieties of Newari are judged primarily on a standard/nonstandard dimension: the standard is Kathmandu, and the nonstandard Bhaktapur, Kirtipur, and Lalitpur (named for the four major cities). Speakers of nonstandard varieties are all considered *gaman* 'villagers', and thus uncouth, subservient, rude, vulgar, naive, and less intelligent than standard speakers. They are thought to share the positive virtues of honesty, frankness, humility, and helpfulness. Speakers of the standard are judged educated, rich, intelligent, refined, and progressive, but also more cunning, selfish, arrogant, and dishonest than nonstandard speakers. A resident who lives in or near one of the other three cities will adopt the standard Kathmandu variety if he or she becomes educated.

Most sociolinguistic research on regional and social varieties equates 'standard' and 'prestige', but the relationship of these dimensions may be much more complex. In a study of varieties of Arabic spoken in Jordan, for instance, Abd-el-Jawad (1987) reports how speakers of a standard variety used in a rural community may switch to a nonstandard variety that is used in an urban area which has higher prestige. The function of such switchng is to identify with the dominant urban group and avoid the stigma of the rural group membership.

Quantitative measures, including the matched guise technique, have been used to establish the reliability of such personality judgements in a variety of speech communities. An interesting question which often remains unexplored, however, is *why* speakers believe they associate such traits with varieties of language.

Reasons given by native speakers include social and physical factors, as well as historical circumstances:

In Iran, Tehrani is reportedly prestigious because it is spoken in the capital, where life is to be enjoyed 'and there are opportunities for everything and everybody'; Shirazi is good-sounding because it has a great literary heritage, and has been the native dialect of many poets and musicians.

In Saudi Arabia, speakers of the Najdi variety are perceived as strong and pure because it is associated with the highly valued desert life. Additionally, it is the dialect spoken by the royal family.

In Indonesia, speakers of Hoakiau (Chinese) Malay are perceived as money-minded and hard working because of their traditional role as businessmen in the economy.

In the United States, a southern 'drawl' is associated by northerners with slow movement and laziness in men, though it is often admired in women.

Personality traits are also associated with phonetic forms in Japan, where Zuzu Ben speakers are considered disagreeable because their variety of Japanese is unclear and nasalized, while the 'friendly and gentle' Osaka variety makes use of a distinctive set of respectful verbs, and 'the tones of these expressions are softer, and more aesthetically proper to feminine speech'.

This is also true in Javanese, where degrees of gentleness or softness are associated with relative speed and volume perceived typical of different varieties, and with different degrees of frankness or directness. One Indonesian reports:

As the language becomes less and less *alus* 'gentle' as we move eastward from Solo, so are the people. Generally speaking, a Javanese from Surabaya (the capital of the East Java province) is less *alus* than one from Solo or Jogjakarta, in that the former tends to talk faster and louder as well as to be more frank and straightforward than the latter.

These relationships between form and attibutes may be considered a type of phonetic symbolism. A key example is provided by Fischer (1965) in his analysis of the differential development of a sandhi rule in Ponape and Truk, two Pacific islands, and the differential perceptions of personality traits in speakers of each. In Ponapean, homorganic stops dissimilate to nasal plus stop, and speakers are judged as more refined, formal, and as placing greater value on precision and quality of speech. In Trukese, a nasal assimilates to the following homorganic stop resulting in more fortis articulation. These speakers are perceived as more aggressive, informal, and as placing greater value on fluency and quantity. The same perceptions are held by members of both speech communities towards themselves and the others, and they may shift for effect; Fischer reports a Ponapean chief omitted sandhi to express aggression, and in Trukese there is some tendency to omit sandhi in polite speech. A completely analogous phenomenon is reported for the related dialects of Batak Toba and Batak Mandailing (Sirait).

Similarly, Navajo speakers in the western part of their reservation normally use an articulation with stronger aspiration and glottal release than do those in the eastern part, and they are judged to be 'harsher' in personality; eastern Navajos may choose to use more fortis articulation to mark intensification without increasing volume. The relationship between fortis articulation and the attribution of forceful personality traits should be explored as a possible universal.

Other areas of attitude research which have recieved considerable attention are how speakers of one language feel about other languages as entities in themselves, and how they feel about non-native or 'accented' varieties of their own. Many of these perceptions are also based on phonetic features, as the English view that German is 'gutteral', and the German response that 'All Americans say [jæææ]'. British English is perceived by German speakers to be more like their own language because final consonants are articulated, while Americans 'slow down at the end'. According to a Japanese saying, 'One gets upset in German, romantic in French, mischievous in Spanish.' The French view their own language as particularly well suited for expressing precision of thought (*Ce qui n'est pas clair n'est pas français* 'What is not clear is not French'), and Japanese their own as excellent for literature, but ill suited to law or science.

> Japanese people do not ordinarily think of the meanings of terms in legal provisions with any precision; they are content with a general and hazy understanding. . . . In Japan lack of clarity and definition is accepted; that the meanings of terms are unclear, unlimited, and unfixed is considered natural and even desirable. (Kawashima 1979)

Foreign accented English is generally well tolerated – even potentially prestigious, if fluent – although the native language of the speaker is a critical variable. Attitudes toward such non-native varieties as Indian English or Nigerian English, however, may be far less accepting. Kachru claims:

> such attitudes are not essentially based on linguistic value judgement but various other factors play an important role, one being a native speaker's fear of seeing *his* language disintegrate in the hands of (or shall we say, through the lips of) non-native users. (1980)

Still, speakers of English, French, German, Russian, Italian, and Spanish think it is entirely appropriate for others to learn their languages, and English speakers especially seem to operate on the assumption that they will do so. Dutch speakers, on the other hand, feel their language is very difficult for others to learn, but that it is quite appropriate for them to speak at least French, German, and English.

> The Dutch seem almost irritated at having to put up with the cumbersome process of talking to a stammering 'learner of Dutch'. Instead, they prefer to show off their superior knowledge of foreign languages. . . . If the foreigner is to overcome this obstacle of the negative attitude towards his trying to communicate in Dutch, he must try to eradicate any signals that could be interpreted as an inability to function fully in that language. One of the clearest of these signals is an accent, and this must undoubtedly influence his efforts to lose his native accent in speaking Dutch. (Schatz)

Other negative attitudes I have heard expressed toward English speakers' trying to communicate in an incompletely learned foreign language include the response of a Turkish taxi driver who insisted 'Americans are supposed to speak English', and that of a Chinese student who was insulted by the implication that she could not communicate adequately in English (which my attempt to use Chinese conveyed). Such attitudes present a formidable barrier for foreign language learners, but the American and British assumption that anyone will welcome another's trying to use their language is ethnocentric.

STEREOTYPING

Making judgements about people according to linguistic features is a common form of stereotyping; it is possible because of the highly 'visible' nature of the markers in language which are correlated with extralinguistic categories in a society, such as race, sex, age, social class, religion, and ethnicity (discussed in Chapter 3). The social categories in turn carry with them traditional attitudes and expectations which strongly influence all communication, and which govern what Goffman (1967) calls 'interaction ritual'.

Social 'typing' or categorization is probably a necessary part of our procedures for coping with the outside world. It allows us to quickly define our orientation to other individuals, and is a basis for our cultural sense of 'manners' and other conventions of interpersonal relations. It is a means for establishing preliminary relationships (Abrahams 1972). If we did not 'know' how to relate appropriately to different groups of people before we were acquainted with them personally, we would be socially ineffective to say the least, and perhaps even unable to function normally in a society. 'Social structure is the sum total of these typifications and of the recurrent patterns of interaction established by means of them' (Berger and Luckmann 1967:33).

Social typing should thereby be seen as a potentially positive and in any case inevitable process. The typing may assume negative aspects, however, and then it ceases to be just a mode of socialization. It may become a means of disaffiliation or rejection, or of rationalizing prejudice, and it is this negative connotation that is usually associated with the term 'stereotyping'. Further, the process of stereotyping involves 'an exaggerated belief associated with a category. Its function is to justify (rationalize) our conduct in relation to that category' (Allport 1954:187).

Because of their negative connotations and consequences, we might like to claim that stereotypes have no basis at all in observable reality, but they often do. Tannen's (1979a) contrast of New York Jewish and Los Angeles non-Jewish conversational style, for instance, documents that New York Jewish speakers talk more, interrupt (overlap) other speakers, and use 'machine-gun' questions, all of which supports common stereotypes about the way 'they' talk. Stereotyping departs from observable reality, however, when such attributes as 'pushy' or 'rude' are inferred from these conversational strategies: i.e. judgements not about how people talk, but about what kind of people they are. From the perspective of the Jewish speakers in the study, the conversational strategies are intended as positive moves to develop rapport.

Another claim we might like to make about stereotyping is that it operates between members of different groups only at initial or superifical contact, and does not survive repeated interaction. Unfortunately, this does not necessarily lead to 'better understanding'.

> On the contrary, it tends to reinforce mistaken judgements of the other's intentions and tends to increase expectations that the other will behave in a certain way. . . . Misjudgement is calcified by the conviction of repeated experience. (Tannen 1979a:161)

Stereotypic expectations may well become self-fulfilling prophesies. Our preconceptions of how a doctor 'should talk', for instance, are usually met; if not, patients may be suspicious of the doctor's credentials or professional competence. I know from years of residence in the state of Texas that most Texans do not actually say *Howdy* in greeting, but the stereotype is reinforced each time I step up to the counter of a Texas-based airline in other parts of the country and hear *Howdy, Ma'am* (which is probably used intentionally to reinforce the corporate Texas image). The stereotype of southerners speaking more slowly than northerners, on the other hand, is generally not supported by objective observational data; it is evidently a misinterpretation of their typical 'breaking' of vowels as a slower rate of speech.

Another type of stereotyping is not based on observable traits at all, but is a negation of the values held by the group which is typing. In this case, the traits which are attributed are not specific to the language or culture of the target group, but tend to be the same for all 'others' (Abrahams 1972). These are universally dehumanizing, imputing childish or animalistic behavior, immorality, and absence of manners, rules, or laws: i.e. absence of culture. The group doing this kind of stereotyping defines culture in terms of its own beliefs and practices, and then interprets all differences as deficiencies. Information about these judgements provides no insights about those being typed, but may be interesting and useful with respect to understanding the values of the source group.

When groups remain at a distance from one another, stereotypes have little effect. Similarly, the stereotypes which a subordinate group holds toward the dominant group in a society have little or no effect on that group, although it clearly affects intergroup communication. In both cases, the stereotyping serves to strengthen group boundaries and emphasize group unity. Stereotypes which the dominant group in a society holds toward subordinate groups, on the other hand, are often adopted by those groups as part of their own self-image.

Recognition of the stereotypes which are held by and about a speech community as such are relevant for ethnographic description in at least three important respects: (1) as a dimension of the attitudes related to language which are part of the content of the description; (2) as part of the framework of sociocultural expectations within which communicative behavior must be interpreted by participants or observers; and (3) as a check on the reliability of reported data when doing research in a community other than one's own. When ethnographers are working in their own speech community, stereotypes must be recognized so that they will not bias perceptions, and so they can be brought under conscious control.

APPROPRIATENESS

Many studies of attitudes toward language use (including, but not limited to stereotypes) have not been toward language in general, but what language or variety of language is considered more appropriate in a specific context. This is basic to all sociolinguistic survey procedures, and has included studies of Spanish and English (e.g. Fishman et al. 1971), varieties of Arabic and English (El-Dash and Tucker 1975), varieties of Norwegian (Blom and Gumperz 1972), and Black English (Hoover 1975). Findings generally show that attitudes towards the appropriate use of codes in a speech community have a very high correlation with their functional distribution, and the relative social status of their speakers.

Many of the attitudes reported relate to which language or variety is considered appropriate for formal education, as opposed to informal interaction. These attitudes are particularly strong in areas where creoles are for the first time being considered viable media for instruction, at least in primary grades. The following quotation is from a letter to the editor of the Trinidad *Guardian* in response to a report on a Language Arts syllabus which includes recognition that English is not the native language of most Trinidadians:

> If the language of the barrack yard and the market is to be the accepted mode of expression in the school-room . . . there would be no need for teachers . . . we could save the high wages of these experts and set them free to go and plant peas . . . where they can give full vent to this dialect stuff. . . . What if not broken English is this dialect? . . . I feel that such discussions should be banned from our news media as a most damaging . . . exercise. (Reported by Sealey)

Conversely, Trinidadian Creole is considered the most appropriate code in events associated with local culture, conversation between intimates, joking, and 'liming'. According to Sealey, a person telling a joke in Standard English in her speech community will be a laughing stock, and calypsoes sung in a variety of English nearer to the standard end of the creole continuum are marked as being 'for export': i.e. not for the people. At the same time, many parents can be heard telling their creole-speaking children to 'speak properly'; the notion that somehow the creole code is improper is instilled from early childhood in the home, and is reinforced in the schools.

Although Cape Verdean Creole has been introduced in bilingual programs in New England, there is a residual attitude among native speakers that it, too, is not appropriate for written communication. In its African context (the Republic of Cape Verde), Crioulo was the Low variety in a diglossic situation, and Portuguese the High. Even if proficiency in Standard Portuguese was not achieved, all written communication, regardless of its nature, was produced in some attempt at Standard Portuguese. This attitude is clearly reflected in Silva's recollection of an experience in Massachusetts:

My cousin's younger sister, having come to the U.S. before starting school and having to leave her sister a note, since the older sister did not know any English, resorted to writing the note in Crioulo. The mere fact that Crioulo was used to communicate the written message produced laughter among Crioulo speakers.

The addition of English for the immigrant speech community has resulted in a trilingual situation. The high and low functions of Standard Portuguese and Crioulo remain essentially the same as they were in Cape Verde, with English used without a strict allocation to domain. According to Silva, rejection of Crioulo in favor of Portuguese is interpreted as more of a rejection of the cultural values and identity of the community than is symbolized by the use of English. The recent influx of Cape Verdeans from Portugal and other former Portuguese colonies has accentuated this situation.

Another reference to the High variety of a language being associated with writing is reported by an Indonesian, where *bahasa resmi* is the official/standard language associated with education, and *bahasa sehari-hari* the daily/colloquial language associated with conversations with intimates, instructions to servants, etc. Although the High variety is more prestigious, a speaker who uses it exclusively is considered pedantic, or worse, 'putting on airs'. Gunarwan reports:

I remember one occasion when, during a casual conversation, a friend made a mistake of using the literary word *semalam* 'last night' instead of the everyday word *tadi malam*. Another friend responded mockingly, saying *Si Didi belajar membaca* 'Didi learns to read', referring to a reading series formerly used in the elementary school.

There has been only minimal acceptance of native language literacy within the Navajo speech community, where Navajo generally functions for oral communication and English for written. Even in a single communicative situation, such as a meeting of tribal representatives, business is conducted in Navajo and minutes recorded in English. Unlike the cases of Cape Verde and Indonesia, relative prestige is not a factor in considering Navajo inappropriate for literacy: Navajo is currently accorded at least as much prestige as English, although that was not always so. Spolsky and Irvine suggest the reason is that 'when the introduction of literacy is associated with a second language, an alien culture, and modern, technological functions, literacy in these new domains is preferred in the alien, second, or standard language' (1982:76). Resisting native language literacy in this instance might thus be seen as a means of protecting traditional culture from the modernizing (and more public) influence of writing.

The appropriateness of one language or variety in a multilingual, international context is even more complex, but rules for selection are quite distinct, and strong negative attitudes often accompany inappropriate language selection.

Speakers generally have some positive feelings about their native language, at least for expressive purposes in intimate or informal contexts with members of the same group. Attitudes toward acceptability and appropriateness for other functions can be understood only in relation to a complex of social and historical factors. Since these include the language in which questions about them are being asked, and the ethnic and linguistic identity of interviewers or observers, data on this aspect of language attitudes are particularly susceptible to biases in elicitation and interpretation.

LANGUAGE AND IDENTITY

Positive feelings about one's own language are often engendered by the role it plays as a marker of desired group identity, and negative feelings if such identity is rejected. Code alternation or shifting often signals changing feelings about group identity for an individual in different contexts, or as different emotions are aroused during a single communicative event.

One dimension of language-related attitudes which is central to the ethnographic description of a speech community is the extent to which linguistic identity is a criterion for group membership. Many American Indians who have lost their ancestral languages in the process of assimilation to English express profound regret and sense of deculturation, expressing the feeling that 'We can't be Indians without an Indian language'. So do many immigrants, yet many other 'hyphen-ated' Americans who speak only English after two or more generations of residence in this country retain ethnic identity only through preservation of a little folklore, with perhaps a few traditional foods or celebrations, and express few regrets about losing ancestral languages. Others who cannot speak the language of their grandparents or great-grandparents have still inherited their linguistic values, which language attitudes out-lasting the language itself, while still others have fully 'melted'.

The diverse attitudes about language and identity are very salient in teaching or learning a second language. Most students value their own group membership; some reject their own group and wish to change; many may wish or need to function as members of more than one group and be 'bicultural' as well as bilingual. Any of these attitudes can be compatible with learning a second language, but they are often viewed in a negative light. Those who value their own group membership and do not wish to acculturate to the dominant group may be treated as not 'well adjusted' to that society. As I said earlier, those who reject their own group and wish to change may be viewed as disloyal to family and old friends. Those who wish to belong to more than one group may be mistrusted by both.

Whatever choice is made regarding group membership, language is a key factor – an identification badge – for both self and outside perception, and this has significant implications for education. The standard middle-class English speech patterns presented as a model in our schools are likely to be considered effeminate and thus rejected by lower-class boys approaching adolescence, especially when these patterns are used by female teachers. The English of male teachers or of older boys would be much more likely to be adopted by boys wanting to establish a male identity. Studies of the acquisition of English by Puerto Rican adolescents in New York and Mexican Americans in Chicago document that the variety being learned and used is not the language taught in English classes, but the language of the dominant peer group in the communities – which in these cases is Black English (Wolfram 1973). A similar phenomenon is reported by Harrington (1978:3) in New York City:

> I was once observing an ESL [English as a Second Language] classroom in which the students were predominantly Spanish-speaking. The teacher's sole job was to try to get the children to speak English. An Egyptian child came to the school who spoke neither Spanish nor English. . . . After a month in the ESL classroom, the Egyptian child was speaking Spanish.

Even very young children are aware of the function of language in establishing group identity, and use the appropriate variety to identify with friends. One six-year-old child I knew developed a lisp when a best friend lost his front teeth, and many middle-class Anglo parents found during the early years of integration in southern states that their children were adding the nonstandard forms of some Black and Spanish-speaking classmates. Middle-class Black parents were often distressed in turn that their standard-English-speaking children were being influenced by the non-standard speech of lower-class White students.

Preadolescence is the age when children in the US are most influenced by peer norms, however. This perhaps accounts for Labov *et al.* (1968) finding that junior high school (12 to 14 year old) boys use more of the stigmatized features of Black English than they did when in the fifth or sixth grade (10 to 11 years old). This social fact of maximal peer influence is as likely as neurological factors to explain certain psychological consequences:

> For example, one can become confused about one's personal identity, or begin to behave as though one actually were inadequate and inferior. As these sentiments

spread through a social system, members of the system may be prone to give and accept one's 'inferior' fate, at the same time as they ready themselves to counter-react in the sense of rejecting the accepted image of one's group, starting often with an exploration of the opposite view – that one's own group is as good if not better than the high prestige group. As the counter-reaction gains social force, the relative attractiveness and status of the two or more ethno-linguistic groups in the society can change. (Lambert 1979)

Lambert further suggests it was this type of reaction that triggered the French Canadian 'revolt' of the 1960s, and the demands exerted by minority groups in the United States at about the same time for bilingual and multicultural education.

Temporary shifts are common in the process of intergroup communication, and research on their occurrence and effect is providing additional insight about language and identity. Giles *et al.* (1973) attribute linguistic *convergence*, or the modification of language toward the variety used by other speakers in an encounter, to a desire for listeners' social approval. Linguistic *divergence*, on the other hand, occurs when a speaker wishes to dissociate himself from listeners. This may be an unconsicous emotional response, but can be 'a deliberate tactic of ethnic dissociation and psychological distinctiveness' (Bourhis *et al.* 1979). Both experimental and naturalistic studies are being conducted on convergence/divergence phenomena in various languages and contexts, and include analyses of verbal codes, prosodic features such as pitch contours and rate of speech, kinesics, and other indicators of interactional synchrony (cf. Erickson 1976; Kempton 1979).

Convergence need not be perceived positively, of course, since the listener may not want to have the speaker identify with him, or may interpret the process as mocking or condescending if his own group is lower in prestige. Also, divergence may not be negative, but merely a sign of less formality and decreased monitoring of speech. In social situations where speakers of American, British, and Australian

English are represented, for instance, the dialect differences often increase as speakers become better acquainted and more relaxed.

The relationship between language and identity along this dimension is thus bidirectional: feelings of closeness or distance may trigger similarity or dissimilarity in language patterns; conversely, the feeling of being on the same linguistic 'wave length' is likely to promote solidarity.

Language may also serve an important function in political or national identification. The resurgence of pride in ethnicity (and associated languages) in the United States is very threatening to many citizens of the country as a symbol of disunity and separatism; to speak a language other than English is considered un-American. Even greater intolerance may be shown toward other languages in the process of nation-building, as evidenced by the social sanctions against the use of Yiddish in Israel. The process of selecting an official language in developing multilingual countries often involves identifying which subgroup is most powerful or prestigious. Nigeria officially continues to use English in large part because to select Hausa, Igbo, or Yoruba would give preeminence to the segment of the country which identifies with that language and exclude the others. In this case English was a neutral choice, a language with which no one identified. The functions of Yoruba are expanding, however, with continuing national development. It is particularly interesting to note ways in which Yoruba is being integrated with English for ceremonial purposes. Bamgbose reports, for instance, that

> the wedding reception which used to be an opportunity for displaying 'big grammar' is now almost invariably conducted in Yoruba with the well-educated bridegroom making an effort to speak a brand of Yoruba sprinkled with English. (1986:30)

The relationship of language and identity is very complex, and important clues to its nature may be found in changing patterns of language distribution and use through time, as well as in synchronic phemonema.

LANGUAGE MAINTENANCE, SHIFT, AND SPREAD

A basic assumption in most theories of culture change is that there are always two counterfaces operating in a society: one for change and one for persistence, stability, or maintenance of the status quo. Especially in culture contact situations, the possible outcomes for the multiple languages or language varieties involved include their maintenance as separate entities, changes in one or both language systems under influence from the other, or the abandonment of one in favor of the other: i.e. one of the counterforces prevails. Of central interest is how different attitudes toward language may determine linguistic fate.

One important factor is the instrumental versus affective functions which a language is felt to serve in the community. Yiddish and Ladino are cases in point. Yiddish made it possible for Ashkenazic Jews from all over Europe to communicate with one another regardless of their national language, serving for both ethnic and religious identification. A similar function was served by Ladino (or Judeo-Spanish) for Sephardic Jews, who were widely dispersed throughout the Middle East and Latin America. With Hebrew serving religious functions, and with its selection as the national and official language of Israel, Yiddish and Ladino lost much of their raison d'être. Harris (1979) reports over three-fourths of her Ladino informants in New York and Israel could think of no valid reasons why the language should be passed on to the next generation, even though they themselves might feel a strong sentimental attachment to it. Not a single one of their grandchildren in either location can speak the language.

In contrast, the Armenian language is still maintained in the United States and Syria, coexisting with English and Arabic, respectively. One reason this has continued is the need to know the language in order to participate in religious services, since the prevailing attitude is that Armenian is the appropriate medium for worship. Armenians who reside in the United States and have visited relatives in the Soviet Union report that religious ties there are considerably weaker, and that use of the Armenian language there seems to be in a state of rapid decline. Similar attitudes toward the use of language in religion are also largely responsible for the survival of Assyrian in immigrant communities in the US and Europe, and at least the marginal existence of Geez in Ethiopia.

The surest symptom of impending language loss is, as with Ladino, when parents no longer see a reason to transmit it to their children, and may even view it as a handicap to their children's education and advancement. As summarized by Dorian (1980):

> Language loyalty persists so long as the economic and social circumstances are conducive to it; but if some other language proves to have greater value, a shift to that other language begins.

Stability of multiple languages in contact, on the other hand, occurs where each has a unique domain (cf. Fishman 1972; 1985), and is thus reserved a continuing function in society. The reason why bilingual education is as likely to result in more rapid linguistic assimilation of minority groups as in minority language maintenance is that it tends to break down the diglossic language distribution between the domains of home and school.

A second major consideration in language maintenance, shift, and spread is the social organization and ecology of the community or communities involved, and attitudes related to these factors. This may include the nature of their boundary mechanisms and political organization, as reported in Barth's (1964a) study of language shift between Pashto and Baluchi speakers in Pakistan. In this case, both groups are part of a single ecological region, with intergroup mobility and a common culture, but with the two languages in differing relationships to social organization. Among the Pathan, Pashto is required for full political participation, but the structure of the Baluch tribes allows bilingual participation, and thus more easily assimilates non-Baluchi speakers. For complex historical reasons, this has contributed to the spread of Baluchi at the expense of Pashto in the region.

The capacity of the US economic and political structures to assimilate waves of immigrants of diverse ethnic origins is a significant factor in their concomitant assimilation to English, but the process has not applied equally to all. It is not coincidental that the more 'visible' minorities, who have encountered negative attitudes towards their assimilation from the dominant groups, are most likely to have maintained separate linguistic and cultural identity.

Attempts at forced assimilation may also support language maintenance, as evidenced in Dozier's (1956) contrast of linguistic acculturation among the Yaqui Indians of Northern Mexico and Arizona and the Tewa Indians of New Mexico. The Yaqui were subject to quite tolerant early colonization by the Spanish, relatively free of friction, and the Yaqui language and culture readily adopted Hispanic traits (about 65 per cent of the lexicon is Spanish-derived). But when the colonizers became less permissive, a crystallization occurred, and no further assimilation took place. The Tewa language and culture remain relatively free of Spanish influence, in large part because of strong coercive attempts to repress them. The Tewa language is now in more danger from English 'because their attitudes toward Anglo-Americans are generally more favorable than toward Spanish-Americans' (Dozier 1956:149).

Imperialistic expansion may also result in language spread, as evidenced in history by periods of expansion and then contraction of Turkish, Quechua, Nahuatl, and Portuguese, and more recently the spread of English and Russian. The contraction phase of Quechua and Nahuatl (languages of the former Inca and Aztec empires, respectively) is attributable to Spanish military conquest and subsequent political and economic domination. The continuing process of replacement of Nahuatl by Spanish has been analyzed by Hill and Hill (1980; 1986), who attribute the shift to a narrowing range of functions for the indigenous language. Nahuatl is still highly valued for identification and solidarity, but Spanish is highly valued for its political and economic functions as the 'language of power' (cf. Brown and Gilman 1960). Unlike the case of Tewa, the functional differentiation of Nahuatl *vis-à-*

vis Spanish is not remaining stable, for solidarity is apparently losing ground to power and prestige. The present situation, therefore, 'is probably a transitory stage which will lead rapidly to language obsolescence' (Hill and Hill 1980:345).

When the dominated area has a strong cultural tradition and feelings of cultural superiority, the indigenous language may prevail: e.g. Greek under Roman rule, and the adoption of French by Norsemen. The spread of religions has also resulted in language spread. This is especially true for Arabic with the rapid spread of Islam because of the firmly rooted belief that it is impossible to translate the Koran into another language.

Patterns of marriage and kinship may also be factors in maintenance or shift. McLendon (1978), for instance, attributes much of the rapid shift among Eastern Pomo speakers (a native California language) to exogamous marriage patterns, and extended family residence and child care is a strong force for language maintenance. Attitudes toward the value of family and group versus individual welfare and achievement also appear to be significant factors.

The role of women in the community is also significant. Where they are uneducated and remain in the home they tend to remain monolingual and contribute to maintenance of the 'mother' tongue; where they are educated, bilingual, and participate in trade or other external activities, exactly the opposite has been observed (cf. Gal 1978, Austro-Hungarian border; Trudgill and Tzavaras 1977, Greeks of Albanian descent; and Wilhite 1977, Mayan in Highland Guatemala).

Language shift may be concomitant with the change in the nature and identity of the entire speech community:

> Frequently the community itself is transformed along with the linguistic switch. That is, only as the community is surrounded and absorbed into a larger community, does it tend to drop its old language and to take on that of a larger group (Swadesh 1948:234)

Geographic or social segregation, on the other hand, contributes to maintenance. Isolated communities in Central

Texas which were settled by immigrant groups in the nineteenth century still preserve conservative varieties of Polish, German, and Alsatian French, which have been lost for generations to those who immigrated to heterogeneous cities, and Spolksy (1971) reports that the proximity of a paved road has a significant effect on Navajo maintenance or loss. The spread of modern technology and mass media are additional forces for social and linguistic integration. On this dimension, attitudes toward the desirability of change play a major role.

The social stratification of a community is also relevant, including the degree of access that speakers of low prestige languages and varieties have to those which are more prestigious, and to jobs which require their use. The key here is motivation and opportunity, as well as the acceptability of assimilation by the dominant group mentioned above.

A third major area of consideration is values and world view. In a broad sense, this includes attitudes toward borrowing foreign words, and the value placed on uniqueness versus homogeneity. The effect of the latter is illustrated by Hamp (1978) in his discussion of the maintenance of Albanian by settlers in Italy, where localisms are valued, versus its loss by settlers in Greece, which exclusively values all things Greek. The pattern persists through immigration to the United States, as Italian-Americans quickly assimilate to the local language, and Greek-Americans cling tenaciously to Greek style for generations, even when they are speaking English (cf. Tannen 1981). Robert DiPietro has made the interesting observation that Albanian has been preserved within the Italian immigrant community in Wisconsin, with the Italian language (and values) probably serving as a buffer zone against English.

The social valuation of linguistic features is important to Labov's view of the 'linguistic variable' as a unit of change. He analyzed the subjective attitudes of residents of Martha's Vineyard (1963) toward such matters as summer tourists, unemployment compensation, work on the mainland, and other aspects of island life, finding typical 'Vineyarder attitudes' most closely associated with the occurrence of particular phonetic variables. In studies of both New York City and Martha's Vineyard, Labov finds self-identity at the root of linguistic change (1972).

Another interesting value dimension in language contact situations is how evaluation of a linguistic variable in one language is susceptible to the evaluation of variants in the dominant competing languages. Examples from Jakobson (1938) and Weinreich (1953) are the merger of /l/ and /lʲ/ in Czech, which is attributable to urban speech which was tinged with a 'fashionable' German accent, and the merger of /š, tš/ with /s, ts/ in Croatian, which is attributed to the foreign accent of native speakers of Venetian Italian. Campbell (1976) adds an example from Teotepeque Pipil, Mexico, in which a change from /š/ to /ř/ is attributed to a social evaluation of stigmatized pronunciation in Spanish.

It seems reasonable to assume that most attitudes toward language and identity also fit in this category, with positive feelings for one's own group contributing to maintenance, and negative feelings to loss. One somewhat surprising finding is that positive attitudes toward a language apart from pragmatic functions do not seem to enhance chances for its survival. As Fishman notes:

in summarizing my findings concerning current language maintenance among pre-World War I arrivals in the United States coming from rural Eastern and Southern European backgrounds, I reported a long-term distinction between attitudes and use, namely, an increased esteem for non-English mother tongues concomitant with the increased relegation of these languages to few and narrower domains of language use. . . . Younger second and third generation individuals were found to view these mother tongues (almost always via translations) with less emotion but with even more positive valence. Instead of a 'third generation return' there seemed to be an 'attitudinal halo-ization' within large segments of all generations, albeit unaccompanied by increased usage. (1964)

Fasold (1975) offers corroboration in the finding that adolescents who are not learning Tiwa along with English still express very positive attitudes toward their language, but this has not prevented the encroachment of English into previously Tiwa domains, and is ultimately unlikely to save the language from extinction. A similar situation pertains in Ireland, where it was found that 'strong sentimental attachments to Irish were not accompanied by language *use*, nor by desire to actively promote it' (Edwards 1985:51, citing the Committee on Irish Language Attitudes Research 1975; emphasis his).

Miller (1970) studied the attitudes of Pima children living on the Salt River reservation toward which of the languages used in their community is best. The majority expressed preference for English with such practical explanations as 'most people speak it', although several chose Pima because it is spoken by parents or grandparents and for ethnic identity: Pima is 'best for Pimas'. It is interesting to note there is an increasing preference for English with age. Miller concludes:

> younger children are more influenced by the standards and language of the home and still largely unaware of attitudes and school and the outside world. With the gradual influence of the school and one's peers, the older child becomes more and more impressed with the success on the outside and the practicality of identifying with the affluent majority. (1970:54–5)

It seems quite likely that linguistic awareness and influence for conformity with the 'outside world' may come at a much younger age and much less gradually if a child is exposed primarily to children from the dominant language group. In the US, bilingual parents who speak other languages at home often report their children wanting to speak only English at home once they begin school; some children exacerbate this situation by insisting that their parents also speak English, or expressing feelings of shame if they cannot or will not. Children in bilingual school programs, however, exhibit much less of this home language rejection.

School programs in themselves, however, cannot be counted on to develop or maintain minority language use among children if there is not both need for the language in the community and support among the children's peers. Evidence for this comes from study of a French-language elementary school in Canada, for instance, where it was determined that the school (St-Michel)

> has not been able to impose its goals and its conventions on its students: the experiences of children outside school, and the influence of their peer group networks evidently constrain the extent to which schools can be depended upon to be the source of language maintenance and cultural continuity in a minority community . . . (Heller nd:13)

In a longitudinal study of over three hundred children of foreign graduate students and visiting faculty in the US (Kleifgen, *et al.* 1986), we found a dramatic shift to English dominance in spite of support for native language maintenace at both home and school. If children had arrived in this country at age five or less, they typically had difficulty communicating in their native language after two years in residence; only those who arrived at age seven or more generally maintained productive balance between their native language and English after that period of time.

Our database included children from a number of different countries, and there were some intergroup differences which illustrate some of the social factors that are involved. Japanese and Korean children experienced the least shift. Most importantly, they seldom stayed in this country for more than a year; their parents expressed concern about keeping children in the US longer for fear they would get behind in their own school curricula, and they were less likely to bring with them older children who were at a more 'critical' period of school than were parents from other countries. Also, the Japanese and Korean mothers generally spoke little or no English themselves, and the time their children were at home was frequently spent almost exclusively with other speakers of the same language background. These two groups had large and well organized support networks in the university community, including baby-sitting pools which insured consistent native language input to young children even when mothers were absent from the home. No similar network existed for the other groups in the sample.

There were also group differences in child rearing practices which must be taken into account, and in the value accorded learning English versus developing and maintaining native language skills. The faster rate of shift among Arabic children, for instance, can be attributed in part to the greater opportunity they had to play with children from other backgrounds in the community context, and in part to the value parents generally placed on their children learning English.

The most notable change among children who first encountered English at age five or less was the effect it had on their pronunciation. Young Arabic speakers lost post-velar and pharyngeal articulation, for instance, and young Chinese speakers used incorrect tones. The general impression of our collaborators who speak the children's languages natively was that they spoke with a foreign (American) accent.

First language attrition for older children who were in the US two or more years was limited almost entirely to loss of productive vocabularly; tests we gave (including translations of the Peabody Picture Vocabulary Test and sentence repetition tasks) indicated relatively little attrition in their receptive competence. These children expressed a feeling of awkwardness in using their native language by that time, however, and a preference for English.

Evidence can also be found in the very limited success of 'language recovery' programs in American Indian communities where the school has tried to develop ancestral language competence in children who have not been taught that language at home. To repeat, the surest symptom of impending language loss is when parents no longer see a reason to transmit it to their children. These same parents apparently cannot then expect the school to give it back to the children and the community, except in unusual cases and limited domains.

214 ATTITUDES TOWARD COMMUNICATIVE PERFORMANCE

An interesting situation is created when a child's parents speak two different languages. In the case of different American Indian languages, Miller (1970) reports there is almost always loss of one Indian language in mixed marriages, and often both, with children speaking only English. (For similar loss in 'Anglo-ethnic' marriages in Australia, see Clyne 1982.) Among the Tucano in the Amazon region, however, where exogamous marriage restrictions result in wives' primary languages being different from their husbands', Sorensen (1967) reports both languages are usually maintained. Most Tucano grow up at least bilingual, and often speak several languages. There are individual cases where it appears that neither language is fully developed for children in this situation, however. Plausible accounts of this fortunately rare phenomenon come from teachers in isolated villages in Alaska, for instance, where the father in a family may speak only English (but is seldom home to provide input for the child), and insists that the mother not use the Eskimo language of the community (which is her dominant tongue). Children raised in a home with the impoverished language input which results reportedly cannot function effectively either in the English-medium school or in the Eskimo community. I know of no case of this nature which has been adequately documented by a sociolinguist, but I do not believe the possibility of 'semilingualism' under such social conditions should be discounted merely on theoretical or philosophical grounds (also discussed in Chapter 2; cf. Martin-Jones and Romaine 1986).

When language loss is occurring at a community level, 'there are some individuals [at lower levels of "semispeaker" proficiency] who actually say very little yet continue to interact in a highly successful fashion with fluent speakers' (Dorian 1982:33). This is because such individuals have receptive competence in the language and are always younger than the fluent speakers, and thus not expected to take a more active role. They participate appropriately in the interaction by using a few words when that is called for, and by following community norms for nonverbal behavior and silence. Dorian contrasts these aspects of the semispeakers' communicative competence with the foreign language learner who may have more verbal fluency, but 'betrays his nonmembership in the speech community by social failures in the use of the language: speaking when he should be silent, asking "rude" questions, failing to recognize a situation in which greetings are obligatory, and the like' (Dorian 1982: 33–4). Even when languages have been completely lost, as in some American Indian communities, indigenous 'ways of speaking' may be maintained which continue to differentiate community members from the dominant English speech community whose language forms they have adopted.

Sometimes the issue is not why languages die, but why they do not. My own research on the Alabama–Coushatta (Koasati) reservation in Texas has provided more questions than answers about why the language of that community is being maintained. Why is a small (less than 200 member) tribe continuing to transmit its language to children? All attend English medium schools, and all monetary rewards are attached to the use of English, yet monolingual Alabama–Koasati speakers are still present in each generation of children. Clearly the relationship between attitudes and language maintenance, shift, and spread remains a viable topic for investigation.

TABOOS AND EUPHEMISMS

Attitudes toward language considered taboo in a speech community are extremely strong, and violations may be sanctioned by imputations of immorality, social ostracism, and even illness or death. No topic is universally forbidden: what cannot be said in one language can in another and vice versa. Neither are linguistic taboos arbitrary: they relate integrally to culture-specific beliefs and practices in religion or magic, decorum, and social control.

Taboos related to religion or magic may affect a wide range of linguistic phenomena, and include animal-name avoidances in many speech communities. It may be believed that animals or spirits understand human language, and that mentioning their names would either drive them away (undesirable if one is hunting), or attract them near where they might inflict harm. Related are the restriction in the former Bangalam Upper Congo against using men's names at home while they are fishing (Frazer 1922); replacing an animal name with a semantically unrelated word which begins with the same sound (e.g. *zag*ʷ*ára* 'leopard' becomes *zamb*ʷ*ára* 'disc of wood to cut bread') in Ethiopia (Leslau 1959); and the substitution of a metaphorical expression for the animal terms (e.g. calling a wolf 'uncle' or 'nice little dog') by peasants in the Ukraine (Smal-Stocki 1950).

In some cases a broader scope of the linguistic system is involved, as among Faroese fishermen who use *sjómal* 'sea language' for protection from spirits and to conceal their business and destination (Lockwood 1956), or where everyday language is considered unworthy of sacred use, as in Zuñi prayers and songs in New Mexico (Newman 1955). Complimenting children is thought to be very dangerous to their health in Turkey because it may attract the evil eye, but this danger may be lessened considerably by immediately repeating the ritual phrase *maşallah* 'what God hath wrought'.

Language is perhaps most awesome when words themselves are accorded power, as in speech communities where a curse literally invokes supernatural wrath, where to be in possession of individuals' names gives control over their well-being, or where to speak or write down a name will allow the soul to escape. In these cases names are concealed, or replaced, for self-protection.

All language may be banned under certain circumstances. When sacrifices are made by Igbo speakers, for instance, the officiating priest usually imposes the observance of strict silence, particularly when the purpose is diverting the attention of malevolent spirits from the carrier. If the silence is violated (a rare occurrence), the sacrifice must be repeated, and the offender has to make an additional sacrifice. Greetings were also taboo between Igbo from different villages during times when there were smallpox epidemics, because of the belief that disease can take human form. Without a greeting, no encounter has taken place (Nwoye 1985).

Taboos which relate to decorum include avoidance of terms or euphemistic reference for aesthetic or moral reasons (often for body parts or bodily functions), interlingual taboos, and respect forms.

A wide range of euphemisms in America intended to soften the verbal impact of dying, death and burial was collected by Pound (1936). These include categories of general literary and figurative expressions (*is out of his misery, climbed the golden stair*), metaphors of sleep and rest (*laid to rest, called to the eternal sleep*), metaphors of departature (*crossed over the Great Divide, gone to the Great Beyond*), metaphors from occupations (*answered the last muster, gave up the ship*), and metaphors from sports (*ran the good race, struck out*). The material adjuncts are also renamed, as the dead (*the deceased, the late lamented*), the cemetry (*the Marble City, memorial park*), the coffin (*casket, eternity box*), the grave (*long home, deep six*), and the funeral (*planting, cold meat party*).

Grimes (1977) illustrates the range of euphemistic processes used in Mexican Spanish to refer to body parts and functions, such as metaphor (*cortar flores* 'to cut flowers' = to defecate), metonymy (*el de hacer niños* 'the thing for making children' = penis), generic expressions (*hacerlo* 'to do it' = to urinate [the same phrase means 'to fornicate' in English]), infantile expressions (*hacer caca* 'to defecate'), proper names (*Doña Josefa* 'vagina'), and borrowing (*cuita* ‹ Nahuatl *cuitlatl* 'feces'). Use of scientific or 'cultured' terms, as in the above translations, may also be considered a euphemistic process. It was common practice for nineteenth-century scholars translating Greek and Roman tales, or recording the folklore of 'primitive' groups, to switch to Latin for the passages which violated English language taboos.

Linguistic taboos are often related to language change: e.g. the word 'bear' probably disappeared in Slavic, Baltic, and Germanic languages because of animal-name avoidance (cf. Slavic 'honeyeater', Baltic 'one who licks', and Germanic 'brown'), and Tonkawa (an indigenous language of Texas) underwent rapid and extensive lexical change because of the practice of changing words which sounded like the names of people who died. Scholars do not know what the original word for 'God' was in Hebrew because of the restriction against using it. Euphemisms have also caused semantic shift, as in Mexican Spanish where *huevos* 'eggs' was used for 'testicles', and *blanquillos* 'little white ones' took over its reference function for 'eggs'.

Interlingual taboos occur in multilingual contexts, where an acceptable word in one language sounds like one which is taboo in another. Haas (1975) describes the dilemma of Thai students trying to avoid using words in their own language which they know sound like obscene words in English. In reverse, many students learning English as a foreign language refuse to pronounce some words 'correctly' because of phonetic similarity to obscene words in their native language (e.g. Turkish speakers do not want to say English *peach*). A useful dictionary of *Dangerous English* (Claire 1980) is available for foreign students, including words which English speakers consider 'vulgar', along with their meanings (illustrated) and appropriate euphemisms; a reverse guide to English words which are obscene in other languages is still needed, and would undoubtedly explain some resistant pronunciation 'problems' in English as a foreign language classes.

Personal names create one of the most common problems in this area, with English-speaking professors unwilling or embarrassed to call on any student named *Fucks*, and *Jesús* is usually rechristened *Jessie* by the second week of class.

Taboos associated with respect forms include avoidance of the name of a ruler, a husband, the aged, or a mother-in-law, or silence in their presence. Total silence is observed by widows in some communities (Cohen 1956).

Perhaps the most stringent linguistic form of social control is social ostracism, where collective or group silence is a weapon. Among the Igbo, for instance, this is accomplished by passing a law which makes it punishable by some stipulated penalities for any member of a village to greet, accept greetings, or be aided by the person considered deviant. This extreme measure is resorted to only when all other measures adopted to bring the offender to repentance and submission to the will of the people have failed. When this happens, the entire village – men, women, and children –

are forbidden to talk to him and members of his immediate family. When he re-establishes himself in the good graces of the community, the embargo on speech is lifted and he becomes a full member of the society again (Nwoye 1985).

A similar communication taboo (called 'shunning') is practiced by the Amish communitity in the United States, and informally by anyone who is 'not on speaking terms' with someone who has displeased them, or who refuses to talk to an errant spouse or child.

Knowing what *not* to do or say is obviously of great interest and importance for the ethnographer, but by their nature, taboos are difficult to elicit. Since many are sex-specific, or applicable only in cross-sex contexts, it is useful for a male and female to work as a team in collecting data. But violations may have such serious consequences for the prospects of continued acceptability in a community, sensitivity to areas where questions should *not* be asked is often more important that finding the answers.

6

Acquisition of Communicative Competence

Child language acquisition has been an object of study for philosophers, educators, psychologists, and linguists for at least two centuries (cf. Bar-Adon and Leopold 1971). Observational reports and analyses over this period reflect a history of changing foci of interest within these several fields as well as shifting theories on the nature of language itself. Such studies provide a useful background for our perspective on language learning in the inclusive sense of the acquisition of the rules and skills which enable a member of a speech community to demonstrate and interpret appropriate communicative behavior in a wide range of social contexts.

As in descriptive and historical linguistics generally, the study of language acquisition in the past century has in turn focused primarily on phonology, syntax, and semantics/pragmatics. As recently as the 1960s and early 1970s, theories of language acquisition were emphasizing the biological or innate factors in the process, and were relegating the social context of language learning to an amorphous sociolinguistic milieu from which children somehow constructed their language via primarily cognitive processes. Attention has now shifted to such topics as the functions language serves for children, what communicative strategies they use, and how these are developed and how input is structured in the processes of social interaction: in short, the acquisition of communicative competence.

Ethnographic modes of investigation would seem to be essential if such basic factors of language acquisition as these are to be adequately described and explained. We can begin to understand how language is learned only if we examine the process within its immediate social and cultural setting, and in the context of conscious or unconscious socialization or enculturation. We must ask about the nature of linguistic input and sociolinguistic training, how and for what purposes children acquire particular communicative strategies, and how language relates to the definition of stages in the life cycle and to recognized role-relationships in the society. We must seek to identify the differential influences of family, peers, and formal education, and consider such matters as the beliefs which the community itself (including its children) holds about the nature of language origin and development. In this chapter we shall consider some of these questions.

EARLY LINGUISTIC ENVIRONMENT

Just as some innate language development capabilities must be posited to explain the rate and sequence of children's acquisition of phonology and syntax, we must also assume that all human infants are born with the capacity to develop patterned rules for appropriate language use from whatever input is provided within their native speech community. Even before a child has acquired language rules, infants evidently are able to deduce a detailed nonverbal, cognitive 'script' for how events are structured or organized: e.g. 'what happens when grandma visits, or how to have breakfast with father' (Kessen and Nelson 1976).

Some commonalities may be found in the sources and nature of input, although content is of course, culture-specific. Children are essentially participant-observers of communication, like small ethnographers, learning and in-ductively developing the rules of their speech community through processes of observation and interaction.

Sources of input for children vary depending on cultural and social factors. Mother's talk (discussed in Chapter 3) is often assumed to be universally the most important source of early input, but wealthier social classes in many cultures delegate most caretaking tasks to servants, and older siblings have major childrearing responsibilities in many societies, especially where women must do work which takes them away from home. The structure and relative influence of the peer group is also culturally determined, as is that of institutions for formal education. The trend to share house-keeping as well as wage-earning responsibilities as part of the 'women's liberation' movement among the middle classes in Western societies and the related concept of a shared 'parenting' role for both male and female, suggests additional attention must be paid to the role of father's language as well. In early studies the father was a primary source of linguistic input in societies such as that of the Trobriand Islanders (Malinowski 1926) and the Hopi (Dennis 1940), where he had a warm and friendly relationship with his children and the mother's brother was chiefly responsible for their behavior. Among the Manus (Mead 1930), the father had the principal role in childrearing and hence might have had more linguistic influence.

In some countries, including the People's Republic of China and the USSR, family members may have a relatively minor role in child care, with primary responsibility residing in a collective nursery. To a lesser degree, day care facilities in Western Europe and the United States effect a similar transfer in primary caretaking (and linguistic input), which adds yet another dimension for investigation. When early child care is thus institutionalized, syntactic and phonological development appear to be about the same in both rate and sequence as when it is not, but the vocabulary learned may reflect differences in experience from home care (Spiro 1958). There may also be differences in communicative strategies acquired by children who attend a nursery school, as I found in my own work with kindergarten age children (particularly in the strategies used to control or manipulate other children), as well as in the domains in which vocabulary and concepts are known.

Among upper classes where the primary caretaker is not a parent, but a servant who is often a speaker of a low prestige variety of the language or even another language entirely, it is interesting to note that children still acquire the more prestigious language of their family. In both Africa and Latin

America the servant caring for the children is often an immigrant from rural areas in the country. Upper-class Africans and Latin Americans report that they learned to understand the language of servants, and could use it when playing with servants' children, but they were strictly reminded of their family identity and language if lower prestige forms were used in inappropriate contexts – such as with their parents or other family members. Conversely, when a caretaker is perceived to speak a prestige language, such as a French governess in an English speech community, her language is frequently acquired and maintained by children even if it is not used by their parents.

Linguistic input is also affected by family structure, and by residential patterns, including who lives in the same house and what their role is in the caretaking process. The presence of a grandparent in the home of immigrant families in the United States, for instance, may be a primary determinant of what language young children will learn first. Even in monolingual English-speaking families, the proximity of one or more grandparents influences the type of linguistic input to children, particularly in the degree to which traditional lore is transmitted in the form of stories, proverbs, songs, and rhymes.

The quantitative aspect of language use to which children are socialized –the taciturnity/loquacity dimension – is also obviously related to their linguistic environment. Birdwhistell (1974) compared the median amount of talk per day in Pennsylvania Dutch and Philadelphia Jewish homes. He found that the former talked two and a half minutes a day and the latter between six and twelve hours, although the amounts of actual new information transmitted in the two types of families did not differ appreciably. Clearly the children in these contexts were being socialized to very different styles, and to some extent, functions, of speaking.

Children in lower social classes in the United States tend to have relatively more verbal input from other children than they do from adults. This does not seem to retard overall linguistic development, but when children are removed from adult native language models for long periods of time, their linguistic maturation may be prematurely ossified. This is the case for Navajo students attending boarding schools where only English is spoken by the staff. They reach adolescence without acquiring mature language forms, and may always continue to speak what is sometimes referred to as 'baby Navajo'. Many rural Appalachian children also retain immature forms, perhaps because they are isolated and have few contacts outside the immediate family (Stewart 1967).

Despite numerous statements in the linguistic literature to the contrary, it is now being recognized that when children have limited input from any source, communicative development may indeed be retarded, though this may be overcome in later childhood. Cultural and social differences sometimes are evident here. I have worked with girls from Mexican American migrant labor families, who were restricted to the house (both because of their responsibility to care for younger siblings and for their own safety) until they entered school. They were found to have limited ability to express themselves in either Spanish or English upon school entry, whereas boys from the same families, who had been allowed to have a broader range of social contacts, were far more fluent in Spanish. (Cases of similar impoverished input in some cross-language marriages where one language is negatively valued were discussed in Chapter 5.)

Many deaf children of hearing parents have also been subjected to this very limited linguistic environment, particularly during the years when educational and medical authorities discouraged parents from using or teaching sign language. Adults were instructed to talk to deaf children all the time, whether the children understood or not. In these cases first language (sign) acquisition was generally delayed until children learned it from peers at school. Hearing children of deaf parents do not suffer the same communicative deprivation, since they generally learn sign at home and acquire speech as a second channel at school or from outside contacts.

Social and cultural factors affect verbal input qualitatively and functionally, as well as quantitatively, but an important caveat needs to be raised concerning the interpretation of cultural and social class differences in mother–child interaction which are reported. All such claims need to be questioned because, unless observer effect has been carefully controlled, they could be the result of differential responses to the investigator or to the research situation – in itself a sociolinguistically and ethnographically interesting circum-stance. It has been found that White, middle class, English-speaking mothers produce twice the amount of speech when they are aware of being observed as when they are not, for instance, although the proportion of utterance types (e.g. declaratives, imperatives, questions) is similar (Graves and Glick 1978). They use far more indirect directives when aware of observation, however, saying such things as 'Can you put the elephant on top?' rather than the direct imperative 'Put the elephant on top' (ibid). This indirect strategy may be the reason Laosa (1977) and others report questions being used with greater frequency by more educated groups, if the researchers are classifying utterances according to grammatical form rather than by pragmatic intent. Utterances classified according to different criteria might well contradict such findings.

SOCIAL INTERACTION

Although language acquisition is generally considered to be primarily a cognitive process, it is clearly a social process as well, and one which must take place within the context of social interaction. Furthermore, children's role in their own learning appears to be far more active than models which focused on either conditioning or innate capacity led us to believe.

All components of a communicative event are potential input to children in their construction of meaning from language, with the social identity of participants evidently the most salient (Slobin 1967). Halliday's (1975) funtional-interactional approach is consonant with this view, claiming that children learn the meaning of language because of the systematic relation between what they hear and what is going on around them. Children's intent to communicate arises naturally out of the system of shared assumptions and understandings which result from the regularities and rituals of their early socialization (Cook-Gumperz 1977). Children begin to use language within this framework of presupposed knowledge, where verbalizations are only part of the message communicated by them or by adults. Halliday's treatment of acquisition considers such factors as the language which the child is reacting to and its meaning potential, the situational environment of interaction (including the roles and statuses of participants), the variety or register of language used in any specific communicative event, the linguistic system itself (both its potential and how it is constructed by the child), and the social structure within which the interaction is taking place. The salience which the identity of participants in a communicative event has for children is underscored by studies of code-switching in even very young bilinguals; this is the most important contextual feature in determining language choice (McClure 1974).

I have recorded similar phenomena in the style-shifting of monolingual children. For example, the following directives/requests were all uttered by one English-speaking boy (age 3 years 7 months) during the course of a single outdoor play period in nursery school. They are categorized according to the role and status of the individual he was speaking to, and it is clear that his communicative competence already includes variability for different levels of politeness and formality.

To peers:
> *Stop that. You're gonna get a swat.*
> *Let's go fishin'.*
> *Come on you guys. Come on. Green slime.*
> *Fix my wheelers.*
> *Let me see what's that.*

To a girl he wanted to persuade to play with him:
> *You can pull me in there too. OK, Michelle?*
> *You get in the back and I'll drive, OK?*
> *You pull me now, OK?*
> *Let's go to see a show Michelle, OK?*
> *Michelle, do you wanna come with me to the show?*
> *Let's go get a . . . this time you wanna go get a ice cream*
> *   cone? Wanna go to Baskin-Robbins?*

To adult caretakers:
Would you go get Stevie a bike?
Would you put on my shoes?

In a study of language socialization in Japan, Clancy also documents that indirection in directives begins to be used in the third year. The mothers she observed used a wide variety of directives with their two-year-old children (including indirect questions and hints), and they provided direct translations of the indirect, polite speech of others. She concludes that 'the primary means by which these children could be learning how to interpret indirection is through the pairing of indirect and direct utterances having the same communicative intent' (1986:229).

There has been significant disagreement about how, at what age, and to what extent children use language to interact with others. The disagreement reflects at least in part differences in social and cultural influences on communicative behavior which would result in differential answers to these questions. Piaget (1926) claimed that children's speech is primarily egocentric, with early conversation essentially collective monologue, and such interactional linguistic forms as commands and requests a later development. He reported that even at six-and-a-half years of age, more than half of children's utterances are egocentric: repetition, monologue, and collective monologue. The social factors involved are illustrated by Keenan's (1974) challenge to Piaget's conclusions in reporting that her twins exhibited such interactional strategies as turn-taking before the age of three, but also by Garvey's (1977) lack of success in replicating Keenan's results with young children who were not acquainted. The code-switching and style-shifting in accordance with participant role-relationships which I reported above add weight to Keenan's arguments that children may be sensitive to the interactional context of language use from a much earlier age than that suggested by Piaget.

While all language is learned in the process of social interaction, different linguistic forms are considered 'typical' or appropriate between adults and children. English-speaking mothers regularly use questions to stimulate interaction with children, and then react to the children's answers as if they were worthy of interest and further verbal response. In contrast, Javanese mothers often use question forms with children, but furnish the answers themselves. This is a way of teaching a child to respect an older person not only because of age, but also because of knowledge; the child learns to control his behavior, to be quiet in the presence of someone who is older and respected. Blount (1972) reports a very low frequency of questions addressed to children in Samoan and Luo societies. In large part this is a cultural difference in adult–child conversational status; English speakers may give children the status of social peer, asking opinions, and allowing children to initiate conversational rounds.

Children's questions to adults are also influenced by cultural factors. In an English speech community, children are generally encouraged to use question forms to request permission or gain information, and they may legitimately use questions (especially 'Why?') to prolong conversation, challenge authority, or hold the floor. Navajo children learn to use more indirect request forms at an early age, especially statements of wishing something would be so, and their questions for information are discouraged by such adult responses as 'Use your eyes'. English-speaking children use questions with another child as a turn-taking device, and also for competitive functions, such as an opening to display knowledge they have that the other does not. (This is similar to riddling in many societies.)

Much of the earlier research on acquisition in the process of adult–child interaction focused on the importance of children's repetition of adult speech. While this is totally inadequate to account for language learning, there are speech communities where mimicry is very common, and considered the most appropriate form of social interaction between adults and young children. Just as Tallensi children in Ghana reportedly learn other social behaviors primarily by looking and copying, for instance, the Tallensi theory of how language is learned is that 'They learn little by little . . . they accompany us and listen to what we say' (Fortes 1938). This belief within the speech community influences the linguistic behavior of adults toward a child; they frequently mimic its babblings and expect repetition in return. Hoġbin (1946) reports a similar prevalence of mimicry in the learning style of Wogeo children in New Guinea. With respect to language learning he reports: 'I often used to hear children repeating their parent's pet phrases and characteristic intonations with remarkable accuracy. Adoption is common, and the natives have a saying, "Use your eyes to find out who begot a strange child and your ears to discover who is rearing it."'

Mead described the use of repetition in the spontaneous native teaching of Tok Pisin to young children by older children in New Guinea:

> Young men who have been away to work for the white man return to their villages and teach the younger boys, who in turn teach the very small boys. . . . It is a common spectacle to see two or three twelve-year-old boys gathered about a three- or four-year-old little boy, 'schooling him'. An older boy gives the cues: 'I think he can.' 'I think he no can'. 'Me like good fellow kai kai (food).' 'Me like kai kai fish.' 'One time along taro.' And the child repeats the lines in his piping little voice without any grasp of their significance. But as it fits in so well with the game of repetition for repetition's sake neither teacher nor pupil tires easily, and the result is that boys of thirteen and fourteen speak perfect pidgin although they have never been out of their isolated villages. (1930:42)

A variety of beliefs and practices are also related to enhancing language development in children who are considered 'delayed' in some respect. Among the Huli (also of New Guinea), for instance, a frog may be lightly tapped on the child's lips, teeth, and tongue (organs associated with articulation) while a chant is repeated. Goldman reports that 'The rationale behind this practice involves the cultural association of frogs (*yago*) and talk' (1987:453). What constitutes language 'delay' is of course culture-specific, as well as the 'remedy'.

An interesting, but less common, focus in research has been on the influence which children themselves have on adult communicative behavior. Von Raffler-Engel and Rea (1978) report that much of the interaction between adults and children is nonverbal, or paralinguistic, with children often confirming understanding or triggering repetitions or paraphrase with grunts, facial expressions, or head nods, which also suggests the need to expand the scope of interaction phenomena which are to be explored and described.

The essential assumption of the interactions model is that the acquisition of communicative competence is the result of interaction processes within a sociocultural context, and not just the unfolding of innate, preprogrammed behavior. Descriptive data from a wide variety of speech communities clearly support this perspective.

LANGUAGE AND ENCULTURATION

Language learning for children is an integral part of their enculturation from three perspectives: (1) language is part of culture, and thus part of the body of knowledge, attitudes, and skills which is transmitted from one generation to the next; (2) language is a primary medium through which other aspects of culture are transmitted; and (3) language is a tool which children may use to explore (and sometimes manipulate) the social environment and establish their status and role-relationships within it. Partially as a result of differential social environments, language learning for a child is thus also learning to be a male, or a female, or rich, or poor, or Black, or English, or Chinese, or Muslim, or Buddhist, or to identify with dozens of other social roles and statuses into which he or she is being enculturated.

The relative importance of verbal explication in the socialization process is not the same in all speech communities, nor in transmitting different aspects of culture within the same community, but the whole of the transmission must be considered communication in its broadest sense. Specific modes of transmission correspond to overall patterns in culture, and to patterns of childrearing in each culture. Hall's (1959) distinction among *formal, informal,* and *technical* levels of culture and types of learning provides a useful framework for illustrating these differences.

Formal learning takes place through precept and admonition, and transmits those aspects of culture which are not to be questioned. Verbal clues that this level is involved include corrections such as 'Boys don't do that' or 'That's not *our* way', and, if these reproofs are challenged by children, appeals to authority may be invoked such as 'Because it is' or 'Because I said so'. It is difficult to imagine most questions regarding the origin or meaning of words being dealt with in any other way, although attempts to do so may account for some of our folk etymologies. When a child asks 'Why is that a *chair*?', the response is likely to be it is a *chair* 'Because it is'. At an older age, the appeal to authority becomes 'Because it says so in the dictionary'. Research (Peal and Lambert 1962) suggests that bilinguals are much less likely to identify words with objects uniquely, but possess a more detached perspective on the arbitrariness of the association between words and the world of experience.

Verbalizations of formal aspects of culture often include the expression of the traditional wisdom of a community in the form of proverbs or other aphorisms. They may be contradictory (depending on the situation), but like other formal aspects of culture, their truth value is not a relevant dimension.

Hopi parents also use a predominantly formal mode of enculturation in their consistent admonition to children to 'Listen to the old people – they are wise', or 'Our old uncles taught us that way – it is the *right* way' (Eggan 1956). Bernstein's (1972:486) examples of positional appeals would also be considered formal in nature:

You should be able to do that by now (age status rule).
Little boys don't cry (sex status rule).
People like us don't behave like that (subcultural rule).
Daddy doesn't expect to be spoken to like that (age relation rule).

The behavior which adults expect of children may be determined at least in part by their language development, and not corrected until adults believe children can understand formal verbal directives. English-speaking adults may say 'No, no' before they believe more complex directives or explanations will be understood, but this is disapproved of in speech communities where adults feel such commands are useless, or may frighten a young child.

Informal learning takes place primarily through nonverbal channels of communication, with the chief agent a model used for imitation. Hall estimates there are hundreds of thousands of details passed from generation to generation for which no one can give rules for what is happening, and may not even know there are any rules involved. These are transmitted informally, and their existence is often apparent only if they are broken.

Much of children's verbal behavior is also learned at this level, with rules unconsciously formulated in some way on the basis of informal observation. By the age of three or four, for instance, English-speaking children have acquired the rule for giving first names and respond to foreign names as 'funny', or break the rule in making up 'silly' names in play. Language-specific grammatical structures are learned primarily by informal means in early childhood, since any correction usually focuses on errors in lexical choice, or 'improper' speech. Pragmatic competence is also acquired informally: English-speaking children are not told explicitly that a surface-form question such as 'Wouldn't you like to put your toys away now?' is not asking for information, and that a direct 'No' would be considered an inappropriate or even rude response. Appropriate indirect responses are also learned (but not taught), and these same children soon develop the competence to respond 'Can I finish this first?' or 'I don't feel very good' as strategies to avoid complying with such a question/directive.

Technical learning is at an explicitly formulated, conscious level, and includes all that children find out in school about the grammar they have already acquired formally; rules are explained by adults, reasons given, and deviations usually corrected without emotional and moral involvement (although instructors may adopt a moralistic attitude toward 'errors' and sanctions may be imposed for violations). Written language skills are most likely to be taught in a technical mode, and more advanced oral rhetorical skills may also be developed at this level. 'Etiquette' is also transmitted technically, with a number of books and even daily newspaper columns in English devoted to explaining rules for 'proper' behavior: e.g who to introduce or present to whom, appropriate forms for invitations for particular social occasions, what clothes to wear to particular occasions, etc.

All cultures make use of all three of these modes of enculturation to some degree, but formal learning tends to be prominent where authority in the family is strictly ordered in a hierarchy, in cultures where the supernatural is a pervasive control on behavior, and where there is a great respect for tradition. On the other hand, children are more likely to be taught on a technical level in a knowledge-oriented society which values information and cognitive skills, and where the mental capacities of youth are accorded great respect.

Personality development is related in many respects to the acquisition of language and culture and should also be considered in the ethnography of communication, at least insofar as its association with verbal behavior or constraints on such behavior is concerned. Data on this point can sometimes provide valuable clues to norms and tolerated variability in particular speech communities. I noted earlier that children may be characterized as 'good' or 'bad' at least partly in terms of their language use, including not only the employment of politeness rules and 'proper' vocabulary, but also features of pronunciation (cf. Fischer 1958). Even expressions of pain and stress are culturally patterned, and may be taught quite early to children. Navajos endure pain quietly, for instance, and the extent of their illness or injury may not be apparent to anyone from a different cultural background. A nurse working in a clinic on the Navajo reservation observed mothers admonishing sick infants and young children to silence their cries, and I have seen five- and six-year-old Navajo children accept vaccinations without any facial or verbal sign of discomfort.

Cultural and social information is encoded in all channels of communication, and in all dimensions of each channel. One of the most obvious carriers of differential experiences within a language group is vocabulary, especially in the relatively limited lexicon of young children. This is evident in Sherk's (1973) comparison of the spontaneous speaking vocabulary of about 500 four-, five-, and six-year-old lower-class (mostly Black) children in Missouri (L) and middle-class (mostly White) children in New England (M). He reported the following differences in frequencies of lexical occurrences:

	L	M
apron	1	743
vegetables	6	165
trash	52	0
whip	23	3
party	9	800

Regional and ethnic differences in experience rather than social class are responsible for Sherk finding only the L group using *chitlins, skillet, lingo, shoats* 'poor people', *pokey, okra, greens*, and *fetch*, but these are no less sociocultural in nature than are different economic levels. (An invalid conclusion was drawn from these data that the differences in lexical use indicate differences in topics which are of interest to the two groups.)

Vocabulary development (and by implication, knowledge of the domains to which the vocabulary pertains) reflects to a significant degree the ordering of priorities within a culture. In the US, schools generally do not introduce *north, east, south*, and *west* until about the forth or fifth grade level (to ten- or eleven-year-olds), but the terms and concepts have been mastered by Navajo children before they come to kindergarten because of the importance of the cardinal directions in the religious beliefs and practices of the community. It would be of interest to know at what age Eskimo children acquire differential terms for snow, Aymara (Bolivia) children different terms for potatoes, and Marshallese (Polynesian) children different terms for stages in the development of coconuts. The development of semantic categories, and indeed of all situated meaning in language, is dependent on the dictates of cultural experience (cf. Cook-Gumperz 1977). Vocabulary knowledge thus becomes a means, as well as an index, of enculturation.

From the perspective of the child within a speech community, the role of language in enculturation is both for personal growth (to communicate information, express feelings, satisfy needs, acquire knowledge, interpret the world) and for socialization (to activate, structure, and maintain social intercourse, gain acceptance, status, and identity within the group). From the perspective of the community as a whole, creating conformity and effecting transmission of the culture are the primary functions of language learning: i.e. successful socialization (see Schieffelin and Ochs 1986a for a review of literature).

DEFINITION OF STAGES AND ROLES

Children learn the social structure of their culture as they learn language, and learning to use appropriate forms when there is a choice is part of learning one's place in society. The set of roles learned first through family interaction, then peer group and wider community, involves age, sex, and social class. Taking a somewhat Whorfian perspective, social forces influence the development of ways of speaking; these in turn influence what is social and psychological reality for a child at various stages and in whatever roles are open to him or her in the community. To learn the complex vertical hierarchies of a society like Bali, for instance, 'As [children] learn to speak, they learn that the words addressed to them by their elders and superiors are never the words in which they may answer . . .' (Mead 1955:42).

Of particular relevance to ethnographers are questions such as how speech to or by children differs with sex or social status, what aspects of speaking might be related to concepts of the ideal or typical man, woman, or child, how speech may be instrumental in marking stages in the life cycle, and how family patterns of organization (authority, rights, responsibilities) are expressed in language.

While most sex role differentiation is in response to social and cultural influences, some differences in male–female language development appear to be innate. McGuinness (1979) reports, for instance, that while the rate of babbling by infants and the number of vocalizations by young boys and girls are apparently the same, girls between two and a half to five years talk 50 per cent more, and boys make twice as many play 'noises'. Girls are better able to hear high frequency sounds, and are more sensitive than boys to sound intensity. Even at the age of one week there is some evidence that females can distinguish between another infant's cry and meaningless noise of the same volume, while males cannot. McGuinness speculates that 'Even before they can understand language, females may be better than males at discerning the emotional content of an utterance' (1979:85).

Differences in language use by adults to boys versus girls in different cultures remain largely unstudied. A survey of various aspects of socialization in 110 cultures (Barry, Bacon, and Child 1957) concludes there is little differentiation by sex in infancy, but in childhood girls have more emphasis put on nurturance, obedience, and responsibility, and boys more on self-reliance and achievement striving; we can assume this is related to differential language use to older children, but there is no explicit reference to this dimension of socialization. Blount does report (1972) that East African Luo adult males use a higher percentage of imperatives to young girls than to young boys, which would be consonant with the trend to train girls more to obedience in most cultures, and with the Luo social structure, which allows males to issue demands to females. Similar male dominance can be inferred from answers to a question asked of 126 Kamba adults in Kenya: 'What is the most important thing for parents to teach a toddler?' Over 80 per cent of the respondents said, 'To say the word "father"'' (Edgerton 1971:114).

Some information on appropriate use of language according to sex is to be found in the folklore and traditional literature. In Thai culture, female 'good manners' entail gentleness, sweet words, and graceful movements, as expressed in the *Suphasit Son Ying* (Bhu *c.* 1803). In addition to ways of speaking, smiling, and walking prescribed in this poetry, girls are to limit topics of conversation only to what is pleasant, and women must never argue with their husbands. In spite of some significant changes in Thai women's actual roles in the last two centuries, the ideal persists, and is still generally considered the appropriate cultural model for girls to emulate. The traditional folk tales of northern Europe similarly present females as hard working, unassertive, and soft spoken in roles like *Snow White, Sleeping Beauty*, and *Cinderella*, while males tend to be active and adventurous like *Jack and the Beanstalk* and *Robin Hood*. Males climb things, shout, leap around; females work quietly by the hearth or sleep.

In many societies differential attitudes toward the ways males and females should talk are realized in different speech training. In Burundi:

> From about the tenth year, boys in the upper social strata are given formal speech training. The 'curriculum' includes . . . formulas for petitioning a superior for a gift; . . . quick-witted, self-defensive rhetoric intended to deflect an accusation or the anger of a superior. . . . Girls in the upper caste are also carefully trained, but to artful silence and evasiveness and to careful listening that will enable them to repeat nearly verbatim what has been said by visitors or neighbors. (Albert 1972)

The Abbey community (in the Ivory Coast) also has clearly formulated ideas of appropriate ways of speaking based on sex. 'Speaking as a woman' refers to everyday informal speech spoken most of the time by anyone (male or female), while 'speaking as a man' is the high variety of language, full of proverbs, symbols, and metaphors, with a loud but gentle voice, using big gestures, and avoiding hesitations. 'Speaking as a child' refers to a very low variety. No normal adult would use it except to identify with children in a setting where most of the participants are quite young (Hepié). This is reminiscent of St Paul's observation. 'When I was a child I spoke as a child, but when I became a man I spoke as a man, and put away childish things.'

In Farsi, a child becomes sociolinguistically 'competent' at three years. At that time he is expected to have picked up such rules as not speaking in the presence of elders unless asked to, requesting properly, and using *shoma* (formal second person pronoun) and the correctly conjugated verb form when addressing an older person. He should also know appropriate forms of address for family members by then. In Nepal, Newar children under six are allowed the latitude of asking or saying anything for they are still considered 'ignorant babies'; but once past the age of six or seven, children are strictly monitored on what they say and how they behave in social gatherings. They are not expected to use respect forms or honorifics in normal interactions until they are around twelve or fourteen, however. While even infants in Bali are fully 'competent' because of belief in reincarnation, they are expected to do nothing for themselves; words are put into their mouths and spoken on their behalf by adults, who even form the infants' hands into appropriate gestures (Mead 1955).

A number of rites of passage observed in different cultures involve receiving a new name, or new terms of address. Different given names are often bestowed at christening or puberty rites, and different family names and titles with marriage. In some communities, teachers switch from using students' first name to title plus last name at about the time they begin secondary school, and in university academic circles in the US students may be invited to call professors by first name after they successfully defend their dissertation. Some nicknames are considered appropriate only for children, and continued use by family may cause considerable embarrassment. Similarly, diminutive forms of names may be dropped with age, especially for males, as Johnny, Billy, and Tommy to John, Bill, and Tom. Names may also be changed because of noteworthy events or achievements by the child, or because the death of someone possessing the same name makes it taboo. Some groups believe that names are a determining factor in children's ultimate deeds in life, including Momaday (1976), a Kiowa Indian who reports that his own name affirmed his life. It was given to him by a storyteller who believed 'a man's life proceeds from his name, in a way that a river proceeds from its source'. Reviews of naming practices and their relation to cultural factors in a wide variety of speech communities have been compiled by Akinnaso (1980) and Bean (1980).

Differential naming practices have led to some problems in keeping track of informants in ethnographic research; the Navajo practice of changing names proved so confusing (perhaps the 'real' one was never given an outsider), that census numbers have been the only sure means of identification for someone from outside the tribe; to use this is particularly significant in charting family relationships, since when American Indian groups were directed to choose 'family' names in the early nineteenth century, brothers often chose (or were assigned) different ones, making relationships unclear.

Naming is usually considerd quite personal within a speech community, but the act clearly identifies children as belonging to their group. If a child later chooses to change group allegiance, changing names is often the most obvious sign of reaffiliation.

COMMUNICATIVE STRATEGIES

Children begin to learn communicative options and to select those appropriate for a given situation at a very early age, and their repertoire changes both quantitatively and qualitatively as they mature. Early stages appear to be primarily nonverbal (and very obvious to others), while those of older children are more often verbal (and may be quite subtle). For instance, aggression is often expressed physically by young children (at least among English speakers), but this behavior comes to be supplemented with verbal taunts and chants by the age of five, and may develop into one of the complex verbal dueling forms of later childhood and adolescence. To get attention, the young child who may hold its breath or bang its head against the wall develops competence in more mature forms of nonverbal behavior (e.g. raising a hand) and appropriate verbalizations (e.g. calls, shifts in intonation, solicitation routines).

Children use language to create and maintain a social hierarchy in their peer group, often with routines known to all in the group which have predetermined responses and are thus controlled by the initiator. Weininger (1978) describes 'knock-knock' routines started by socially subordinate children in a Texas kindergarten, which then forced higher ranking children to respond and interact with them. Directives are often used by children to establish a power position, with compliance by others interpreted as their accepting lesser status. English-speaking children use fewer imperative forms between equals than do adults, but direct more to subordinates (Mitchell-Kernan and Kernan 1977). This does not appear to represent a developmental stage in acquiring adult communicative competence, but rather a difference in linguistic strategies. There also appear to be differences in features in the social context which identify a power role for adults versus children; age and size are more salient determinants of power for children than are social or economic status (Owens 1979).

There is a growing body of cross-cultural information on when and how children learn to request, direct, insult, comment, and summon, and thus to what extent such acquisition may be tied to development factors or to cultural experiences. It seems clear that even quite young children may use language to control adult behavior, as well as that of other children, in order to get what they want, to escape punishment, to gain approval. One three-and-a-half-year old has learned to make a request without risking refusal or negative response by giving the addressee the option, 'If you want to play house with me you can', and DiPietro (1975) reports his son acquired a verbal strategy by age four which attempts to put the adult in a double bind. The child would challenge, 'I bet I know what you'll say if I ask you something', and he can't really lose. If the adult answers 'No', the child wins the verbal match with, 'See I knew you'd say that'; if the adult answers 'yes', the child wins by getting what he wants.

FORMULAIC EXPRESSIONS

While receptive competence clearly precedes production in most areas of communicative development, the reverse is often true of the acquisition of routines and polite formulas. Even infants of six or seven months are taught to wave and say *bye-bye* 'good-bye'. This, plus *please* and *thank you* are usually the first routines taught to English-speaking children. Perhaps the first sign of acquired meaning comes when a child looks sad or cries when parents say *bye-bye* before going away for a few hours, but this stage generally comes several months later than the first production.

Bauman (1976) reports a similar production-to-comprehension order in the acquisition of riddles as solicitational routines. The developmental sequence at age five begins with descriptive routines: proper form, but no misleading element as 'what's red, round, and good to eat' (an apple), or 'what's round and bounces' (a ball). This progresses to power and control aspects; children understand the puzzling nature of riddles, but consider answers arbitrary, and do not understand the ambiguity involved. They do understand that the poser is always right, as in 'What color is blood?' 'Red.' 'No, it's blue and black.' Competence at age seven includes recognition of the riddle as a traditional form, and routines are memorized as fixed forms, but with flaws that indicate ambiguities are still not fully comprehended. Correct preformance of riddles, according to Bauman, becomes increasingly prevalent at about age eight.

The process through which children acquire ritual competence (which would include polite formulas) is 'perhaps the most fundamental socialization of all since they thereby learn about the nature they are to have as actors' (Goffman 1971:157). If a child neglects to use the proper formula, an adult may halt the sequence and prompt, 'What do you say?'

What evidence there is on the acquisition of ritual forms in other speech communities suggests that mimicry or this prompting of young children are both common phenomena. Four- to six-year-old Newar children in Nepal, for instance, are taught to interact socially by repeating greetings or leavetakings. The parent, while greeting a visitor, turns to the child and says 'Say *namaste*', and the child utters the greetings with the appropriate gesture (i.e. palms of hands together with fingers pointing upward and a slight bowing of the head).

Some routines, although common to all adults in a speech community, may not be learned until after childhood. Where greeting or leavetaking routines are complex (as in Arabic and Indonesian), competence in full forms is not expected of children, and condolence routines are also generally delayed even though the deaths of friends and family may be experienced from infancy.

At later stages of childhood, prompting in teaching ritual verbal performances may range from Boy Scout pledges, to oaths of allegiance to the flag, to recitals of religious creeds – all aspects of continued enculturation. Comparable socialization (and prompting) may continue into post-adolescence in marriage vows, legal oaths, and occupation or military domains.

NONVERBAL COMMUNICATION

Communicatively significant nonverbal behaviors develop along with the verbal in young children, and in some apsects precede it. Before Thai children can talk, for instance, they learn to use the *wai* gesture (described in Chapter 4 and for Newar children above) when the parents or caretakers tell them to greet or say good-bye to someone. Before giving the children something to eat, the caretakers ask, 'What would you do first?', and receive a *wai* in response (Ekasingh).

Unlike the culture-specific *wai*, some nonverbal behaviors appear to be 'natural' to all young humans, and are perhaps even shared by higher order primates. Darwin (1872) was the first to suggest there are facial expressions which universally convey the same emotion, and to some extent he has been supported by subsequent research (cf. Harper, Wiens, and Matarazzo 1978). Most features of nonverbal communication are language/culture-specific, however, and are learned in the same way language/culture-specific elements of verbal behavior are learned. In the case of the few universal behaviors (generally expressing emotion), cultural learning often takes the form of constraining gestures or facial expressions in terms of how and when they may be used: i.e. 'display rules' (Ekman 1972) are language/culture-specific. Cultural constraints must also be acquired whenever nonverbal behavior appropriate for children is not considered appropriate for adults, or when different behavior is appropriate for males and females in a society.

In cross-cultural research, Von Raffler-Engel (1977) describes Japanese and English children being socialized into the suppression of most hand gestures, and finds early evidence of culture-specific body movement. A Japanese girl videotaped at two years three months, for instance, bows to a pretend addressee over a toy telephone when saying good-bye, just as her mother makes a toy kangaroo bow to her on 'leaving'. Birdwhistell (1970) has also noted the emergence of nonverbal behaviors which are sex-specific by the age of two; American male–female differences include posture, eye behavior, and the angle of arms and legs to the body.

One of the most interesting questions in the acquisition of communicative competence is how children learn when *not* to talk, and what silence means in their speech community.

In part, the relative silence of some children (e.g. Chinese, Japanese, and Hopi) over others (e.g. British and American) may be related to childrearing practices and values regarding the relative value of individual achievement and initiative; children in societies which value individual achievement generally talk more. Additionally, the cultural experience of children who will be less verbal about their needs and wishes seems to include closer physical contact with early caretakers, and expectations that adults or older siblings will care for them without need for verbalization. This also relates to attitudes even in the adult speech community that people should not, and should not have to, ask directly for what they want. In Clancy's observations of mothers interacting with two-year olds in Japan, she noted that they would attribute speech to individuals who had actually remained silent in order to heighten children's awareness of what others' feelings might be, or provide 'lessons in how to guess what others are thinking and feeling [i.e. inferencing] even when they have not spoken' (1986:235).

Training young children to silence and heightened non-verbal perception may be considered part of the transmission of world view, as in this example reported by Locke (1980):

A Colville Indian child from the Northwest Coast is trained to perceive with all of his senses before he learns to speak so that he may become sensitive to the world around him. A grandparent will say 'Wighst' and slap his hand on a solid surface. The child who is crawling on the floor will stop playing or daydreaming or whatever he is doing and become alert at the sound of that word and will try to feel through his body and his feet the vibrations of the stream or animals walking or people walking about him. The child sharpens his peripheral vision. He listens to all the sounds about him, he focuses all his senses, including that other sense, that is sensitive to the vibrations of the earth. The training is constant. . . . Thus he is prepared to relate to other two-leggeds, four-leggeds, the winged creatures, the crawling ones, the finned ones, the rooted ones, and all of life, all of our relations.

Other potentially relevant cultural differences in childrearing practices are suggested by Wang (1977):

In order to keep the children from saying or doing something disapproved of by the authorities, Asian parents teach them to be obedient and to honor their families. Everything is arranged and decided for them. They are not given any choices; therefore, they do not have to make choices and justify their actions verbally.

Silence is praised, and talkativeness is scolded. They are taught not to express their feelings.

As with other areas of sociolinguistic training, proverbs and stories may also be used to teach children to be silent. Some of these proverbs have been cited in the discussion of attitudes toward language (Chapter 5). Additionally, Confucius is quoted as saying 'The wise man desires to be slow to speak but quick to act', and teachers in Taiwan warn students who talk too much that 'Disaster comes in through the mouth' and 'One who talks too much will fail' (Wang 1977). One line from a Javanese pedagogical song-poem by W. S. Rendra reads: *Tumumgkula yen dipun dukani* 'Just look down if you are reprimanded'.

Children's learning of appropriate silence, like other communicative strategies, is not necessarily developing competence in adult norms for sociolinguistic behavior, but may involve quite different rules for adults and children. Slavey children in Canada are allowed to be relatively voluble, and yet become taciturn in old age (Christian and Gardner 1977), for instance, and in many societies it may be appropriate for children to talk freely with other children but be expected to be silent in the presence of adults.

Silent slots in discourse may also have different meanings for adult and child members of the same speech community. In contrast to the claim that silence is an appropriate response to inappropriate questions for adults (Lakoff 1973), English-speaking children usually consider a reply mandatory. In many cases, the same contexts which call for a formal style from adult speakers require silence of children. Formal style or verbal rituals may appropriately replace silence as they are acquired, or as the speech community feels children are old enough to use them.

Perhaps because so much of nonverbal competence is acquired during early childhood, it is learned primarily through informal and formal means and less often at a technical level. This is perhaps also the reason that appropriate nonverbal behavior is often unconscious, and why it is seldom completely mastered in a second language.

PEER INFLUENCE AND EXTENDED ACQUISITION

There has traditionally been less attention paid to continuing acquisition and refinement of language skills in later years of childhood, and into adulthood, than to early language acquisition. It has been well established that extended language acquisition must be qualitatively different because of neurological changes, such as the vastly diminished amount of uncommitted cortex (Penfield 1965), but we must also recognize that different stages of communicative development involve very different aspects of socialization, and different primary sociocultural influences. Although this basic generalization may not hold true for all cultures, young children are usually most dependent on and influenced by family, adolescents by peers, and adults by such social institutions as their workplace. We are particularly interested in knowing what verbal strategies are not learned until after childhood, how they are acquired, and what functions they have for members of a particular speech community.

Peer group relations and influence play a very important part in the socialization of most older children and adolescents, but who or what constitutes a peer group, and the relative influence which that group has on members, is quite culture-specific. In the mainstream, middle class of the United States, a 'peer group' is defined primarily by age, and there is little latitude in this respect. A child from this group who plays with, or even enjoys, the company of children several years younger or older is often considered 'odd'. In contrast, members of the peer groups in many subcultures in the country include children in the neighborhood within a wide range of ages, particularly when older children have primary caretaking reponsibilities for their younger siblings. The influence of this age-mixing is clearly seen in the language development of bilingual children; those in the care of older brothers and sisters and thus in contact with a wider range of neighborhood children usually know more English on school entry than do the oldest children of these families, or others where primary care is provided by adults at home. In other societies, such as Mexico, it is commonplace to see older children and teenagers spontaneously playing with young children in the community.

A very different kind of situation is reported in Cat Harbour, Newfoundland, where there is virtually no influence from peers. This is apparently part of a pattern of socialization to values of formality, inhibition, caution, and reserve. 'Children are taught to avoid close relationships with their peers, that emotional expression is to be avoided, and that any exposure can lead to exploitation' (Faris 1968).

The function of language in establishing and regulating peer relations has been analyzed among Israeli children, where it includes participating appropriately in verbal exchanges which focus on sharing treats. Developing competence in the rules which govern these exchanges is related to children's moral development (Katriel 1987), and plays a role in their enculturation to the moral order of their society. A second type of peer exchange involves *brogez*, which 'functions as a standardized mechanism for the regulation of conflicts among Israeli children . . . [allowing for] both the expression and the containment of aggression' (Katriel 1985:485). An interesting aspect of events such as these which regulate interaction in peer culture is the extent to which the rules for appropriate conduct are often developed, transmitted, and maintained with little encouragement or interference from adult members of the community. Naturalistic studies of child disputing and negotiation events in other cultures include Adger (1986), Boggs (1978), Emihovich (1986), Maynard (1985), and Saville-Troike (1986).

In complex societies, occupational socialization (and thus the acquisition of occupation-specific communicative competence) seldom begins until well after childhood. Often a unique vocabulary (jargon) must be learned, which may be acquired through technical education, informal 'on the job' observation and imitation, or a combination of both.

Prospective linguists, for instance, must learn not only a specialized vocabulary, but appropriate argumentation structures (cf. Perlmutter and Soames 1979), appropriate written style to be published in professional journals, and currently appropriate examples to use in oral and written presentations.

New government employees in the United States enter the bureaucratic subculture; in addition to the acquisition of new vocabulary, they must also learn to recognize and generate acronyms, and process and produce idiomatic expressions which are unique to that domain. New patterns of language use must be learned, including new forms of address, new ways to answer telephones, and often even new ways to formulate requests, invitations, jokes, and insults. (These and other specialized varieties associated with purpose are discussed in Chapter 3.)

In a few societies, training in occupational rituals may begin in early childhood. The Cagaba (Chibchan speakers in Colombia) select their leaders through divination, and apprenticeship usually begins as soon as a chosen boy is weaned and lasts 19 years. During this time, the boy is secluded from all except the current leader (often his father) and other apprentices (Lagacé 1977). Early informal training is more common, where children who are expected to assume the role which a parent or grandparent holds are encouraged to observe, and may practice in role-playing contexts with their peers. Some Navajo boys who are expected to become medicine men have already assumed the role of storyteller among their peers by the age of five or six, and conduct play ceremonials. In these contexts the boys may exhibit skills in using voice qualities appropriate for characterizing animal voices, or intoned speech, which are generally considered far beyond the productive competence of children that age.

Part of the delay that does occur in aspects of communicative development may be attributed to the level of cognitive maturity required to acquire some concepts or functions; when this is the reason, rather than differential social requirements or experience, we should of course find little cultural variation. One area where this is a factor is the development of competence in figurative language, including the interpretation of puns, jokes, riddles, similies, metaphors, and irony (Gardner *et al.* 1978). While children are sensitive to some types of figurative language in early childhood (e.g. they may designate the *nose, mouth,* or *feet* on a picture of a mountain), speakers can really use language figuratively only after they have acquired considerable competence in its literal structure, and are at a cognitive level to process it more abstractly.

It is possible that the usual delayed acquisition of competence in a function like condoling is due to combined factors of required cognitive maturity and attitudes within a community about which events are appropriate for child participation and which not. In Saudi Arabia, for instance, condoling requires highly ritualized formulaic language including both prescribed verbal and nonverbal behavior. It is not appropriate for males to participate until they are about fourteen years old, and never appropriate for females. On the other hand, in some societies it may be considered appropriate for much younger children to participate in condoling. Hogbin (1946) reports Wogeo (New Guinea) parents at funerals instruct children of about three years to do their share of weeping, and Pukapukan (Polynesia) children commonly play burying games after the death of someone in the community in order to experience fringe-level participation in the funeral wake and burial (Beaglehole 1941). Even though Abbey children in the Ivory Coast do not speak at formal funeral events, they have a spectator role, and how they walk and gesture is considered very important.

English-speaking children are generally not present at wakes and funerals to learn informally by observation, but they are still expected to somehow know the 'right thing to say' to the bereaved when they are old enough to participate, even for the first time. Except for priests, ministers, and funeral directors, who do learn appropriate formulas as part of their professional training, most English speakers remain quite insecure of their own competence in this situation.

In general, then, it appears that: (1) where complex ritual forms are prescribed, children are expected to be silent, but are often allowed to observe so they have the opportunity to acquire the appropriate behaviors informally; (2) when ritual forms are used but it is considered inappropriate for children to observe them, direct instruction is required at a later stage in their enculturation; (3) where there is more flexibility in the choice of language, but still strong feelings of propriety about the choices which are made, even adult members in the community may feel linguistically insecure.

The most difficult situations for speakers probably occur when change is in progress, where old rules no longer hold but new ones have not yet codified (cf. Paulston 1976 for examples of sociolinguistic change in Sweden); and where rules are not explicit or are dependent on complex contextual conditions, as those governing use of terms of address in the United States, particularly toward persons of higher rank and/or advanced age (cf. Ervin-Tripp 1972 for formulation of rules in her region). Speakers are generally expected to acquire such rules informally, by observing others and abstracting the appropriate patterns; boundaries for correct behavior are more likely to be clearly marked when it is controlled formally.

SPEECH PLAY

One of the greatest influences the peer group has on the acquisition of communicative competence in many languages comes through various kinds of speech play. Some of these contribute directly to the development of the child's control of the linguistic code (lexicon, phonology, and grammar), while others include games which provide license for children to play roles not appropriate in nonplay contexts, games which allow nonviolent modes for the expression of aggression and hostility, and games which reinforce cultural knowledge and values.

Regarding development of the linguistic code, Sanches and Kirshenblatt-Gimblett see

> the foci of children's speech play – that is, whether the individual form is mainly dominated by phonological, grammatical, semantic, or sociolinguistic structure – as reflecting an exercise in whatever part of the structure the child is currently mastering. (1971:43)

Counting rhymes such as 'One, two, buckle my shoe; Three, four, shut the door' are found in many languages, generally focusing on sound, as well as serving as mnemonic devices for learning the lexical sequence. Chinese children chant numbers as they walk or play, which involves a tonal as well as lexical sequence to be learned, and Bambara children in Mali recite puns which rely on alliterations and homophones (spoken or sung by boys, usually sung by girls), such as the following:

Kelen, kerekete kelen	(one, one snail)
Fila, filanin-ko	(two, a twins' business)
Saba, afala	(three, a snake-killer)
Nari, Nanògòlen	(four, dirty sauce)

Using the same phonological processes, Bambara counting puns may also be maxims which convey traditional wisdom:

Duru, dugu tè sigi masakè kò (five, there is no town
without a chief)
Wòrò, hòronya nin kadi bè ye(six, we all like freedom)

Speech play involving counting is widely used for turn selection in children's games. Cultural diffusion is evident in the form of some of these events: e.g., children in the Philippines and Korea recite numbers in Japanese, although they are generally perceived to be nonsense routines without meaning (reported by Ablanque and Park-Mun). Another selection game which has diffused is 'paper, scissors, stone', in which children chant rhythmically for three beats and then commit to a handshape on the fourth which represents one of the three named objects and determines order of play (scissors cuts paper, stone breaks scissors, and paper covers stone). Children on the islands of Visayan and Mindanao in the Philippines call this event *dyangkingkoy*, which has no referential meaning for them (Ablanque), although the chant can again be traced to a Japanese language source.

Another form of speech play contributing to both phonology and lexicon is practiced by deaf children, who tell stories (in sign) with words in alphabetical order. The game is complicated by older children, and additional manual skill developed, by signing two different words simultaneously with the left and right hands.

Some play is designed to test verbal competence quite

consciously, as in a Newar question and answer game, in which the respondent must answer quickly and in a form which rhymes with the question. A sing-song effect is created and hesitation disqualifies a participant. As in many other cases, such play is performance, and this test always has an audience. A similar pattern is found among US Blacks, where the form given by the challenger must be appropriately rhymed by the person challenged.

Riddling is a common form of speech play in many communities. Among Quechua children this does not begin until near puberty, and then contributes to sexual socialization as well as language development. Isbell and Fernandez (1977) speculate such verbal play involves the exploration of ambiguous semantic categories, the development of meta-phorical concepts and skills, and thus increased flexibility and creativity in language use.

Children's verbal play can yield information on a far broader scope of their socialization processes than just language development, and provides insights into the culture they are learning and the social structure of which they are a part. According to Bernstein, this is so because children's speech play influences organization of experience and behavior. It makes 'the child sensitive to role and status and also to the customary relationships connecting and legitimizing the social positions within his peer group' (1960:180). Adult ways of speaking may be practiced in make-believe roles, such as giving tea parties and offering 'One lump or two', or playing school and assuming the mannerisms and speech of teacher and principal.

Insults yield particularly valuable cultural information, because a comment on a cultural value is always one of their defining features. Mitchell-Kernan and Kernan (1977) report they have been able to ascertain that children have acquired particular cultural values by examining their insults. They can rank the strength of the insult, and thus the strength of the cultural value underlying it, by analyzing the nature of the response to that insult in comparison with others (a procedure that will work for adult insults as well). In a cross-cultural comparison of insults, for instance, Mitchell-Kernan and

Kernan find Black American children insulting primarily with comments on appearance and intellectual capacity (e.g. accusing others of being babies), while the most serious insult for Samoan children is a comment on generosity. In Korea, children's insults generally concern the honor of the family name (directed at mother first, then father). Illegitimacy is often suggested, and the likelihood that the family achieved its status by cheating.

Insults are just one type of verbal contest used by children. Abrahams describes one of their general functions as 'trying-on' mature roles within the safe confines of the peer group while arming the children with verbal weapons which will be useful in adult life. Among Black males, these contests include categories labeled *rapping* (often competitive repartee between male and female), *shucking* and *jiving* (flattering and cajoling), and *signifying* (goading) (see Kochman 1972, especially pp. 241–64, for descriptions and illustrations of these categories).

A verbal contest unique to young (8 to 11 year old) Black females is *stepping* (organized competitive 'spelling', foot stepping, and hand clapping), in which the body is used to iconically represent the shape of letters, following the spelling *M I Crooked Letter Crooked Letter I Crooked Letter Crooked Letter I Hump Back Hump Back I* for 'Mississippi'. Skilled performers are called *kookalaters* (‹crooked letter). Gilmore (1981) reports that *stepping* has been banned from the public schools in Philadelphia because of its frequent sexual explicitness. One version given by Gilmore is as follows:

M for the money
 I if ya give it to me
S sock it (to me)
S sock it
 I if I buy if from ya
S sock it
S sock it
 I if I take it from you
P pump it
P push it
 I :::

The following is an example of *playing the dozens*, another Black male verbal contest in which insults typically involve obscene reference to the addressee's mother:

I fucked your mother from house to house
she thought my dick was Mighty Mouse.

(Hannerz 1969:130)

While some may be simple one liners (e.g. 'Your mother smokes a pipe', or even just 'Your mother'), the more elaborate ones rhyme. Very similar is the *verbal dueling* of Turkish boys. One example reported by Dundes, Leach, and Özkök (1972:144–5) begins with insult:

Ananın   amı.
[mother-your's cunt]
(Your mother's cunt.)

The verbal retort must rhyme, as:

Babamin   kıllı damı.
[father-my's hairy roof]
(My father's hairy roof.)

Although it rhymes, the response is not considered a very successful one, which may warrant a further counterattack:

Uyduramadın   yancığına
[Make-up-couldn't-you side-its-to-of-it]
(You didn't make a very good rhyme.)

Bin   devenin kancığına
[ride camel's female-to]
(You ride a female camel.)

East Javanese children also quarrel using rhymes, although the content of theirs is seldom obscene. This event may be between two individuals, but more often is between two groups of children. It is not uncommon for the duel to begin with:

Kambang ecèng-ecèng,	(Eceng-eceng flowers,
Kembangé suradadu,	The flowers of soldiers,
Beyèn rèntèng-rèntèng,	We used to walk hand in hand,
Saiki ngajak satru.	But now we become enemies.)

The point is to throw as many insulting rhymes as possible at the opponent, and strict turn-taking is not observed. Delays occur when one group discusses what rhyme to say next or waits for prompting from older children or relatives. When children become more and more excited, they start to use ordinary language (no rhymes), but rarely end in a physical fight.

A clear example of speech play reinforcing cultural knowledge and values is found in Saudi Arabia, where preschool boys or girls participate in competitive individual and group recitation of Koranic verses. When in a group, children raise their voices over others if they know the verse well and mumble along if they do not; each child tries to recite verses the others do not know. The event is not considered prayer because it is not accompanied by other acts required in prayer. But it is considered religious training and, additionally, practice in Classical Arabic as a kind of reading-readiness exercise. Again, the audience is an important factor in this play-performance, which in this case includes attentive and approving adults.

Another example comes from China, where traditional social roles are still transmitted to children in this mode. In the following pattern (which may be extended to great length), P1 is an older child or adult and P2 is two or three years of age. The young child is only required to repeat 'inside sits' (prompted by P1 as needed) and provide an address term, while the older participant supplies the role function and rhyme (Jin).

P1 *Ji dan ji dan ke ke,*
    (Egg egg shell,)
P2 *Li tou zuoge ge-ge.*
    (Inside sits a brother.)
P1 *Ge-ge chu lai mai cai.*
    (Brother comes out to buy things.)

P2   *Li tou zuoge nai-nai.*
     (Inside sits a grandmother.)
P1   *Nai-nai chu lai shao xiang.*
     (Grandmother comes out to light incense.)
P2   *Li tou zuoge gu-niang.*
     (Inside sits a girl.)
P1   *Gu-niang chu lai dian deng.*
     (The girl comes out to light a candle.)

One final example comes from Venezuela, where children in the preschool educational program are taught a game called *Matare*. The game begins when two children choose a name to call another child. They start by calling out an 'ugly' name, which other children sing that they won't accept, and continue in this manner until a 'good' name is picked and accepted by the group. Conveyed are cutural notions of the status of different occupations and appropriate sex roles: e.g. only boys can be called a name like 'shoemaker' and 'carpenter', and only girls one like 'servant' and 'cook'.

FORMAL EDUCATION

In considering the place of formal education in children's acquisition of communicative competence, ethnographers are primarily concerned with what patterns of speaking are developed and used primarily as a consequence of schooling.

To begin with, some speech events are unique to the context of school. One of the first performance routines learned by kindergarten students in the United States is 'Show and Tell', which is usually considered a major step toward more complex public speaking, and has several new rules for appropriate speaking which are either learned from observing others or through explicit correction of errors (teachers are given very explicit instruction in how to teach this routine to children):

1   Appropriate topics are limited by other children's interest and the teacher's sense of propriety. Part of developing

competence is learning what *not* to tell, and how to leave out details of a lengthy narrative.

2 Explicit and decontextualized language is encouraged, with the teacher and other children making a conscious effort to elicit more facts with WH-questions or prompting if too much shared information is being assumed.

3 Nonverbal behavior is also prescribed, with children told to stand on two feet, face their audience, and take their hand from in front of their mouth.

Other classroom-specific communicative phenomena are rigid turn-taking, with a raised hand to request a turn; the spatial arrangement, with children seated in rows of desks or around tables; and peer interaction which is initiated and controlled by an adult.

In educational programs where the language of instruction is essentially the same code which the children have learned at home, the oral language development which takes place through formal education is primarily new vocabulary, new rules for speaking, practice in interpretation and use of a more formal style, and skills for public performance. Most emphasis is placed on acquiring a new channel of communication (writing), and on the skills and conventions involved in its interpretation and use. At the earliest stages of schooling, this includes letter or character formation, directionality, and locating what is considered the top and front of a book. (All of these conventions are of course arbitrary, and relative to which writing system is being learned.) Some pictorial conventions of nonverbal communication are also taught at this level for the interpretation of accompanying illustrations (e.g. balloons around words indicate dialogue, elongated spots on the face means that the person is crying, etc.).

In many speech communities formal education is conducted in a linguistic code quite different from the one children have acquired at home, but it is still true that the development of communicative competence in these settings emphasizes a formal style, reading and writing skills, and ways of speaking often unique to the school. Educational anthropologists have focused more on traditional education than formal schooling, but the comparative studies that do exist suggest there may be more commonality cross-nationally in ways of using language in this cultural domain than in any other, in large part because formal schooling in most of the world today stems from the same European traditions. This leads to differential discontinuity in ways of speaking at home versus school, and an important area of ethnographic research.

Formal education is carried out largely through the medium of language, and the children who succeed are those who 'learn how to learn' through abstract linguistically mediated instruction. Scribner and Cole (1973) suggest that the linguistic activities, especially the use of decontextualized language, lead to cognitive skills of abstraction and generalization which are rarely found among traditionally educated individuals. Western-type formal schooling, including the learning of reading and writing, may thus result in the development of qualitatively different cognitive abilities from those usually found in traditional societies. Ethnographers should be aware of and sensitive to this possibility in their research.

Emphasis on writing begins on school entry in most parts of the world, including the development of physical and artistic skills for producing written forms: spelling and penmanship are considered critical subjects in most Latin American schools; traditional Chinese and Japanese education values competence in calligraphy, and children still practice regularly with a brush and ink block beginning with their first year of school; and grading in Australian schools is normally based exclusively on written work, with frequent oral contributions often penalized.

Oral language competence is also stressed in some societies, but this often means competence in reciting what was written by others: Yugoslavian elementary school students reportedly must memorize great quantities of poetry, and are then graded on the fluency, smoothness, and dramatic appropriateness of their oral interpretation to the class; and Chinese education based on Confucian traditions emphasized memorization and recitation of the Four Books, with the target civil service examination measuring the same competence.

Questions and answers occur in almost all classrooms of the world, in all languages, but they have quite differing functions. Teachers most commonly ask questions to test student knowledge rather than to gain information on the ostensible topic, since the 'right' answer is already prescribed. Former students from such diverse countries as the USSR, Taiwan, Germany, and Indonesia report being highly praised if they gave the expected response, but reprimanded for not being diligent enough if they could not. Learning not to volunteer answers may be learning to avoid potential reprimands, but may also be learning to be properly humble in not seeking attention or praise. That this is learned behavior is illustrated by the fact that in Japanese elementary schools children appear to be quite willing to answer questions before they are called on, but few Japanese students volunteer answers by the high school level. Teachers from the English speech community often think students from other cultures do not volunteer answers because they are 'shy', but this is an ethnocentric interpretation. Asian students in classes with English speakers generally consider their classmates who do volunteer freely as being rude, inconsiderate of the teacher, and wasting class time. Latin American students frequently misinterpret the relative informality in US classrooms as lack of teacher disciplinary control, particularly at the junior high and high school levels, which accounts for teachers' return misinterpretation of their behavior as 'undisciplined'.

Although it is seldom listed as such, one important function of language for students in academic contexts is to convey a 'proper attitude' toward school. A list of behaviors related to school success which Wallat (1981) has extracted from the literature includes:

Speak positively to others.
Make positive comments to the teacher.
Speak positively about academic materials.
Answer or try to answer questions.
Initiate contacts about work assignments.

Even more indicators of 'proper attitude' that she lists involve nonverbal communicative behaviors, including:

Sit up straight.
Smile at the teacher.
Use your body to show attention.
Use your body, or face, to show self-control.
Nod in agreement as the teacher speaks.

Because schools are major socializing institutions for the society in which they function, they must generally transmit the values and beliefs of those who control them. The choice of language for education is a major consideration in multilingual contexts, and reflects the power structure in the country, attitudes toward group identities, and educational philosophy and priorities. Japan was forced to change its basic curricular framework after World War II to the American pattern as 'progressive' educational principles were imposed along with military occupation, but with return to Japanese control, methods again changed from 'learning by doing' to renewed heavy emphasis on memorization, repetition, and reading and responding in unison. Even educational practices of long standing may be changed as part of the process of social revolution, however, as evidenced by successful attempts to institute educational change in the People's Republic of China and in Turkey. The attempt in Turkey included even changing the name of the institution itself from *mektep*, which designated the traditional Koranic school, to *okul*, an invented term based on *oku-* 'to read'. However the curriculum is designed and whatever the methods of instruction, language constitutes the center of formal education, as both object and medium of instruction.

MULTILINGUAL CONTEXTS

Children in multilingual speech communities must, in addition to multiple language codes, acquire skills in switching and more complex rules for appropriate usage.

One of the earliest ethnographic studies of children in a bilingual community was Barker's (1947) research in Tucson, Arizona. The situation there was quite typical of the Southwestern United States at that time, with parents using Spanish with children at home, and children learning English at school and using it in formal relations. While Spanish continued to be used for close relationships and ceremonial relationships in the adult community, code-switching was common for informal relationships among younger bilinguals. Two major shifts in patterns of usage seem to be emerging in recent years: because of bilingual education, many children are also acquiring a formal variety of Spanish along with literacy in the process of formal instruction; and the use of code-switching in informal interaction is now common for older as well as younger speakers.

While it is usual for children to learn the official (H) language as a second language in school, in some speech communities it is actually acquired first in the home, and children learn to speak the indigenous language (L) when they are older. This phenomenon has been reported by Rensch (1977) for children in Oaxaca who first learn Spanish and then Chontal, by Tabouret-Keller (1972) for children who learn French before their patois, and by Thompson (1971) for Mexican American children who learn English before Spanish.

The age at which children can functionally differentiate codes depends to a great extent on the context of acquisition, but most have developed the competence to switch appropriately according to the linguistic identity of the addressee by the age of three, and by situation or setting soon after. Switching by topic, or by the role-relationship between speakers other than language of the addressee, comes at a later stage in development. The degree of physical difference associated with language use, or even dress, may be a major factor. In Taiwan, even toddlers who knew only one word of English ('Hi') identified me immediately as someone appropriate to say it to; on the other hand, Spanish-speaking six-year olds in Texas refused to use Spanish with a Mexican American researcher until he took off his coat and tie.

Other interesting questions are which language multilingual

parents choose to use with their children, the children's attitudes towards the different codes, and the different functions assigned to each.

CHILDREN'S BELIEFS ABOUT LANGUAGE

Children themselves often have definite ideas about the nature of language, how it is learned, and how it is used, but while children have been frequent objects of observation by ethnographers, they are seldom interviewed.

The willingness of at least one subgroup to respond can be inferred from the response which *Life* had to a questionnaire it aimed at children from six to twelve years of age (Flaherty 1972). Over 250,000 children returned the questionnaire, and almost 5,000 also submitted letters to elaborate on their opinions. One question that related to language was whether or not they felt parents listened to them; 85 per cent answered affirmatively, although there were a few negative comments:

> Only when I'm being funny.
> My parents only listen when they're mad at me.
> Did you know that parents and teachers can scream at you, but you cannot scream at them? We have feelings too.

The conclusion was that children in this speech community want – and expect – to be asked what they think, and to have adults listen. Such attitudes are also part of learned communicative competence.

Other questions asked of children in the United States have included what they call their teachers, and how they think they learned the address rule. All of the six- to twelve-year olds interviewed by Bruhn (1975) used title plus last name; younger children did not know why, but those eight years and older formulated reasons.

> I guess that's just the way we learned to do it.
> They won't let you call them anything else.

It's just that little kids don't do that. . . . The teachers
call each other the first names.
In most schools you're not allowed to call people by the
first name.

I observed a six-year old who was transferred to a school in
which her mother was teaching, greet her in the hall with
'Good morning, Mrs X', much to her mother's surprise.
When I asked the child why she had used that form of
address, she answered quite simply, 'Because the other kids
do'.

Children can often be observed talking to dolls, animals,
and infants, but do they believe their addressees can
understand them? There are undoubtedly different beliefs
underlying similar behavior depending on cultural experiences,
just as there are for adults. When Miller (1970) asked Pima
children 'Do animals have a language?' and 'Do they
understand our language?', the age distribution of affirmative
responses was particularly interesting. Of the children under
eight, 75 per cent believes animals have a language but none
think they understand ours; 90 per cent of the ten-year olds
believe animals have a language and 70 per cent that they
understand ours; and the eleven-year olds responded with 100
per cent affirmative answers to animals understanding our
language. Since much of the Pima folklore contains animal
characters who possess speech, the increasing belief in this
capacity probably reflects learning of the traditional stories of
the tribe. (It would be very interesting to know to what extent
this belief is retained in older children and among adults.)

Young children's beliefs concerning the ability of infants to
talk might be particularly interesting to explore because of
their intermediate status, but we cannot assume answers even
of young children will always be truthful. Since they have
already acquired some communicative strategies, they may
know how to use the intermediate role as interpreters to their
advantage. One three-year old who was babbling with her
baby sister was asked what the infant was saying, and she
responded, 'She says she wants ice cream.' Of course both
were rewarded. At the age of four, my own daughter

carefully trained her younger brother to include among his first phrases, 'I did it', whenever something was broken.

Children also have opinions about how language is being used by adults. Viorst (1976) consulted her experts from kindergarten and first and second grade, plus her own children, on the subject 'What's a Good Mommy?' Several of the 'good mommy' behaviors reported had to do with her use of language, such as:

> A good mommy runs when you get hurt. . . . She doesn't just say, 'Oh, no, what is it now?'
> (When you cry in the night) She always says, 'damn', but she always comes.
> (When you fall out of the car) She wouldn't scream, 'Stupid, I said not to lean on the door.'

Some of the children's responses also evidenced their own increasing competence in pragmatics:

> When she starts to act real weird, you have to look scared and serious. Don't giggle. When mommies are mad, they get madder when children giggle.
> If you have some flowers and your mommy looks like she's going to give you a spanking, sometimes a good thing to do is give her the flowers.

One child explained mothers were allowed to get angry, however, when they pulled such linguistic jokes as asking if she could make a ham and cheese sandwich and after it was made saying, 'I never told you I *wanted* ham and cheese. I only asked could you *make* one.' The child further explained, 'If she didn't get mad, she wouldn't be a good mommy. She'd be a dumb mommy.'

Clearly, all ethnographers who study the acquisition of communicative competence, should not neglect to elicit in their interviews the perceptions of the children themselves.

7

Directions and Applications

Much of human existence – both individual and corporate – is mediated through communication, linguistic as well as non-linguistic. It attends the individual's entry into a society and his or her departure from it. Through it, everything from dyadic interactions to the operation of complex nation-states is managed. Language and other aspects of communication serve many ends, from the gratification of individual desires to the organization of massive cooperative efforts. Beauty and destruction, altruism and venality, the profound and the trivial, are all accomplished within the frameworks of often unconscious bodies of social conventions which guide and constrain the possibilities of communicative action.

It is the task of the ethnography of communication to elucidate these conventions in different societies, and to understand the dynamics of their representation and reflection in the constitutive enactment of situated events. But the effort to fulfill this task may barely be said to have begun. The reasons undoubtedly have to do with the inertia of established disciplines, and the difficulties of transcending disciplinary boundaries. The field of inquiry lies at the intersection of linguistics and anthropology, sociology and hermeneutics, folklore and political science, speech and social psychology, and like Kurdistan, remains a *terra incognita* divided among competing states.

As Hymes has pointed out, the traditional focus of linguistics on abstract code characteristics to the neglect of function, and the traditional focus of anthropology and sociology on the abstract patterns of cultural and social organization to the neglect of details of their enactment, has left us largely ignorant of the role of language and other modes of communication in the realization of social life. While the humanistic disciplines have long dealt with such issues, often in great depth, they have usually done so within the largely unexamined context of a single cultural tradition, and so have not provided the tools required for concomitant analysis of the taken-for-granted context itself. The recognition and definition of a new field of study, falling between existing paradigms and not fully contained within any of them, requires a major intellectual reorientation of perspective, to see that there exists something truly new and significant to study, which cannot be conveniently reduced to some existing set of concepts and methods of analysis. We must come to realize, in other words, that the elephant is a valid and interesting species worthy of examination in its own right, and not merely an accidental assemblage of rubber hoses, ropes, and tree trunks.

In discussing the concepts, methods, and perspectives of the ethnography of communication, I have cited numerous examples of its application – especially to the study of language variation and multilingualism, folklore and ritual events, and child language acquisition. In 1975, discussing the prospects for future directions in the field, Bauman and Sherzer said that 'perhaps the most important lies in its potential for the clarification and solution of practical social problems' (1975: 115); to a limited extent, that potential is gradually being realized.

Some of the most socially important research has been conducted on events in legal, medical, and educational settings. It has generally focused on the power relationships that exist in them, and on issues of justice or equity in the delivery of social services. O'Barr (1982), for instance, reports how different verbal strategies influence jury decisions about credibility, and Wodak-Engel (1984) describes how social class differences in rules of speaking lead to discrimination against working class defendants. The power dimension is largely a factor of the social role-relationships that participants bring with them to an encounter, but as is demonstrated in the case of a medical interview (e.g.

Treichler, Frankel, and Kramarae, *et al.* 1984), it is also a dynamic negotiated product of interaction.

Strategies of negotiating power relationships are also the focus of Erickson and Schultz's (1982) study of *The Counselor as Gatekeeper*. Their analysis is important both in positing universals in communication ('tell each other the context' and 'interdependent of action') and in describing the miscommunication which can result from different communicative behaviors, even when participants share linguistic rules of phonology, grammar, and vocabulary use. The social implications of their findings are especially significant because gatekeeping encounters between students and school officials, or between job applicants and job counselors, often determine access to career paths – and thus to future power. Gatekeeping is directly related to the process of segregating students for socialization and limiting the transmission of knowledge, as a scarce and valuable commodity, to a chosen few.

Segregated socialization may also involve exclusive learning of the language of transmission so that others cannot understand the content (thereby maintaining the aura of mystery, and the power that control of it brings), as described by Philips (1982) with respect to the training of lawyers to the 'cant'. (But conversely, see Maley 1987 for a positive exposition of the legal legislative style and Keller-Cohen 1987 on potential benefits of bureaucratic texts.)

A strong call for the application of ethnography of communication to educational issues was voiced by Hymes in his Introduction to *Functions of Language in the Classroom* (Cazden, John, and Hymes 1972:xiv–xv). The unifying principle of that collection is one of 'starting where the children are', and speaking 'to their condition'. For Hymes, research and application involve a two-way sharing of knowledge – the investigator contributing scientific modes of inquiry, and participants providing the requisite knowledge and perspective of the particular community contexts. To repeat what I said earlier, the issue is one of ethics as much as one of science. 'If linguistics and ethnography are to contribute to a democratic way of life, their knowledge and perspective must be gained and used in democratic ways. . . .

Both inquiry and application are processes that involve mutuality and sharing of knowledge; neither can succeed as a one-way application' (Hymes 1972:xv). Within this (1972) volume, very important contributions were made to the understanding of differential rules for classroom language use with respect to ability level (e.g. Gumperz and Hernández-Chávez) and to culture (e.g. Boggs, Dumont, and Philips).

The findings of Philips that cultural differences relate to different structure of classroom interaction and control have subsequently been extended by research in a variety of situations, including that of Au (1980) and Erickson and Mohatt (1982). Microanalysis of ways of speaking in the classroom has further identified paralinguistic features which may create barriers to teaching and learning (e.g. Barnhardt 1982; Michaels 1981), and pragmatic phenomena that lead to stereotyping and miscommunication (e.g. Gumperz 1981).

Much of the ethnographic research on sociolinguistic diversity in classrooms has focused on how teacher–student interaction patterns vary in relation to student achievement level (or teacher expectations), social identity, and cultural background. These types of contrast are particularly relevant to issues of organization and control of classes which are tracked for ability level. Differences in student–teacher and peer interaction patterns are also found between entire schools when their student bodies represent different social group membership – perhaps due to teachers' lower expectations of students with lower social status, or to their fear of losing control. Anyon (1981), for instance, dramatically illustrates how classrooms situated in different socioeconomic areas of a single city differ not only in the processes of teacher–student interaction, but also qualitatively in terms of the types of educational knowledge being transmitted in them.

These and other studies of differential interaction in classrooms indicate that while no discrimination may be intended, some groups of students are being given less opportunity to learn than others. Furthermore, the communication–achievement/expectation relationship becomes a vicious cycle. Teachers' attitudes and expectations not only influence communicative patterns; they are transmitted through those patterns to students and may become self-fulfilling prophecies. While most of the research which documents this barrier to the education of subordinated minority groups has been conducted with Spanish speakers, Blacks, and Native Americans in the US, it is a common obstacle as well for Aborigines in Australia, Quechua speakers in Peru and Bolivia, and immigrant Turkish speakers in Germany and the Netherlands. Netherlands.

Most research on classroom communication has been quite narrowly focused on detailed analysis of what takes place just within the classroom itself ('microethnographic' in nature). While it has yielded much interesting and useful information, it may also be faulted for not taking into account the social and cultural ecology within which education is taking place (e.g. Ogbu 1981; Rist 1980), including the home background of students. The value of examining patterns of communication ethnographically in a larger context ('macroethnography') is illustrated in the work of Heath (1983), who made a comprehensive analysis of patterns in language use by preschool children and their parents in two Carolina communities in the US. Her study provides a paradigmatic model in its demonstration of how children's socialization into rules for speaking related differentially to eventual success in school, and how the application of knowlege about the methods and findings of the ethnography of communication can contribute to the improvement of children's educational opportunities.

A second example of the scope of macroethnographic research is provided by Hornberger (1987), who evaluates and interprets Quechua language use in a bilingual education program in Peru in part on the basis of classroom observations there, but also in relation to community observations and interviews, and on the ways in which the communicative patterns observed in school reflect economics, politics, and other social factors.

Other areas in which significant applications of the ethnography of communication are being made include the study of (1) literacy as involving socially-constituted communicative events (e.g. Cook-Gumperz 1986; Schieffelin and Gilmore 1986; Whiteman 1981), (2) foreign language teaching (e.g. Munby 1977; 1978; Savignon 1983) and testing (e.g. Rivera 1983), (3) translation (e.g. Nida 1977; Xu 1987), (4) cross-cultural communication (e.g. Gumperz 1979; 1982; Scollon and Scollon 1981), and (5) the accomplishment of inequality/discrimination (e.g. Chick 1985; Wolfson and Manes 1985). Many examples and references can also be found that are not drawn from purely ethnographic studies, but that exemplify methods and dimensions that should be incorporated in an adequate ethnography of communication (e.g. papers in Ensink, et al. 1986; Fisher and Todd 1986).

Thus far there have been very few studies focused on the ethnography of communication itself, so that much of the existing data is partial and anecdotal. A true approach to the ethnographic study of communication in a community must follow the standards for in-depth research established in ethnographic field work generally, and must combine it with a level of sensitivity to linguistic phenomena characteristic of the best work in sociolinguistics and folklore. Shortcuts and 'blitzkrieg' techniques can only serve to produce superficial data and trivial results.

While the ethnographer of communication must work with as open a mind as possible, anthropologists have long known that no investigator is a *tabula rasa*, free of preconceptions and expectations based on previous experience. It has therefore been a major aim of this book to present a wide range of possibilities regarding the occurrence and interpretation of various communication-related phenomena, in order to sensitize the reader to potential aspects to be encountered in undertaking fieldwork. Because the subject is still relatively new, we remain very far from the point where any definitive summation can be attempted. Every new study will undoubtedly continue to provide new insights and illuminate new dimensions to guide future research.

Like any science, the ethnography of communication must be cumulative if it is to increasingly deepen our understanding of human behavior. In addition (as Hymes called for in an ethnology of communication), it must become comparative in nature, and seek to formulate cross-cultural generalizations and hypotheses which can be further tested in new settings. While it is basically empirical and naturalistic, it must reach beyond the existential and phenomenological and accept findings from quantitative and experimental studies which are not immediately apparent or accessible from qualitative observational approaches. It must be holistic in its orientation, and guard against the risks of reductionism inherent in isolating and analyzing a segment of the total society or a specific aspect of behavior. Finally, it must be open to new ideas and insights from all sides, and avoid the premature adoption of models or orthodoxies for the analysis of data. Only in this way can we be certain that the ethnography of communication will realize its potential for contributing, alongside other established disciplines, to our greater understanding of the human condition.

References

SOURCES OF UNPUBLISHED EXAMPLES

Students at Georgetown University in the years 1974–80 and at the University of Illinois in the years 1980–8 have provided me with many of the unpublished examples in this book. Where an example or quotation appears in the text with a name but no date, reference is made to oral information, unpublished essays or research from such sources. The students, whether specifically named in the text or not, are listed here under the language, group, or country on which they have provided information:

Abbey (Ivory Coast): Marcellin Hepié
Amharic (Ethiopia): Demissie Manahlot, Mulugeta Seyoum
Arabic: Mohammed Al-Rusan, Saud Assubaiai, Atteya El-Noory, Sulaiman G. Elwedyani, Youssef Mahmoud, Ahmed Mouakket, William B. Royer, Jr
Bambara (Mali): Issiaka Ly
Batak (Indonesia): Bistok Sirait
Belgium: Marcel Van Thillo
Berber (northwest Africa): Omar Boukella, Ghada Mardini
Bukadon (Philippines): Genoveva M. Ablanque
Cape Verdian Creole: Izione Silva
Chinese: Rey-Mei Chen, Hong-Gang Jin, Cher-Leng Lee
Czechoslovakia: Vessna Vuchichevich
(Deaf) Sign Language: Virginia Covington, Barbara M. Kannapell, William Rudner
Dutch: Henriette Frederica Schatz
English: Carolyn T. Adger, Cheri Bridgeforth, Leonie Cottrill, Lou A. Daly, John K. Donaldson, Jr, Mary Owens, Katherine A. Spaar, Susan Van Coevern
Farsi (Iran): Ali A. Aghbar, A. Javad Jafarpur, Ahmed A. Thabet

German: Helga Kansy, Sebine Koschorreck, Karin Steinhaus
Greek: William Alatis, Margaret Heliotis
Hebrew: Amy Aidman, Channa Seikevicz
Igbo (Nigeria): Gregory Nwoye
Indonesian/Javanese: Asim Gunarwan, Siti A. Suprapto
Japanese: Midori Chiba, Tetsuo Kumatoriya, Takashi Matsunaga, Eri B. Shinoda, Aoi Tsuda, Harumi Williams
Kaingáng (Brazil): Gloria Kindell
Korean: Yong-Hwan Jo, Soon-Bok Kim, Hyun-Hee Kim Oh, Jun-Eon Park, Mae-Ran Park-Mun
Mixe-Zoque (Mexico): Linda Hudson O'Neill
Newari (Nepal): Jyoti Tuladhar
Quechua (Ecuador): Lucinda Hart-González
Spanish: Isabel Castellanos, María D. Clark, Carmen Simich-Dudgeon, Annette Silverio-Borges
Sranan/Dutch: Annemarie Jong A. Kiem, Robby Morroy
Tamil (India): Francis Britto
Tanzania: Robert Jalbert
Thai: Namtip Aksornkool, Tiraporn Bunnag, Suphatcharee Ekasingh, Penchusee Lerdtadsin, Premchitra Satyavanija, Pornthip Virapongse
Tongan: Michael Wimberly
Trinidadian Creole: Wendy Sealey

BOOKS AND ARTICLES

Abd-el-Jawad, Hassan R. 1987. Cross-dialectal variation in Arabic: competing prestigious forms. *Language in Society* 16:359–68.
Aberle, David. 1966. *The Peyote Religion among the Navaho*. London: Aldine.
Abrahams, Roger D. 1972. Stereotyping and beyond. In Roger D. Abrahams and Rudolph C. Troike, eds, *Language and Cultural Diversity in American Education*, pp. 19–29. Englewood Cliffs, NJ: Prentice-Hall.
——— 1973. Toward a Black rhetoric: being a survey of Afro-American communication styles and role-relationships. Texas working papers in sociolinguistics No. 15.
——— 1983. *The Man-of-Words in the West Indies: Performance and the Emergence of Creole Culture*. Baltimore: Johns Hopkins University Press.

Adger, Carolyn Temple. 1986. When difference does not conflict: successful arguments between Black and Vietnamese classmates. *Text* 6:223–37.

Akinnaso, F. Niyi. 1980. The sociolinguistic basis of Yoruba personal names. *Anthropological Linguistics* 22(7): 275–304.

Albert, Ethel M. 1972. Culture patterning of speech behavior in Burundi. In John J. Gumperz and D. Hymes, eds. *Directions in Sociolinguistics: The Ethnography of Communication*, pp. 72–105. New York: Holt, Rinehart & Winston.

Allport, Gordon. 1954. *The Nature of Prejudice*. Cambridge: Mass.: Addison-Wesley.

Anyon, Jean. 1981. Social class and school knowledge. *Curriculum Inquiry* 11:3–42.

Atkins, J. D. C. 1887. Annual report of the commissioner of Indian affairs. In House Executive Document No. 1, 50th Congress, 1st session, serial 2542, pp. 19–21.

Attinasi, John, Pedro Pedraza, Shana Poplack, and Alicia Pousada. 1982. *Intergenerational Perspectives on Bilingualism: From Community to Classroom*. New York: Center for Puerto Rican Studies, City University of New York.

Au, Kathryn H. 1980. On participation structures in reading lessons. *Anthropology and Education Quarterly* 11:91–115.

Awbery, G. M. 1984. *Cardiff Working Papers in Welsh Linguistics* 3:1–19. (Cited in T. Arwyn Watkins. 1985. Welsh Studies: Language. *The Year's Work in Modern Language Studies* 46.)

Bailey, Charles-James N. 1976. The state of non-state linguistics. *Annual Review of Anthropology* 5:93–106.

Bailey, Guy and Natalie Maynor. 1987. Decreolization? *Language in Society* 16:449–73.

Bamgboṣe, Ayọ. 1986. *Yoruba: A Language in Transition*. Lagos: J. F. Odunjo Memorial Lectures Organizing Committee.

Bar-Adon, Aaron and Werner F. Leopold, eds. 1971. *Child Language: A Book of Readings*: Englewood Cliffs, NJ: Prentice-Hall.

Barker, George C. 1947. Social functions of language in a Mexican-American community. *Acta Americana* 5:185–202.

Barkin, Florence and Elizabeth Brandt, eds. 1980. *Speaking, Singing and Teaching: A Multidisciplinary Approach to Language Variation*. Anthropological Research Papers No. 20. Tempe: Arizona State University.

Barnhardt, Carol. 1982. Tuning-in: Athabaskan teachers and

Athabaskan students. Paper presented at the Annual Meeting of the American Anthropological Association, Washington, DC. (Cited in Judith Preissle Goetz and Margaret Diane LeCompte. 1984. *Ethnography and Qualitative Design in Educational Research*. New York: Academic Press.)

Barry, Herbert III, Margaret K. Bacon, and Irvin L. Child. 1957. A cross-cultural survey of some sex differences in socialization. *The Journal of Abnormal and Social Psychology* 55:327–32.

Barth, Fredrik. 1964a. Ethnic processes on the Pathan-Baluch boundary. In Georges Redard, ed., *Indo-Iranica. Mélanges preséntés à Georg Morgenstierne à l'occaision de son soixante-dixième anniversaire*. Wiesbaden: Otto Harrassowitz. (Reprinted in Gumperz and Hymes (1972), pp. 454–64.)

1964b. *Nomads of South Persia: The Basseri Tribe of the Khamesh Confederacy*. London: Allen and Unwin.

1966. *Models of Social Organization*. Occasional Papers of the Royal Anthropological Institute of Great Britain and Ireland No. 23.

Basso, Keith. 1970. To give up on words: silence in the Western Apache culture. *Southwestern Journal of Anthropology* 26:213–30.

1979. *Portraits of 'The Whiteman': Linguistic Play and Cultural Symbols among the Western Apache*. London: Cambridge University Press.

and H. A. Selby, eds. 1976. *Meaning in Anthropology*. Albuquerque: University of New Mexico Press.

Bateson, Gregory. 1955. A theory of play and phantasy. *Psychiatric Research Reports* 2:39–51. American Psychiatric Association. (Reprinted in *Steps to an Ecology of Mind* (1972), pp. 177–93. New York: Ballantine.)

Baugh, John. 1983. *Black Street Speech: Its History, Structure, and Survival*. Austin, TX: University of Texas Press.

and Joel Sherzer, eds. 1984. *Language in Use: Readings in Sociolinguistics*. Englewood Cliffs, NJ: Prentice-Hall.

Bauman, Richard. 1974. Speaking in the light: the role of the Quaker minister. In Richard Bauman and Joel Sherzer, eds, *Explorations in the Ethnography of Speaking*, pp. 144–60. London: Cambridge University Press.

1976. The development of competence in the use of solicitational routines: children's folklore and informal learning. Texas working papers in sociolinguistics No. 34.

1977. Linguistics, anthropology, and verbal art: toward a unified perspective with a special discussion of children's folklore. In M. Saville-Troike, ed., *Linguistics and Anthropology*, pp. 13–36. Washington, DC: Georgetown University Press.

1983. *Let Your Words Be Few: Symbolism of Speaking and Silence among Seventeenth-Century Quakers*. London: Cambridge University Press.

and Joel Sherzer, eds. 1974. *Explorations in the Ethnography of Speaking*. London: Cambridge University Press.

1975. The ethnography of speaking. *Annual Review of Anthropology* 4:95–119.

Beaglehole, Ernest and Pearl. 1941. Personality development in Pukapukan children. In Leslie Spier, A. Irving Hallowell, and Stanley Newman, eds, *Language, Culture, and Personality*, pp. 282–98. Menasha, WI: Sapir Memorial Publication Fund.

Bean, Susan S. 1980. Ethnology and the study of proper names, *Anthropological Linguistics* 22(7):305–16.

Bell, Michael J. 1983. *The World from Brown's Lounge: An Ethnography of Black Middle-Class Play*. Urbana: University of Illinois Press.

Benedict, Ruth. 1934. *Patterns of Culture*. Boston: Houghton Mifflin.

Bereiter, Carl and Siegfried Engelman. 1966. *Teaching Disadvantaged Children in the Preschool*. Englewood Cliffs, NJ: Prentice-Hall.

Berger, Peter and Thomas Luckmann. 1967. *The Social Construction of Reality*. New York: Doubleday.

Berk-Seligson, Susan. 1986. Linguistic constraints on intrasentential code-switching: a study of Spanish/Hebrew bilingualism. *Language in Society* 15:313–48.

Bernstein, Basil. 1960. Review of *The Lore and Language of School Children*, by Iona and Peter Opie. *British Journal of Sociology* 11:178–81.

1971. *Class, Codes and Control*. London: Routledge & Kegan Paul.

1972. A sociolinguistic approach to socialization; with some reference to educability. In John J. Gumperz and D. Hymes, eds. *Directions in Sociolinguistics: The Ethnography of Communication*, pp. 465–97. New York: Holt, Rinehart & Winston.

Berry J. W. 1969. On cross-cultural comparability. *International Journal of Psychology* 4:119–28.

Bhatia, V. K. 1987. Language of the law. *Language Teaching* 20:227–34.

Bhu, Sunthorn. *c.* 1803. *Suphasit Son Ying.* (Published in 1973 by Silpa Bannakarn of Bangkok; translation provided by Namtip Aksornkool.)

Birdwhistell, Ray L. 1952. *Introduction to Kinesics: An Annotation System for Analysis of Body Motion and Gesture.* Louisville, KY: University of Louisville Press.

1970. *Kinesics and Context: Essays in Body Motion Communication.* Philadelphia: University of Pennsylvania Press.

1974. The language of the body: the natural environment. In Albert Silverstein, ed., *Human Communication: Theoretcial Explorations*, pp. 203–20. New York: John Wiley & Sons.

Bloch, Maurice. 1974. Symbols, song, dance and features of articulation: is relation an extreme form of traditional authority? *Archives Européennes de Sociologie* 15(1): 55–71.

ed. 1975. *Political Language and Oratory in Traditional Society.* New York: Academic Press.

1976. The past and the present in the present. (The Malinowski Memorial Lecture, delivered at the London School of Ecnomics and Political Science.) *Man* 12:278–92.

Blom, Jan-Petter and John J. Gumperz. 1972. Social meaning in linguistic structure: code-switching in Norway. In John J. Gumperz and D. Hymes, eds. *Directions in Sociolinguistics: The Ethnography of Communication*, pp. 407–34. New York: Holt, Rinehart & Winston.

Bloomfield, Leonard. 1927. Literate and illiterate speech. *American Speech* 10:432–9. (Reprinted in Hymes (1964), pp. 391–6.)

1933. *Language.* New York: Holt.

Blount, Ben G. 1972. Parental speech and language acquisition: some Luo and Samoan examples. *Anthropological Linguistics* 14(4):119–30.

1977. Parental speech to children: cultural patterns. In M. Saville-Troike, ed., *Linguistics and Anthropology*, pp. 117–38. Washington, DC: Georgetown University Press.

Boas, Franz. 1911. Introduction. *Handbook of American Indian Languages*, pp. 1–83. Bureau of American Ethnology Bulletin 40. Washington, DC: Government Printing Office.

Boggs, Stephen T. 1978. The development of verbal disputing in part-Hawaiian children. *Language in Society* 7:325–44.

Bourhis, Richard V., Howard Giles, Jacques P. Leyens, and Henri Tajfel. 1979. Psycholinguistic distinctiveness: language divergence in Belgium. In Howard Giles and Robert N. St Clair, eds. *Language and Social Psychology*, pp. 158–85. Oxford: Basil Blackwell.

Brandt, Elizabeth A. 1977. The role of secrecy in Pueblo society. In Stanton Tefft, ed., *Secrecy: A Cross-Cultural Perspective*. New York: Human Sciences Press.

Brewer, William F., D. J. Hendrich, and Stella Vosniadou. In press. A cross-cultural study of children's development of cosmological models. In D. Toppings, V. Kobayashi, and D. Crowell, eds, *Thinking: The Third International Conference*. Hillsdale, NJ: Lawrence Erlbaum.

Briggs, Charles L. 1984. Learning how to ask: native meta-communicative competence and the incompetence of fieldworkers. *Language in Society* 13:1–28.

    1986. *Learning How to Ask: A Sociolinguistic Appraisal of the Role of the Interview in Social Science Research*. London: Cambridge University Press.

Brislin, Richard W., Walter J. Lonner, and Robert M. Thorndike. 1973. *Cross-Cultural Research Methods*. New York: John Wiley & Sons.

Brown, Bruce L., William J. Strong, and Alvin C. Rencher. 1975. Acoustic determinants of perceptions of personality from speech. *International Journal of the Sociology of Language* 6:11–32.

Brown, Penelope and Colin Fraser. 1979. Speech as a marker of situation. In Klaus R. Scherer and Howard Giles, eds, *Social Markers in Speech*, pp. 33–62. London: Cambridge University Press.

    and Stephen Levinson. 1979. Social structure, groups and interaction. In Klaus R. Scherer and Howard Giles, eds. *Social Markers in Speech*, pp. 291–341. London: Cambridge University Press.

Brown, Roger and Albert Gilman. 1960. The pronouns of power and solidarity. In Thomas Sebeok, ed., *Style in Language*, pp. 253–76: Cambridge, Mass.: Massachusetts Institute of Technology.

Bruhn, Thea. 1975. A study of some children's perspectives on socialization. Manuscript, Georgetown University.

Bullock, Henry Allen. 1970. *A History of Negro Education in the South*. New York: Praeger.

Campbell, Lyle. 1976. Language contact and sound change. In William M. Christie, Jr, ed., *Current Progress in Historical Linguistics*. Amsterdam: North Holland.

Castellanos, Isabel Mercedes. 1976. The use of language in Afro-Cuban religion. Dissertation, Georgetown University.

Cazden, Courtney B., Vera P. John, and Dell Hymes, eds. 1972. *Functions of Language in the Classroom.* New York: Teachers College Press.

Chafe, Wallace L., ed. 1980. *The Pear Stories: Cognitive, Cultural and Linguistic Aspects of Narrative Production.* Norwood, NJ: Ablex.

Chick, J. Keith. 1985. The interactional accomplishment of discrimination in South Africa. *Language in Society* 14:299–326.

Chiu, Rosaline K. 1972. Measuring register characteristics: a prerequisite for preparing advanced level TESOL programs.

Chomsky, Noam. 1965. *Aspects of the Theory of Syntax.* Cambridge, Mass.: Massachusetts Institute of Technology.

1968. *Language and Mind.* New York: Harcourt, Brace & World.

Christian, Jane and Peter M. Gardner. 1977. The individual in Northern Dene thought and communication: a study in sharing and diversity. Mercury Series Canadian Ethnology Service Papers No. 35. Ottawa: National Museum of Man.

Cicourel, Aaron V. 1974. *Cognitive Sociology: Learning and Meaning in Social Interaction.* New York: The Free Press.

Claire, Elizabeth. 1980. *A Foreign Student's Guide to Dangerous English.* Rochelle Park, NJ: Eardley.

Clancey, Patricia M. 1986. The acquisition of communicative style in Japanese. In Bambi B. Schieffelin and Elinor Ochs, eds, *Language Socialization Across Cultures,* pp. 213–50. London: Cambridge University Press.

Clyne, M. 1982. *Multilingual Australia.* Melbourne. (Cited in René Appel and Pieter Muysken. 1987. *Language Contact and Bilingualism.* London: Edward Arnold.)

Cohen, Marcel. 1956. *Pour Une Sociologie du Language.* Paris: Paris Educations, Albin Michel.

Cook-Gumperz, Jenny. 1977. Situated instructions: Language socialization of school age children. In Susan M. Ervin-Tripp and Claudia Mitchell-Kernan, eds, *Child Discourse,* pp. 103–21. New York: Academic Press.

ed. 1986. *The Social Construction of Literacy.* London: Cambridge University Press.

Corsaro, William, A. 1978. 'We're friends, right?': children's use of access rituals in a nursery school. Texas working papers in sociolinguistics No. 43.

Cummins, James. 1979. Linguistic interdependence and the educational development of bilingual children. *Review of Educational Research* 49(2):222–51.

d'Anglejan, Alison and G. Richard Tucker. 1973. Sociolinguistic correlates of speech styles in Quebec. In Roger W. Shuy and Ralph W. Fasold, eds, *Language Attitudes: Current Trends and Prospects*, pp. 1–22. Washington, DC: Georgetown University Press.

Darwin, Charles. 1872. *The Expression of the Emotions in Man and Animals*. London: Murray.

Demisse, Teshome and M. Lionel Bender. 1983. An argot of Addis Ababa unattached girls. *Language in Society* 12:339–47.

Dennis, Wayne. 1940. *The Hopi Child*. New York: Wiley & Sons.

Deuchar, Margaret. 1978. Diglossia and British sign language. Texas working papers in sociolinguistics No. 46.

DiPietro, Robert J. 1975. The strategies of language use. Paper presented at the second annual LACUS forum, Toronto.

DiSciullo, Anne-Marie, Pieter Muysken, and Rajendra Singh. 1986. Government and code-mixing. *Journal of Linguistics* 22:1–24.

Dittmar, Norbert. 1977. The acquisition of German syntax by foreign migrant workers: Heidelberger Forschungsprojekt 'Pidgin-Deutsch'. In David Sankoff, ed., *Linguistic variation: Models and Methods*, pp. 1–22. New York: Academic Press.

Dorian, Nancy C. 1980. Language loss and maintenance in language contact situations. Paper presented at the Conference on the Attrition of Language Skills, University of Pennsylvania.

1982. Linguistic models and language death evidence. In Loraine K. Obler and Lise Menn, eds, *Exceptional Language and Linguistics*, pp. 31–48. New York: Academic Press.

Douglas, Mary. 1970. *Natural Symbols: Explorations in Cosmology*. New York: Random House.

1971. Do dogs laugh? A cross-cultural approach to body symbolism. *Journal of Psychosomatic Research* 15:387–90.

ed. 1973. *Rules and Meanings*. Harmondsworth, Mddx: Penguin.

Dozier, Edward P. 1956. Two examples of linguistic acculturation: the Yaqui of Sonora and Arizona and the Tewa of New Mexico. *Language* 32:146–57. (Reprinted in Hymes (1964), pp. 509–20.)

Driver, Beth. 1978. Children's negotiation of answers to questions. Texas working paper in sociolinguistics No. 51.

Duncan, Hugh Dalziel. 1962. *Communication and Social Order*. London: Oxford University Press.

Dundes, Alan, Jerry W. Leach, and Bora Özkök. 1972. The

strategy of Turkish boys' verbal dueling. In John J. Gumperz and D. Hymes, eds. *Directions in Sociolinguistics: The Ethnography of Communication*, pp. 130–60. New York: Holt, Rinehart & Winston.

Duran, Richard P., ed. 1981. *Latino Language and Communicative Behavior*. Norwood, NJ: Ablex.

Duranti, Allesandro. 1986. Sociocultural dimensions of discourse. In Teun A. Van Dijk, ed., *Handbook of Discourse Analysis. Volume 1: Disciplines of Discourse*, pp. 193–230. New York: Academic Press.

1988. Ethnography of speaking: toward a linguistics of the praxis. In Frederick J. Newmeyer, ed., *Language: The Socio-Cultural Context*, pp. 210–28. London: Cambridge University Press.

Edgerton, Robert B. 1971. *The Individual in Cultural Adaptation: A Study of Four East African Peoples*. Berkeley: University of California Press.

Edwards, John R. 1979. Judgements and confidence reactions to disadvantaged speech. In Howard Giles and Robert N. St Clair, eds. *Language and Social Psychology*, pp. 22–44. Oxford: Basil Blackwell.

1985. *Language, Society and Identity*. Oxford: Basil Blackwell.

Eggan, Dorothy. 1956. Instruction and affect in Hopi cultural continuity. *Southwestern Journal of Anthropology* 12(4):347–70.

Eibl-Eibesfeldt, I. 1970. The expressive behavior of the deaf and blind born. In M. von Cranach and I. Vine, eds. *Non-Verbal Behavior and Expressive Movements:* New York: Academic Press.

1972. Similarities and differences between cultures in expressive movements. In Robert A. Hinde, ed., *Non-Verbal Communication*, pp. 297–314. London: Cambridge University Press.

1974. Similarities and differences between cultures in expressive movements. In Shirley Weitz, ed., *Nonverbal Communication: Readings with Commentary*, pp. 20–33. London: Oxford University Press.

Ekman, Paul. 1972. Universal and cultural differences in facial expressions of emotion. In J. K. Cole, ed., *Nebraska Symposium on Motivation (1971)*, pp. 207–83. Lincoln: University of Nebraska Press.

Wallace V. Friesen, and Silvan S. Tomkins. 1971. Facial affect scoring technique: a first validity study. *Semiotica* 3:37–58.

El-Dash, Linda and G. Richard Tucker. 1975. Subjective reactions to various speech styles in Egypt. *International Journal of the*

Sociology of Language 6:33–54.

Eliason, Marcus. 1980. 'Tu' 'Du' or not 'Tu' 'Du'. Associated Press. (Appeared in Champaign-Urbana (IL) *News-Gazette* 18 Sept., p. B1.)

Ellis, D. S. 1967. Speech and social status in America. *Social Forces* 45:431–7.

Emihovich, Catherine. 1986. Argument as status assertion: contextual variations in children's disputes. *Language in Society* 15:485–500.

Enninger, Werner and Joachim Raith. 1982. An ethnography of communication approach to ceremonial situations: a study on communication in institutionalized social contexts: the Old Order Amish church service. *Zeitschrift für Dialektologie und Linguistik Beihefte* Heft 42. Wiesbaden: Franz Steiner Verlag GMBH.

Ensink, T., A. van Essen, and T. vander Geest, eds. 1986. *Discourse Analysis and Public Life: Papers of the Groningen Conference on Medical and Political Discourse.* Dordrecht, Holland: Foris.

Erickson, Frederick, 1976. One function of proxemic shifts in face to face interaction. In A. Kendon, R. Harris, and M. R. Key, eds, *The Organization of Behavior in Face to Face Interaction.* The Hague: Mouton.

and Gerald Mohatt. 1982. Cultural organization of participation structures in two classrooms of Indian students. In George Spindler, ed., *Doing the Ethnography of Schooling*, pp. 132–74. New York: Holt, Rinehart & Winston.

and Jeffrey Shultz. 1979. When is a context?: some issues and methods in the analysis of social competence. Manuscript.

1982. *The Counselor as Gatekeeper: Social Interactions in Interviews.* New York: Academic Press.

Ervin-Tripp, Susan M. 1969. Sociolinguistics. In Leonard Berkowitz, ed., *Advances in Experimental Social Psychology*, pp. 91–165. New York: Academic Press.

1972. On sociolinguistic rules: alternation and co-occurrence. In John J. Gumperz and D. Hymes, eds, *Directions in Sociolinguistics: The Ethnography of Communication*, pp. 213–50. New York: Holt, Rinehart & Winston.

and Claudia Mitchell-Kernan, eds. 1977. *Child Discourse.* New York: Academic Press.

Fang, Hanquan and J. H. Heng. 1983. Social changes and changing address norms in China. *Language in Society* 12:495–507.

Fanshel, David and Freda Moss. 1971. *Playback: A Marriage in*

Jeopardy Examined. New York: Columbia University Press.

Faris, J. C. 1968. Validation in ethnographical description: the lexicon of 'occasions' in Cat Harbour. *Man* 3(1):112–24. (Reprinted in Douglas (1973), pp. 45–59, as 'Occasions' and 'non-Occasions'.)

Fasold, Ralph W. 1975. How to study language maintenance and shift: the case of the Tiwa Indians. Paper presented at the Linguistic Society of America, San Francisco.

Ferguson, Charles A. 1959. Diglossia. *Word* 15:325–40. (Reprinted in Hymes (1964), pp. 429–37.)

1964. Baby talk in six languages. In John J. Gumperz and D. Hymes eds, The Ethnography of Communication, *American Anthropologist* 66(6):103–14.

1977. Baby talk as a simplified register. In Catherine E. Snow and Charles A. Ferguson, eds, *Talking to Children: Language Input and Acquisition,* pp. 219–36. London: Cambridge University Press.

1978. Religious factors in language spread. Paper presented for the Conference on Language Spread, Aberystwyth, Wales.

1986. The study of religious discourse. In Deborah Tannen and James E. Alatis, eds, *Language and Linguistics: The Interdependence of Theory, Data, and Application,* pp. 205–13. Washington, DC: Georgetown University Press.

Firth, Raymond. 1973. *Symbols: Public and Private.* Ithaca, NY: Cornell University Press.

Fischer, John L. 1958. Social influence in the choice of a linguistic variant. *Word* 14:47–56. (Reprinted in Hymes (1964), pp. 483–8.)

1965. The stylistic significance of consonantal sandhi in Trukese and Ponapean. *American Anthropologist* 67:1495–1502. (Reprinted in Gumperz and Hymes (1972), pp. 498–511.)

Fisher, Sue and Alexandra Dundas Todd, eds. 1986. *Discourse and Institutional Authority: Medicine, Education and Law.* Norwood, NJ: Ablex.

Fishman, Joshua A. 1964. Language maintenance and language shift as fields of inquiry. *Linguistics* 9:32–70.

1966. *Language Loyalty in the United States.* The Hague: Mouton.

1971. The links between micro- and macro-sociolinguistics in the study of who speaks what language to whom and when. In Joshua A. Fishman, Robert L. Cooper, and Roxana Ma, *Bilingualism in the Barrio,* pp. 583–604. Bloomington: Indiana

University Publications.

1972. Domains and the relationship between micro and macro-sociolinguistics. In John J. Gumperz and D. Hymes, eds, *Directions in Sociolinguistics: The Ethnography of Communication*. New York: Holt, Rinehart & Winston. (Revised version of 1971.)

1980. Bilingualism and biculturalism as individual and as societal phenomena. *Journal of Multilingual and Multicultural Development* 1(1):3–15.

1985. The societal basis of the intergenerational continuity of additional languages. In Kurt R. Jankowsky, ed., *Scientific and Humanistic Dimensions of Language*, pp. 551–7. Amsterdam: John Benjamins.

Robert L. Cooper, and Roxana Ma. 1971. *Bilingualism in the Barrio*. Bloomington: Indiana University Publications.

Flanders, Ned A. 1970. *Analysing Teaching Behavior*. New York: Addison-Wesley.

Flaherty, Tom. 1972. 250,000 children have their say: 'We don't want to rebel, just be heard'. *Life* 29 Dec.: 87–8D.

Fortes, Meyer, 1938. Social and psychological aspects of education in Taleland. *Africa* 11(4) Supplement. (Reprinted in Middleton (1970), pp. 14–74.)

Frake, Charles O. 1969. Struck by speech: the Yakan concept of litigation. In Laura Nader, ed., *Law in Culture and Society*. Chicago: Aldine. (Reprinted in Gumperz and Hymes (1972), pp. 106–29.)

Franklin, Karl J. 1977. The Kewa language in culture and society. In Stephen A. Wurm, ed., *Language, Culture, Society, and the Modern World* (Fascicle 1). Pacific Linguistics Series C, No. 40: New Guinea Area Languages and Language Study Vol. 3.

Frazer, Sir James George. 1922. *The Golden Bough: A Study in Magic and Religion*. New York: MacMillan.

Frender, R., B. L. Brown, and W. E. Lambert. 1970. The role of speech characteristics in scholastic success. *Canadian Journal of Behavioral Science* 2:299–306.

Friedrich, Paul. 1972. Social context and semantic feature: the Russian pronominal usage. In John J. Gumperz and D. Hymes, eds, *Directions in Sociolinguistics: The Ethnography of Communication*, pp. 270–300. New York: Holt, Rinehart & Winston.

Gal, Susan. 1978. Peasant men can't get wives: language change and sex roles in a bilingual community. *Language in Society* 7(1):1–16.

1979. *Language Shift: Social Determinants of Linguistic Change in Bilingual Austria.* New York: Academic Press.

Gardner, Howard, Ellen Winner, Robin Bechhofer, and Dennie Wolf. 1978. The development of figurative language. In Keith E. Nelson, ed., *Children's Language* Vol. 1, pp. 1–38. New York: Gardner Press.

Gardner, Peter M. 1966. Symmetric respect and memorate knowledge: the structure and ecology of individualistic culture. *Southwestern Journal of Anthropology* 22:398–415.

Garfinkel, Harold. 1967. *Studies in Ethnomethodology.* Englewood Cliffs, NJ: Prentice-Hall.

1972. Remarks on ethnomethodology. In John J. Gumperz and D. Hymes, eds, *Directions in Sociolinguistics: The Ethnography of Communication,* pp. 301–45. New York: Holt, Rinehart & Winston.

Garnica, Olga K. 1977. Some prosodic and paralinguistic features of speech to young children. In Catherine E. Snow and Charles A. Ferguson, eds, *Talking to Children: Language Input and Acquisition,* pp. 63–88. London: Cambridge University Press.

Garvey, Catherine. 1977. Play with language and speech. In Susan M. Ervin-Tripp and Claudia Mitchell-Kernan, eds, *Child Discourse,* pp. 27–47. New York: Academic Press.

Geertz, Clifford. 1973. *The Interpretation of Cultures.* New York: Basic Books.

1976. 'From the native's point of view': on the nature of anthropological understanding. In Keith Basso and H. A. Selby, eds, *Meaning in Anthropology,* pp. 221–37. Albuquerque: University of New Mexico Press.

Giles, Howard. 1979. Ethnicity markers in speech. In Klaus R. Scherer and Howard Giles, eds, *Social Markers in Speech,* pp. 251–90. London: Cambridge University Press.

and Robert N. St Clair, eds. 1979. *Language and Social Pyschology.* Oxford: Basil Blackwell.

K. R. Scherer, and D. M. Taylor. 1979. Speech markers in social interaction. In Klaus R. Scherer and Howard Giles, eds, *Social Markers in Speech,* pp. 343–81. London: Cambridge University Press.

D. M. Taylor, and R. Bourhis. 1973. Towards a theory of interpersonal accommodation through language: some Canadian data. *Language in Society* 2:177–223.

Gilmore, Perry. 1981. Spelling 'Mississippi': recontextualizing a literacy-related speech event. Paper presented at the Second Annual University of Pennsylvania Ethnography in Education Research Forum, Philadelphia.

1985. Silence and sulking: emotional displays in the classroom. In Deborah Tannen and Muriel Saville-Troike, *Perspectives on Silence*, pp. 139–62. Norwood, NJ: Ablex.

Gleason, Jean Berko. 1975. Fathers and other strangers: men's speech to young children. In Daniel P. Dato, ed., *Developmental Psycholinguistics: Theory and Applications*, pp. 289–97. Washington, DC: Georgetown University Press.

1976. Parental judgement of children's language abilities. Paper presented at the Linguistic Society of America, Philadelphia.

Ester Blank Grief, Sandra Weintraub, and Janet Fardella. 1977. Father doesn't know but: parents' awareness of their children's linguistic, cognitive, and affective development. Paper presented at the Biennial Meeting of the Society for Research in Child Development, New Orleans.

and Sandra Weintraub. 1978. Input language and the acquisition of communicative competence. In Keith Nelson, ed., *Children's Language* Vol. 1, pp. 171–222. New York: Gardner Press.

Goffman, Erving. 1963. *Behavior in Public Places: Notes on the Social Organization of Gatherings*. New York: The Free Press.

1967. *Interaction Ritual: Essays on Face-to-Face Behavior*. Garden City, NY: Doubleday.

1971. *Relations in Public: Microstudies of the Public Order*. New York: Harper & Row.

1974. *Frame Analysis*. New York: Harper & Row.

Goldman, Laurence Richard. 1987. Ethnographic interpretations of parent–child discourse in Huli. *Journal of Child Language* 14:447–66.

Goodenough, Ward H. 1957. Cultural anthropology and linguistics. In Paul L. Gavin, ed., *Report of the Seventh Annual Round Table Meeting on Linguistics and Language Study*, pp. 109–173. Washington, DC: Georgetown University Press. (Reprinted in Hymes (1964), pp. 36–9.)

Goodman, Felicitas D. 1969. The acquisition of glossolalia behavior. Paper presented at the American Anthropological Association, New Orleans.

Gottschalk, Louis A. and Coldine C. Gleser. 1969. *The Measure-*

ment of Psychological States through the Content Analysis of Verbal Behavior. Berkeley: University of California Press.

Graves, Zoë R. and Joseph Glick. 1978. The effect of context on mother–child interaction: a progess report. *Institute for Comparative Human Development Newsletter* 2(3):41–6.

Green, Judith L. and Cynthia Wallat, eds. 1981. *Ethnography and Language in Educational Settings*. Norwood, NJ: Ablex.

Grice, H. Paul. 1975. Logic and conversation. In Peter Cole and Jerry L. Morgan, eds, *Syntax and Semantics: Speech Acts* Vol. 3, pp. 41–58. New York: Academic Press.

Grimes, Larry M. 1977. The linguistic taboo: examples from modern Mexican Spanish. *The Bilingual Review/La Revista Bilingüe* 4(1–2):69–80.

Grobsmith, Elizabeth S. 1979. Styles of speaking: an analysis of Lakota communication alternatives. *Anthropological Linguistics* 21(7):355–61.

Gumperz, John J. 1962. Types of linguistic communities. *Anthropological Linguistics* 4(1):28–40.

1970. Sociolinguistics and communication in small groups. Language-Behavior Research Laboratory, Working Paper No. 33. Berkeley: University of California.

1976. The sociolinguistic significance of conversational code-switching. Language-Behavior Research Laboratory, Working Paper No. 46. Berkeley: University of California.

1977. Sociocultural knowledge in conversational inference. In Muriel Saville-Troike, ed., *Linguistics and Anthropology*, pp. 191–212. Washington, DC: Georgetown University Press.

1979. The retrieval of sociocultural knowledge in conversation. *Poetics Today* 1:273–86.

1981. Conversational inference and classroom learning. In Judith Green and Cynthia Wallat, eds, *Ethnography and Language in Educational Settings*, pp. 3–23. Norwood, NJ:Ablex.

1982. *Discourse Strategies*. London: Cambridge University Press.

1984. Communicative competence revisited. In Deborah Schiffrin, ed., *Meaning, Form, and Use in Context: Linguistic Applications*, pp. 278–89. Washington, DC: Georgetown University Press.

and Dell Hymes, eds. 1964. The ethnography of communication. *American Anthropologist* 66(6).

eds. 1972. *Directions in Sociolinguistics: The Ethnography of Communication*. New York: Holt, Rinehart & Winston. (Oxford: Basil Blackwell 1986.)

Haas, Mary R. 1941. Tunica. In Franz Boas, ed., *Handbook of American Indian Languages* Part 4, pp. 1–143. Bureau of American Ethnology Bulletin 40. Washington, DC: Smithsonian Institution.

1944. Men's and women's speech in Koasati. *Language* 20:142–9. (Reprinted in Hymes (1964), pp. 228–33.)

1957. Interlingual word taboos. *American Anthropologist* 53: 338–41. (Reprinted in Hymes (1964), pp. 489–94.)

Hall, Edward T. 1959. *The Silent Language*. Garden City, NY: Doubleday.

1963. A system for the notation of proxemic behavior. *American Anthropologist* 65:1003–26.

Halliday, Michael A. K. 1970. Functional diversity in language as seen from a consideration of modality and mood in English. *Foundations of Language* 6:322–61.

1975. *Learning How to Mean: Explorations in the Development of Language*. London: Edward Arnold.

1978. *Language as a Social Semiotic: The Social Interpretation of Language and Meaning*. London: Edward Arnold.

Hamp, Eric. 1978. Problems of multilingualism in small linguistic communities. In James E. Alatis, ed., *International Dimensions of Bilingual Education*, pp. 155–64. Washington, DC: Georgetown University Press.

Hannerz, Ulf. 1969. *Soulside: Inquiries into Ghetto Culture and Community*, New York: Columbia University Press.

Harper, Robert G., Arthur N. Wiens, and Joseph D. Matarazzo. 1978. *Nonverbal Communication: The State of the Art*. New York: John Wiley & Sons.

Harrrington, Charles. 1978. Bilingual education, social stratification, and cultural pluralism. Equal Opportunity Review (Summer). New York: ERIC Clearinghouse on Urban Education, Teachers College, Columbia University.

Harris, Tracy Kay. 1979. The prognosis for Judeo-Spanish: its description, present status, survival and decline, with implications for the study of language death in general. Dissertation, Georgetown University.

Haviland, J. B. 1979. Guugu Yimidhirr brother-in-law language. *Language in Society* 8(3):365–93.

Heath, Shirley Brice. 1983 *Ways with Words: Language, Life, and Work in Communities and Classrooms*. London: Cambridge University Press.

Helfrich, Hede, 1979. Age markers in speech. In Klaus R. Scherer and Howard Giles, eds, *Social Markers in Speech*, pp. 63–107. London: Cambridge University Press.

Heller, Monica, nd. Language and ethnic identity in a Toronto French-language school. Toronto: Ontario Institute for Studies in Education.

Heritage, John C. 1985. Recent developments in conversation analysis. *Sociolinguistics* 15(1):1–19.

Hill, Jane H. 1988. Language, culture, and world view. In Frederick J. Newmeyer, ed., *Language: The Socio-Cultural Context*, pp. 14–36. London: Cambridge University Press.

and Kenneth C. Hill. 1980. Mixed grammar, purist grammar, and language attitudes in modern Nahuatl. *Language in Society* 9:321–48.

1986. *Speaking Mexicano: Dynamics of Syncretic Language in Central Mexico*. Tucson: University of Arizona Press.

Hobart, Mark. 1975. Orators and patrons: two types of political leader in Balinese village society. In Maurice Bloch, ed., *Political Language and Oratory in Traditional Society*, pp. 65–92. New York: Academic Press.

Hockett, Charles F. 1958. *A Course in Modern Linguistics*. New York: Macmillan.

Hogbin, H. Ian. 1946. A New Guinea childhood: from weaning till the eighth year in Wogeo. *Oceania* 16(4):275–96. (Reprinted in Middleton (1970), pp. 134–62.)

Hoover, Mary Eleanor Rhodes. 1975. Appropriate use of Black English by Black children as rated by parents. Stanford Center for Research and Development in Teaching, Technical Report No. 46.

Hopkins, Nicholas A. 1977. Historical and sociocultural aspects of the distribution of linguistic variants in Highland Chiapas, Mexico. In Ben G. Blount and Mary Sanches, eds, *Socio-cultural Dimensions of Language Change*, pp. 185–226. New York: Academic Press.

Hornberger, Nancy H. 1987. Bilingual education success, but policy failure. *Language in Society* 16:205–26.

Hudson, R. A. 1980. *Sociolinguistics*. Cambridge: Cambridge University Press.

Huspek, Michael R. 1986. Linguistic variation, context and meaning: a case of -*ing*/*in*' variation in North American workers's speech. *Language in Society* 15:149–64.

Hymes, Dell. 1961. Functions of speech: an evolutionary approach. In Frederick C. Gruber, ed., *Anthropology and Education*, pp. 55–83. Philadephia: University of Pennsylvania Press.

—— 1962. The ethnography of speaking. In T. Gladwin and W. C. Sturtevant, eds, *Anthropology and Human Behavior*, pp. 13–53. Washington, DC: Anthropological Society of Washington.

—— ed. 1964. *Language in Culture and Society*. New York: Harper & Row.

—— 1966a. On communicative competence. Paper presented at the Research Planning Conference on Language Development among Disadvantaged Children, Yeshiva University.

—— 1966b. Two types of linguistic relativity. In William Bright, ed., *Sociolinguistics*. The Hague: Mouton.

—— 1967. Models of interaction of language and social setting. *Journal of Social Issues* 33(2):8–28.

—— 1970. Linguistic aspects of comparative political research. In R. Holt and J. Turner, eds, *The Methodology of Comparative Research*, pp 295–341. New York: The Free Press.

—— 1972. Models of the interaction of language and social life. In John J. Gumperz and D. Hymes, eds, *Directions in Sociolinguistics: Ethnography of Communication*, pp. 35–71. New York: Holt, Rinehart & Winston.

—— 1973. On the origins and foundations of inequality among speakers. *Language as a Human Problem*. Special issue of *Daedalus* 102(3):59–85.

—— 1974. *Foundations in Sociolinguistics: An Ethnographic Approach*. Philadelphia: University of Pennsylvania Press.

—— 1978. What is ethnography? Texas working papers in sociolinguistics No. 45.

—— 1979a. How to talk like a bear in Takelma. *International Journal of American Linguistics* 45(2):101–6.

—— 1979b. Sapir, competence, voices. In Charles J. Fillmore, Daniel Kempler, and William S-Y Wang, eds, *Individual Differences in Language Ability and Language Behavior*, pp. 33–45. New York: Academic Press.

—— 1980. Tonkawa poetics: John Rush Buffalo's 'Coyote and Eagle's Daughter'. In Jacques Maquet, ed., *On Linguistic Anthropology: Essays in Honor of Harry Hoijer, 1979*. Malibu, CA: Undena Publications.

—— 1981. *'In Vain I Tried to Tell You': Essays in Native American Ethnopoetics*. Philadelphia: University of Pennsylvania Press.

—— 1987. Communicative competence. In Ulrich Ammon, Norbert

Dittmar, and Klaus J. Mattheier, eds, *Sociolinguistics: An International Handbook of the Science of Language and Society*, pp. 219–29. Berlin: Walter de Gruyter.

Joel Sherzer, Regna Darnell, *et al*, 1967. Outline guide for the ethnographic study of speech use. Manuscript. (Revised by Sherzer and Darnell and published in Gumperz and Hymes (1972), pp. 548–54.)

Irvine, Judith Temkin. 1973. Caste and communication in a Wolof village. Dissertation, University of Pennsylvania.

Isbell, Billie Jean and Fredy A. R. Fernandez. 1977. The ontogenesis of metaphor: riddle games among Quechua speakers seen as cognitive discovery procedures. *Journal of Latin American Lore* 3(1):19–49.

Jackson, Bruce. 1987. *Fieldwork*. Urbana: University of Illinois Press.

Jakobson, Roman. 1938. On the theory of phonological associations among languages. *Proceedings of the Fourth International Congress of Linguists, Copenhagen*, pp. 45–58. (Reprinted in A. Keiler, ed., *A Reader in Historical and Comparative Linguistics* (1972), pp. 241–52. New York: Holt, Rinehart & Winston.

Jefferson, Gail. 1984. On the organization of laughter in talk about troubles. In J. M. Atkinson and John C. Heritage, eds, *Structures of Social Action: Studies in Conversation Analysis*, pp. 347–69. London: Cambridge University Press.

Jenness, Diamond. 1929. The ancient education of a Carrier Indian. National Museum of Canada Bulletin No. 62: Annual Report for 1928, pp. 22–7. Ottawa: F.A. Acland.

Johnson, Mary Canice. 1972. Sequential moves and meaning in classroom discussion: a sociolinguistic survey. Dissertation, University of Texas at Austin. (Revised and published as *Discussion Dynamics: An Analysis of Classroom Teaching* (1979). Rowley, Mass.: Newbury House.)

Kachru, Braj B. 1976. Models of English for the third world: white man's linguistic burden or language pragmatics? *TESOL Quarterly* 10(2):221–39.

1977. Linguistic schizophrenia and language census: a note on the language situation. *Linguistics* 186:17–32.

1980. The pragmatics of non-native varieties of English. In Larry Smith, ed., *English for Cross-Cultural Communication*. London: Macmillan.

1982. The bilingual's linguistic repertoire. In Beverly Hartford,

Albert Valdman, and Charles R. Foster, eds, *Issues in International Bilingual Education: The Role of the Vernacular*, pp. 25–52. New York: Plenum Press.

1983. *The Indianization of English: The English Language in India*. London: Oxford University Press.

1986. *The Alchemy of English: The Spread, Functions and Models of Non-Native Englishes*. Oxford: Pergamon Institute of English.

Kahane, Henry and Renée. 1979. Decline and survival of Western prestige languages. *Language* 55(1):183–98.

Katriel, Tamar. 1985. *Brogez*: ritual and strategy in Israeli children's conflicts. *Language in Society* 14:467–690.

1987 'Bexibùdim!': ritualized sharing among Israeli children. *Language in Society* 16:305–20.

Kawashima, Takeyoshi. 1979. The Japanese linguistic consciousness and the law. *Japan Echo* 6(3):105–14. (Translation from Nihonjin no gengo ishiki to hōtitsu, in *Sekai* (February 1979).

Keenan, Elinor O. 1974. Conversational competence in children. *Journal of Child Language* 1:163–83.

1975. A sliding sense of obligatoriness: the polystructure of Malagasy oratory. In Maurice Bloch, ed., *Political Language and Oratory in Traditional Society*, pp. 93–112. New York: Academic Press.

1976. The universality of conversational postulates. *Language in Society* 5(1):67–80.

Keller-Cohen, Deborah. 1987. Literate practices in a modern credit union. *Language in Society* 16:7–24.

Kempf, Renate. 1985. Pronouns and terms of address in *Neues Deutschland*. *Language in Society* 14:223–37.

Kempton, Willet. 1979. The rhythmic basis of interactional microsynchrony. In M. R. Key, ed., *Verbal and Nonverbal Communication*. The Hague: Mouton.

Kessen, William and Katherine Nelson. 1976. What does the child's world look like? Report of research in the *Carnegie Quarterly* 24(2):1–3.

Kipers, Pamela S. 1987. Gender and topic. *Language in Society* 16:543–57.

Kirshenblatt-Gimblett, Barbara, ed. 1976. *Speech Play: Research and Resources for the Study of Linguistic Creativity*. Philadelphia: University of Pennsylvania Press.

Kleifgen, JoAnne, Soonai Ham, Atteya El Noory, Mary Fritz, and Muriel Saville-Troike. 1986. Shifting patterns of language dominance in bilingual children. Paper presented to the annual convention of the American Educational Research Association, San Francisco, CA.

Kochman, Thomas, ed. 1972. *Rappin' and Stylin' Out: Communication in Urban Black America*. Urbana: University of Illinois Press.

Kroeber, Alfred L. 1935. History and science in anthropology. *American Anthropologist* 37:538–69.

1944. *Configurations of Culture Growth*. Berkeley: University of California Press.

Labov, William. 1963. The social motivation of a sound change. *Word* 19:273–309.

1966, *The Social Stratification of English in New York City*. Washington, DC: Center for Applied Linguistics.

1970. The logic of nonstandard English. In James E. Alatis, ed., *Linguistics and the Teaching of Standard English to Speakers of Other Languages or Dialects*, pp. 1–44. Washington, DC: Georgetown University Press.

1972. On the mechanism of linguistic change. In John J. Gumperz and D. Hymes, eds. *Directions of Sociolinguistics: The Ethnography of Communication*, pp. 512–38. New York: Holt, Rinehart & Winston.

Paul Cohen, Clarence Robins, and John Lewis. 1968. A study of the non-standard English of Negro and Puerto Rican speakers in New York City. USOE Final Report.

and David Fanshel. 1977. *Therapeutic Discourse: Psychotherapy as Convention*. New York: Academic Press.

Lagacé, Robert O., ed. 1977. *Sixty Cultures: A Guide to the HRAF Probability Sample Files* (Part A). New Haven, CN: Human Relations Area Files.

Lakoff, Robin. 1973. Questionable answers and answerable questions. In Braj B. Kachru, *et al.*, eds, *Issues in Linguistics: Papers in Honor of Henry and Renée Kahane*. Urbana: University of Illinois Press.

Lambert, Wallace E. 1979. Language as a factor in intergroup relations. In Howard Giles and Robert H. St Clair, eds, *Language and Social Psychology*, pp. 186–92. Oxford: Basil Blackwell.

H. Frankel, and G. R. Tucker. 1966. Judging personality through speech: a French-Canadian example. *Journal of Communication* 16:305–21.

R. C. Hodgson R. C. Gardner, and S. Fillenbaum. 1960. Evaluational reactions to spoken languages. *Journal of Abnormal and Social Psychology* 60:44–51.

Laosa, Luis M. 1977. Socialization, education, and continuity: the importance of the sociocultural context. *Young Children* 32(5):21–7.

Laughlin, Robert M. 1980. *Of Shoes and Ships and Sealing Wax: Sundries from Zinacantán.* Contributions to Anthropology No. 25. Washington, DC: Smithsonian Institution.

Lavandera, Beatriz R. 1980. Discussion of code-switching. In Florence Barkin and Elizabeth Brandt, eds, *Speaking, Singing and Teaching: A Multidisciplinary Approach to Language Variation*, pp. 368–70. Anthropological Research Papers No. 20, Tempe: Arizona State University.

Laver, John and Peter Trudgill. 1979. Phonetic and linguistic markers in speech. In Klaus R. Scherer and Howard Giles, eds, *Social Markers in Speech*, pp. 1–32. London: Cambridge University Press.

Leach, Edmund. 1976. *Culture and Communication.* London: Cambridge University Press.

Leiter, Kenneth. 1980. *A Primer on Ethnomethodology.* London: Oxford University Press.

Leslau, Wolf. 1959. Taboo expressions in Ethiopia. *American Anthropologist* 61:105–7.

Locke, Patricia. 1980. The nature of the socio-cultural aspects of American Indian language uses. Paper presented at the Conference on Research in American Indian Education, National Institute of Education, Washington, DC.

Lockwood, W. B. 1956. Word taboo in the language of the Faroese fisherman. *Transactions of the Philological Society*, pp. 1–24. London.

Lyons, John, ed. 1970. *New Horizons in Linguistics.* Harmondsworth: Penguin.

Macaulay, Ronald K. S. 1975. Negative prestige, linguistic insecurity, and linguistic self-hatred. *Lingua* 36:147–61.

    1976. Social class and language in Glasgow. *Language in Society* 5(2):173–88.

    and G. D. Trevelyan. 1973. Language, education, and employment in Glasgow. Final report to the SSRC. Edinburgh: The Scottish Council for Research in Education.

McClure, Erica. 1974. The acquisition and use of Spanish and English color terms among Mexican American children. Paper presented to the American Anthropological Association, Mexico City.

1977. Aspects of code-switching in the discourse of bilingual Mexican-American children. In Muriel Saville-Troike, ed., *Linguistics and Anthropology*, pp. 93–116. Washington, DC: Georgetown University Press.

McGuinness, Diane. 1979. How schools discriminate against boys. *Human Nature* February, pp. 82–8.

McLendon, Sally. 1978. How languages die: a social history of unstable bilingualism among the Eastern Pomo. In Margaret Langdon, Shirley Silver, and Kathryn Klar, eds, *American Indian and Indo-European Studies*, pp. 137–50. The Hague: Mouton.

Maher, John. 1986. English for medical purposes. *Language Teaching* 19:112–45.

Maley, Yon. 1987. The language of legislation. *Language in Society* 16:25–48.

Malinowski, Bronislaw. 1923. The problem of meaning in primitive languages. Supplement to C. K. Ogden and I. A. Richards, *The Meaning of Meaning*, pp. 296–336. London: Kegan Paul.

1926. *Crime and Custom in Savage Society*. London: K. Paul, Trench, Trubner.

1935. *Coral Gardens and their Magic: A Study of Agricultural Rites in the Trobriand Islands*. Vol II, *The Language of Magic and Gardening*. New York: American.

Martin-Jones, Marilyn and Suzanne Romaine. 1986. Semilingualism: a half-baked theory of communicative competence. *Applied Linguistics* 7:26–38.

Maurer, David W. 1940. The con man and his lingo. In *The Big Con*. Indianapolis, NY: Bobbs-Merrill.

Maxwell, Madeline M. and Sybil Smith-Todd. 1986. Black sign language and school integration in Texas. *Language in Society* 15:81–94.

Maynard, Douglas W. 1985. How children start arguments. *Langue in Society* 14:1–30.

Mead, Margaret. 1930. *Growing Up in New Guinea: A Comparative Study of Primitive Education*. New York: William Morrow.

1955. Children and ritual in Bali. In Margaret Mead and Martha Wolfenstein, eds, *Childhood in Contemporary Cultures*, pp. 40–51. Chicago: University of Chicago Press.

Michaels, Sarah. 1981. 'Sharing time': children's narrative styles and differential access to literacy. *Language in Society* 10:423–42.

Middleton, John, ed. 1970. *From Child to Adult: Studies in the Anthropology of Education*. Austin: University of Texas Press.

Miller, Mary R. 1970. The language and language beliefs of Indian children. *Anthropological Linguistics* 12(2):51–61.

Milroy, Lesley, 1987a. *Language and Social Networks*. Second Edition. Oxford: Basil Blackwell.

1987b. *Observing and Analysing Natural Language: A Critical Account of Sociolinguistic Method*. Oxford: Basil Blackwell.

Mitchell-Kernan, Claudia and Keith T. Kernan. 1977. Pragmatics of directive choice among children. In Susan M. Ervin-Tripp and Claudia Mitchell-Kernan, eds, *Child Discourse*, pp. 189–208. New York: Academic Press.

Momaday, Scott N. 1976. *The Names*. New York: Harper & Row.

Mueller, Claus. 1973. *The Politics of Communication: A study in the Political Sociology of Language, Socialization and Legitimation*. London: Oxford University Press.

Munby, John. 1977. Applying sociocultural variables in the specification of communicative competence. In Muriel Saville-Troike, ed., *Linguistics and Anthropology*, pp. 231–47. Washington, DC: Georgetown University Press.

1978. *Communicative Syllabus Design*. London: Cambridge University Press.

Newman, Stanley. 1955. Vocabulary levels: Zuñi sacred and slang usage. *Southwestern Journal of Anthropology* 11:345–54.

Nida, Eugene A. 1977. Translating means communicating: a sociolinguistic theory of translation. In Muriel Saville-Troike, ed., *Linguistics and Anthropology*, pp. 213–29. Washington, DC: Georgetown University Press.

Nishimura, Miwa. 1986. Intrasentential code-switching: the case of language assignment. In Jyotsna Vaid, ed., *Language Processing in Bilinguals: Psycholinguistic and Neuropsychological Perspectives*, pp. 123–43. Hillsdale, NJ: Lawrence Erlbaum.

Nketia, J. H. Kwabene. 1972. Surrogate languages of Africa. *The Conch* 42:11–48.

Nwoye, Gregory O. 1985. Eloquent silence among the Igbo of Nigeria. In Deborah Tannen and Muriel Saville-Troike, eds, *Perspectives on Silence*, pp. 185–91. Norwood, NJ: Ablex.

O'Barr, William M. 1982. *Linguistic Evidence: Language, Power, and Strategy in the Courtroom*. New York: Academic Press.

Ogbu, John U. 1981. School ethnography: a multilevel approach. *Anthropology and Education Quarterly* 12:3–29.

Oh, Hyun Hee Kim. 1988. Sociolinguistic and stylistc aspects of code-switching in Korean–English bilingual children: a naturalistic, longitudinal study. Dissertation, University of Illinois at

Urbana–Champaign.

Opler, Morris. 1941. *An Apache Life Way*. Chicago: University of Chicago Press.

Ornstein-Galicia, Jacob, ed. 1984. *Form and Function in Chicano English*. Rowley, Mass.: Newbury House.

Owens, Mary. 1979. Solicitation techniques among English-speaking children in the US: the use of direct and indirect request forms. Dissertation, Georgetown University.

Paulston, Christina Bratt. 1976. Pronouns of address in Swedish: social class semantics and a changing system. *Language in Society* 5(3):359–86.

Peal, Elizabeth and Wallace Lambert. 1962. The relation of bilingualism to intelligence. *Psychological Monographs: General and Applied* 126(27):1–23.

Penfield, Wilder. 1965. Conditioning the uncommited cortex for language learning. *Brain* 88(4):787–98.

Perlmutter, David M. and Scott Soames. 1979. *Syntactic Argumentation and the Structure of English*. Berkeley: University of California Press.

Philips, Susan U. 1970. Acquisition of rules for appropriate speech usage. In James E. Alatis, ed., *Bilingualism and Language Contact: Anthropological, Linguistic, Psychological, and Sociological Aspects*, pp. 77–102. Washington, DC: Georgetown University Press.

1976. Some sources of cultural variability in the regulation of talk. *Language in Society* 5(1):81–95.

1982. The language socialization of lawyers: acquiring the 'cant'. In George Spindler, ed., *Doing the Ethnography of Schooling*, pp. 176–209. New York: Holt, Rinehart & Winston.

1983a. An ethnographic approach to bilingual language proficiency assessment. In Charlene Rivera, ed., *An Ethnographic/Sociolinguistic Approach to Language Proficiency Assessment*, pp. 88–106. Clevedon, Avon: Multilingual Matters.

1983b. *The Invisible Culture: Commuication in Classroom and Community on the Warm Springs Indian Reservation*. New York: Longman.

Philipsen, Gerry and Donal Carbaugh. 1986. A bibliography of fieldwork in the ethnography of communication. *Language in Society* 15:387–98.

Piaget, Jean. 1926. *The Language and Thought of the Child*. New York: Harcourt, Brace & World.

Pliskin, Karen L. 1987. *Silent Boundaries: Cultural Constraints on*

Sickness and Diagnosis of Iranians in Israel. New Haven, CN: Yale University Press.

Poplack, Shana. 1979. 'Sometimes I'll start a sentence in Spanish *y temino en Español*: toward a typology of code-switching,' New York: Centro de Estudios Puertorriqueños.

Pound, Louise. 1936. American euphemisms for dying, death, and burial. *American Speech* 11(3):195–202.

Powell, John, W. 1877. *Introduction to the study of Indian languages*, first edition. Washington, DC: BAE, Smithsonian Institution.

1880. *Introduction to the study of Indian languages*, second edition. Washington, DC: BAE, Smithsonian Institution.

Pye, Clifton. 1986. Quiché Mayan speech to children. *Journal of Child Language* 13:85–100.

Pyles, Thomas. 1959. Bible belt onomastics or some curiosities of anti-pedobaptist nomenclature. *Names* 7(2):84–100.

Rensch, Calvin R. 1977. Situación actual de los estudios lingüísticos de las lenguas de Oaxaca. Paper presented at a conference on the State of Anthropology in the State of Oaxaca, Mexico.

Retmono, R. 1967. The Javanese language before and after independence: an observation of a language in a changing society. Manuscript, University of Texas at Austin.

Rist, Ray C. 1980. Blitzkrieg ethnography: on the transformation of method into a movement. *Educational Researcher* 9(2):8–10.

Robinson, W. Peter. 1979. Speech markers, and social class. In Klaus R. Scherer and Howard Giles, eds, *Social Markers in Speech*, pp. 211–49. London: Cambridge University Press.

Rubin, Joan. 1968. *National Bilingualism in Paraguay*. The Hague: Mouton.

Rudner, William A. and Rochelle Butowsky. 1980. Ameslan signs used by the deaf gay community. *Sign Language Studies* December.

Salmond, Anne, 1975. Mama makes the man: a look at Maori oratory and politics. In Maurice Bloch, ed., *Political Language and Oratory in Traditional Society*, pp. 45–64. New York: Academic Press.

Sanches, Mary and Barbara Kirshenblatt-Gimblett. 1971. Child language and children's traditional speech play. Texas working papers in sociolinguistics No. 5 (Reprinted in Kirshenblatt-Gimblett (1976), pp 65–110.)

Sankoff, David and Shana Poplack. 1981. A formal grammar for code-switching. *Papers in Linguistics* 14:3–46.

Sapir, Edward. 1915. Abnormal types of speech in Nootka. Canada, Geological Survey Memoir 62 Anthropological Series No. 5. Ottawa: Government Printing Bureau. (Reprinted in David G. Mandelbaum, ed., *Selected Writings of Edward Sapir in Language, Culture, Personality*, pp. 179–96 (1958). Berkeley: University of California Press.)

Savignon, Sandra J. 1983. *Communicative Competence: Theory and Classroom Practice*. Reading, Mass.: Addison-Wesley.

Saville-Troike, Muriel, ed. 1977. Linguistics and Anthropology. Washington, DC: Georgetown University Press.

    1978. *A Guide to Culture in the Classroom*. Rosslyn, VA: National Clearinghouse for Bilingual Education.

    1980. *Synchronic Variation in Navajo: Regional, Social, and Developmental Evidence from Child Language*. Final Report to the National Science Foundation. ERIC ED 193 918.

    1985. The place of silence in an integrated theory of communication. In Deborah Tannen and Muriel Saville-Troike, eds, *Perspectives on Silence*, pp. 3–18. Norwood, NJ: Ablex.

    1986. Children's dispute and negotiation strategies: a naturalistic approach. In Joshua A. Fishman, *et al.*, eds, *The Fergusonian Impact. Volume I: From Phonology to Society*, pp. 135–52. Berlin: Mouton de Gruyter.

    1987. Dilingual discourse: communication without a common language. *Linguistics* 25:81–106.

    1988. A note on men's and women's speech in Koasati. *International Journal of American Linguistics* 54:421–2.

    1989. Communicative competence. In William Bright, ed., *Oxford International Encyclopedia of Linguistics*. Oxford: Oxford University Press.

Schegloff, Emanuel A. 1968. Sequencing in conversational openings. *American Anthropologist* 70:1075–95.

    1982. Discourse as an interactional achievement: some uses of 'uh huh' and other things that come between sentences. In Deborah Tannen, ed., *Analyzing Discourse: Text and Talk*, pp. 71–93. Washington, DC: Georgetown University Press.

Scherer, Klaus R. 1979. Personality markers in speech. In Klaus R. Scherer and Howard Giles, eds., *Social Markers in Speech*, pp. 147–209. London: Cambridge University Press.

    and Howard Giles, eds. 1979. *Social Markers in Speech*. London: Cambridge University Press.

Schieffelin, Bambi B. and Perry Gilmore, eds. 1986. *The Aquisition of Literacy: Ethnographic Perspectives*. Norwood, NJ: Albex.

and Elinor Ochs. 1986a. Language socialization. *Annual Review of Anthropology* 15:163–91.

eds. 1986b *Language Socialization Across Cultures*. London: Cambridge University Press.

Scollon, Ronald and Suzanne B. K. Scollon. 1979. *Linguistic Convergence: An Ethnography of Speaking at Fort Chipewyan, Alberta*. New York: Academic Press.

1981. *Narrative, Literacy, and Face in Interethnic Communication*. Norwood, NJ: Ablex.

Scribner, Sylvia and Michael Cole. 1973. Cognitive consequences of formal and informal education. *Science* 182:553–9.

Searle, John. 1969. *Speech Acts*. London: Cambridge University Press.

1977a. A classification of illocutionary acts. In A. Rogers, R. Wall, and J. P. Murphy, eds. *Proceedings of the Texas Conference on Performatives, Presuppositions*, and *Implicatures*, pp. 27–45. Arlington, VA: Center for Applied Linguistics.

1977b. Indirect speech acts. In Peter Cole and Jerry L. Morgan, eds, *Syntax and Semantics: Speech Acts* Vol. 3, pp. 59–82. New York: Academic Press.

Shearer, Lloyd. 1988. Intelligence report. *Parade Magazine*, January 10, p. 16.

Sherk, John K. 1973. A word-count of spoken English of culturally disadvantaged preschool and elementary pupils. Kansas City: University of Missouri.

Sherzer, Joel. 1974. *Namakke, sunmakke, dormakke*: three types of Cuna speech event. In Richard Bauman and Joel Sherzer, eds, *Explorations in the Ethnography of Speaking*, pp. 263–82. London: Cambridge University Press.

1975. Ethnography of Speaking. Manuscript, University of Texas at Austin.

1977. The ethnography of Speaking: a critical appraisal. In Muriel Saville-Troike, ed., *Linguistics and Anthropology*, pp. 43–58. Washington, DC: Georgetown University Press.

1983. *Kuna Ways of Speaking: An Ethnographic Perspective*. Austin: University of Texas Press.

Shimanoff, Susan B. 1980. *Communication Rules: Theory and Research*. Beverly Hills: Sage.

Shuy, Roger W. 1974. Problems of communication in the cross-cultural medical interview. Texas working papers in sociolinguistics No. 19.

1975a. Code-switching in Lady Chatterley's Lover. Texas working papers in sociolinguistics No. 22.

1975b. Variability and the public image of language. Paper presented at the conference on New Ways of Analysing Variation in English (NWAVE) IV, Georgetown University.

Joan C. Baratz, and Walt Wolfram. 1969. Sociolinguistic forces in speech indentification. NIMHR Project Report. Washington, DC: Center for Applied Linguistics.

and Ralph W. Fasold, eds. 1973. *Language Attitudes: Current Trends and Prospects.* Washington, DC: Georgetown University Press.

Silverman, Philip and Robert J. Maxwell. 1978. How do I respect thee? Let me count the ways: deference towards elderly men and women. *Behavior Science Research* 13(2):91–108.

Sjoberg, Andrée F. 1962. Coexistant phonemic systems in Telugu: a socio-cultural perspective. *Word* 18(3):269–79.

Skopek, Lucienne. 1975. Sociolinguistic aspects of the medical interview. Dissertation, Georgetown University.

Slobin, Dan I., ed. 1967. *A Field Manual for Cross-Cultural Study of the Acquisition of Communicative Competence* (second draft). Berkeley: University of California.

Smal-Stocki, Roman. 1950. Taboo on animal names in Ukranian. *Language* 26:489–93.

Smith, Philip M. 1979. Sex markers in speech. In Klaus R. Scherer and Howard Giles, eds. *Social Markers in Speech*, pp. 109–46. London: Cambridge University Press.

Smith, Riley. 1973. Some phonological rules in the Negro speech of East Texas. Dissertation, University of Texas at Austin.

Snow, Catherine E. 1972. Mothers' speech to children learning language. *Child Development* 43:549–65.

and Charles A. Ferguson, eds. 1977. *Talking to Children: Language Input and Acquisition.* London: Cambridge University Press.

Soeffner, Hans-Georg. 1985. Hermeneutic approaches to language. *Sociolinguistics* 15(1):21–4.

Sorenson, Arthur P., Jr 1967. Multilingualism in the Northwest Amazon. *American Anthropologist* 69:670–84.

Spiro, Melford E. 1958. *Children of the Kibbutz.* Cambridge, Mass.: Harvard University Press.

Spolsky, Bernard. 1971. Navajo language maintenance III: accessibility of school and town as a factor in language shift. Navajo Reading Study Progress Report No. 14. Albuquerque: University of New Mexico.

and Patricia Irvine. 1982. Sociolinguistic aspects of the acceptance of literacy in the vernacular. In Florence Barkin, Elizabeth A. Brandt, and Jacob Ornstein-Galicia, eds, *Bilingualism and Language Contact*, pp. 73–9. New York: Teachers College Press.

Spradley, James P. 1979. *The Ethnographic Interview*. New York: Holt, Rinehart & Winston.

1980. *Participant Observation*. New York: Holt, Rinehart & Winston.

Sridhar, S. and K. Sridhar. 1980. The syntax and psycholinguistics of bilingual code-mixing. *Canadian Journal of Psychology/Revue Canadienne de Psychologie* 34:407–16.

Stewart, William A. 1967. *Language and Communication. Problems in Southern Appalachia*. Washington, DC: Center for Applied Linguistics.

Stokoe, William C. 1969. Sign language diglossia. *Studies in Linguistics* 21:27–41.

Stoller, Paul. 1986. The reconstruction of ethnography. In Phyllis Pease Chock and June R. Wyman, eds, *Discourse and the Social Life of Meaning*, pp. 51–74. Washington, DC: Smithsonian Institution Press.

Strathern, Andrew. 1975. Veiled speech in Mount Hagen. In Maurice Bloch, ed., *Political Language and Oratory in Traditional Society*, pp. 185–203. New York: Academic Press.

Subrahamian, K. 1978. My Mrs. is Indian. *Anthropological Linguistics* 20(6):295–6.

Swadesh, Morris. 1948. Sociologic notes on obsolescent language. *International Journal of American Linguistics* 14:226–35.

Tabouret-Keller, Andrée. 1972. A contribution to the sociological study of language maintenance and shift. In Joshua A. Fishman, ed., *Advances in the Sociology of Language* Vol. 2, pp. 364–76. The Hague: Mouton.

Talmy, Leonard. 1976. Communicative aims and means: a synopsis. In Working Papers on Language Universals No. 20, Stanford University.

Tammivaara, Julie and D. Scott Enright. 1986. On eliciting information: dialogues with child informants. *Anthropology and Education Quarterly* 17:218–38.

Tannen, Deborah. 1979a. Processes and consequences of conversational style. Dissertation, University of California at Berkeley.

1979b. What's in a frame? Surface evidence for underlying expectations. In Roy Freedle, ed., *New Dimensions in Discourse*

Processing, pp. 137–81. Norwood, NJ: Ablex.

1980. A comparative analysis of oral narrative structures. Athenian Greek and American English. In Wallace L. Chafe, ed., *The Pear Stories: Cognitive, Cultural and Linguistic Aspects of Narrative Production*, pp. 51–87. Norwood, NJ: Ablex.

1981. Indirectness in discourse: ethnicity as conversation style. *Discourse Processes* 4(3):221–38.

and Muriel Saville-Troike, eds. 1985. *Perspectives on Silence*. Norwood, NJ: Ablex.

Taylor, M. Ean. 1987. Functions of in-house language: observations on data collected from some British financial institutions. *Language in Society* 16:1–6.

Taylor, Steven J. and Robert Bogdan. 1984. *Introduction in Qualitative Research Methods: The Search for Meaning*. Second Edition. New York: John Wiley & Sons.

Thompson, Lawrence C. 1978. Control in Salish grammar. Paper presented to the American Anthropological Association, Los Angeles.

Thompson, Roger M. 1971. Language loyalty in Austin, Texas: a study of a bilingual neighbourhood. Dissertation, University of Texas at Austin.

Tiwary, K. M. 1975. Tuneful weeping: a mode of communication. Texas working papers in sociolinguistics No. 27.

Treichler, Paula A., Richard M. Frankel, Cheris Kramarae, Kathleen Zoppi, and Howard B. Beckman. 1984. Problems and *problems*: power relationships in a medical encounter. In Cheris Kramarae, Muriel Schulz, and William M. O'Barr, eds, *Language and Power*, pp. 62–88. Beverly Hills, CA: Sage.

Troike, Rudolph C. 1970. Receptive competence, productive competence, and performance. In James E. Alatis, ed., *Linguistics and the Teaching of Standard English to Speakers of Other Languages or Dialects*, pp. 63–74. Washington, DC: Georgetown University Press.

and Muriel Saville-Troike. 1988. Video recording for linguistic fieldwork. *Notes on Linguistics* 37:44–51.

Trosset, Carol S. 1986. The social identity of Welsh learners. *Language in Society* 15:165–92.

Trudgill, Peter. 1974. *The Social Differentiation of English in Norwich*. London: Cambridge University Press.

1975. Sex, covert prestige, and linguistic change in the urban British English of Norwich. In Barrie Thorne and Nancy Henley, eds, *Language and Sex: Difference and Dominance*.

Rowley, Mass.: Newbury House.

and G. A. Tzavaras. 1977. Why Albanian-Greeks are not Albanians: language shift in Attica and Biotia. In Howard Giles, ed., *Language, Ethnicity and Intergroup Relations*, pp. 171–84. New York: Academic Press.

Tsuda, Aoi. 1984. *Sales Talk in Japan and the United States*. Washington, DC: Georgetown University Press.

Tsujimura, Toshiki. 1977. Keigo. In Kiyoji Satō, ed., *Kokugogaku Kenkyŭ Jiten*, pp. 191–6. Tokyo: Meiji Shoin.

Turnbull, Colin M. 1961. *The Forest People*. London: Chatto & Windus.

Tway, Patricia. 1975. Workplace isoglosses: Lexical variation and change in a factory setting. *Language in Society* 4(2):171–83.

Tyler, Stephen A. 1972. Context and alternation in Koya kinship terminology. In John J. Gumperz and D. Hymes, eds, *Directions in Sociolinguistics: The Ethnography of Communication*, pp. 251–69. New York: Holt, Rinehart & Winston.

1978. *The Said and the Unsaid: Mind, Meaning, and Culture*. New York: Academic Press.

Van Riper, William R. 1979. Usage preferences of men and women: *did, came,* and *saw. American Speech* 54(4):279–84.

Viorst, Judith. 1976. What's a good mommy? *Catholic Digest* (May), pp. 45–9. (Condensed from *Redbook*.)

von Humboldt, Wilhelm. 1836. *Über die Vershiedenhiet des menschlichen Sprachbaues und ihren Einfluss auf die geistige Entwickelung des Menschengeschlechts*. Royal Academy of Sciences of Berlin. (Reprinted as *Linguistic Variability and Intellectual Development*, translated by George C. Buck and Frithjof A. Raben. 1971. University of Miami Press.)

von Raffler-Engle, Walburga. 1977. The nonverbal adjustment of children's communicative style. In B. N. Laria and D. E. Gulstad, eds, *Papers for the 1977 Mid-America Linguistic Conference*. Columbus: University of Missouri.

1978. A pluri-model communicative approach to language acquisition. In *Development in Verbal and Non-Verbal behavior*. Toyko: Bunka Hyoron.

and Catherine Rea. 1978. The influence of child's communicative style on the conversational behavior of the adult. Paper presented at the First International Congress for the Study of Child Language, Tokyo.

Vosniadou, Stella and William F. Brewer. In press. A cross-cultural investigation of children's acquisition of knowledge in observational astronomy. In H. Mandl, E. de Corte, N. Bennett, and F. H. Friedrich, eds, *Proceedings of the Second European Conference for Research on Learning and Instruction.*

Walker, R. and C. Adelman. 1975. Interaction analysis in informal classrooms: a critical comment on the Flanders' system. *British Journal of Educational Psychology* 45:73–6.

Wallat, Cynthia. 1981. Communicative competence. Paper presented at the National Institute of Education Language Proficiency Assessment Symposium, Warrenton, VA.

Wang, Peter Chin-tang. 1977. The effect of East/West cultural differences on oral language development. Paper presented at the Chinese Languages Teacher's Association, San Francisco.

Watkins, Laurel J. 1979. Pronominal prefixes in Kiowa. Paper presented to the American Anthropological Association, Cincinnati.

Weiniger, Jane C. G. 1978. Communicative strategy among children in a bilingual school environment (K-3). In James E. Redden, ed., Occasional Papers on Linguistics No. 3: *Proceedings of the Second International Conference on Frontiers in Language Proficiency and Dominance Testing*, pp. 117–25. Carbondale: Southern Illinois University.

Weinreich, Uriel. 1953. *Languages in Contact: Findings and Problems.* Publications of the Linguistic Circle of New York No. 1 (Published by Mouton in 1970.)

Werner, Oswald and G. Mark Schoepfle. 1987. *Systematic Fieldwork. Volume 1: Foundations of Ethnography and Interviewing.* Newbury Park: Sage.

White, J. B. c. 1870. A history of the Apache Indians of Arizona territory. Unpublished in the archives of the Smithsonian Institution. BAE ms. 179.

Whiteman, Marcia Farr, ed. 1981. *Variation in Writing: Functional and Linguistic-Cultural Differences.* Volume I of *Writing: The Nature, Development, and Teaching of Written Communication.* Hillsdale, NJ: Lawrence Erlbaum.

Whiting, Beatrice B. and John W. M. Whiting. 1975. *Children of Six Cultures: A Psycho-Cultural Analysis.* Cambridge, Mass.: Harvard University Press.

Whorf, Benjamin Lee. 1940. Science and linguistics. *Technological Review* 42:229–31, 247–8. (Reprinted in John B. Carroll, ed., *Language, Thought, and Reality: Selected Writings of Benjamin Lee Whorf* (1956), pp. 207–19. New York: Wiley.)

Widdowson, H. G. 1973. Directions in the teaching of discourse. In

Corder and Roulet, eds, *Theoretical Linguistic Models in Applied Linguistics*. Brussels: AIMAV; Paris: Didier.

Wierzbicka, Anna. 1985. A semantic metalanguage for a crosscultural comparison of speech acts and speech genres. *Language in Society* 14:491–514.

Wilhite, Margaret. 1977. Marketing and bilingualism: patterns of accommodation in Highland Guatemala. Paper presented at the American Anthropological Association, Houston.

Wilkins, D. A. 1976. *Notional Syllabuses*. London: Oxford University Press.

Williams, Frederick. 1973. Some research notes on dialect attitudes and stereotypes. In Roger W. Shuy and Ralph W. Fasold, eds, *Language Attitudes: Current Trends and Prospects*, pp. 113–28. Washington, DC: Georgetown University Press.

Williams, Thomas Rhys. 1967. *Field Methods in the Study of Culture*. New York: Holt, Rinehart & Winston.

Witherspoon, Gary. 1977. *Language and Art in the Navajo Universe*. Ann Arbor: University of Michigan Press.

Wolfram, Walt. 1973. *Sociolinguistic Aspects of Assimilation: Puerto Rican English in East Harlem*. Washington, DC: Center for Applied Linguistics.

and Todd D. Wolfram. 1977. How come you asked how come? In Ralph W. Fasold and Roger W. Shuy, eds, *Studies in Language Variation: Semantics, Syntax, Phonology, Pragmatics, Social situations, Ethnographic Approaches*. pp. 237–54. Washington, DC: Georgetown University Press.

Wolfson, Nessa and Joan Manes, eds. 1985. *Language of Inequality*. Berlin: Mouton.

Woodward, James C., Jr. 1976. Black southern signing. *Language in Society* 5(2):211–18.

Woolard, Kathryn A. 1987. Code-switching and comedy in Catalonia. *IPRA Papers in Pragmatics* 1:106–22.

Woolford, E. 1983. Bilingual code-switching and syntactic theory. *Linguistic Inquiry* 14:520–36.

Worth, Sol and John Adair. 1975. *Through Navajo Eyes: An Exploration in Film Communication and Anthropology*. Bloomington: Indiana University.

Wright, Richard. 1975. Review of Robbins Burling, *English in Black and White* [1973], New York: Holt, Rinehart & Winston; and William Labov, *Language in the Inner City: Studies in the Black English Vernacular* [1972], Philadelphia: University of Pennsylvania Press. *Language in Society* 4(2):185–98.

Xu, Guo-Zhang. 1987. Code and transmission in cross-cultural discourse: a study of some examples from Chinese and English. In Larry E. Smith, ed., *Discourse Across Cultures: Strategies in World Englishes*, pp. 66–72. New York: Prentice-Hall International.

Zimmerman, Don H. and Candace West. 1975. Sex roles, interruptions, and silences in conversation. In Barrie Thorne and Nancy Henley, eds, *Language and Sex: Difference and Dominance*. Rowley, Mass.: Newbury House.

Index of Languages

Abbey, 139–40, 144, 162–6, 176–7, 237–8, 249
Albanian, 208, 209
American Sign Language, 85, 86–7, 96–7, 224, 251
Amharic, 79, 216
Apache, 6, 33, 188–9
Arabic, 12, 20, 54, 58, 66, 69, 76, 82–3, 144, 185–6, 190–1, 197, 213, 242, 249, 255
Armenian, 19–20, 205–6
Assyrian, 206
Aymara, 235
Aztec, *see* Nahuatl (Aztec)

Bahasa Indonesian, *see* Indonesian
Balinese, 31, 235, 238
Baluchi, 206
Bambara, 95, 155, 161–2, 188, 251
Basseri, 41
Bavarian German, 37; *see also* German
Berber, 93
Black English, 21, 84, 85, 96, 197, 202–3, 234, 252, 253–4; *see also* English
Bokmal, *see* Norwegian

Cagaba, 248
Carrier, 6
Catalan, 69
Chibchan, 248
Chinese, 13, 16, 37–8, 60–1, 63–4, 69, 80, 151–2, 173–5, 188–9, 194,

213, 243, 250, 255–6
Chontal, 261
Creole: Haitian, 54; Trinidadian, 34, 198; Cape Verdean, 198–9; Tok Pisin, 229
Crioulo, *see* Creole: Cape Verdean
Croatian, 210; *see also* Serbo–Croatian
Cuna, San Blas, 34, 36
Czech, 210

Dari, 184
Dutch, 64–5, 68, 193–4

English, 12–13, 17, 31, 34–5, 38, 43, 51–2, 54, 57, 58–67, 69, 71–4, 75, 77–8, 81, 84, 88–9, 90, 93, 94, 99–100, 102, 104–5, 135, 139, 184–5, 187, 193–4, 197, 199–200, 203–4, 207, 211–15, 217–18, 226–8, 232–3, 241; *see also* Black English, Indian English, Old English, Pidgin English, Puerto Rican English
Eskimo, 93, 214, 188–91, 238
Esperanto, 105

Faroese, 216
Farsi, 91, 184, 188–91, 238
Flemish, 55
French, 55, 69, 89, 90, 96, 193, 208, 209, 212, 261

Geez, 76, 206

General Index

Abnormal speech, 101–4
Access, to community, *see* Community access
Acquisition, of communicative competence, 220–64
Act sequence: 144, 152–4
Age, and varieties of language, 98–100
Applications, 266–70
Appropriateness, of language, in specific context, 197–200
Arrangement of data, *see* Data
Artifacts, material, and ethnographic analysis, 114
Artistic data, and ethnographic analysis, 116
Attitude, to language, 181–219

Baby talk, 98–9
Backchannel signals, 148–9
Background information, and ethnographic analysis, 114
Beliefs: about language use, and ethnographic analysis, 116; about language, by children, 262–4
Bilingualism, 55, 201–2, 210–14
Borrowing, versus code-switching, 66–7
Boundaries, of communicative events, 44, 135–6
Boundary functions, of speech communities, 83–4

Categories: social, and language

use, 20; of talk, 30–2
Channels of communication, 23, 52, 145
Child care, and language development, 221–5
Children: and acquisition of language, 220–30; and beliefs about language, 229, 262–4; as participant-observers of communication, 221
Classification of data, *see* Data
Classroom discourse cycle, 175–6
Code-alternation, 58
Code-markers, 58, 70–4
Code-switching, 57–70
Codes, verbal and non–verbal, 22–3, 58, 117, 144–5
Cognitive orientation, 7
Common knowledge, and ethnographic analysis, 116
Communication: channels of, *see* Channels of communication; components of, 24, 138–57; ethnography of, as a discipline, 1–2; ethnography of, and significance for other fields, 8–9; holistic perspective, for study of, 10; patterns of, *see* Patterns of communication
Communicative act, 28–30
Communicative competence, 2–3, 7, 29–35
Communicative event: 27–30, 161–75; components of,

311